THE RIGHT TO A REMEDY AND TO reparation for gross human rights violations

a practitioners' guide

International Commission of Jurists

P.O. Box 91
Rue des Bains 33
CH-1211 Geneva 8
Switzerland
E-mail: info@icj.org
www.icj.org

® The Right to a Remedy and to Reparation for Gross Human Rights Violations – A Practitioners' Guide

ISBN: 92-9037-106-4
Geneva, December 2006
ISBN: 978-958-930771-7
Bogotá, Colombia, June 2007

Photo cover page: @stockphoto/Christine Balderas
Design cover page: Daniel Hincapié- Marta Rojas
Printing: Ediciones Antropos, Bogotá, Colombia

→

THE RIGHT TO A REMEDY AND TO reparation for gross human rights violations

a practitioners' guide

INTERNATIONAL COMMISSION OF JURISTS
2006

This guide was researched and written by Cordula Droege.
Federico Andreu-Guzmán provided legal review
and Anne Philippart de Foy assisted in its production.

This project has been made possible with the support
of the Evangelical Development Service, Germany

TABLE OF CONTENTS

TABLE OF ABBREVIATIONS

ACHR	American Convention on Human Rights
AfrCHPR	African Charter on Human and People's Rights
AfrComHPR	African Commission on Human and People's Rights
CAT	Convention against Torture and other Forms of Cruel, Inhuman or Degrading Treatment or Punishment
CEDAW	Convention on the Elimination of All Forms of Discrimination against Women
CERD	International Convention on the Elimination of All Forms of Racial Discrimination
CoE	Council of Europe
CRC	Convention on the Rights of the Child
ECHR	European Convention on Human Rights
ECtHR	European Court of Human Rights
ECT	Treaty establishing the European Community
ETS	European Treaties Series
G.A	General Assembly
I/ACtHR	Inter-American Court of Human Rights
I/AComHR	Inter-American Commission on Human Rights
ICC	International Criminal Court
ICCPR	International Covenant on Civil and Political Rights
ICESCR	International Covenant on Economic, Social and Cultural Rights
ICJ	International Court of Justice
ICTR	International Tribunal for Rwanda
ICTY	International Tribunal for the Former Yugoslavia
ILC	International Law Commission
MWC	International Convention on the Protection of the Rights of All Migrant Workers and Members of their Families
OAS	Organization of American States
PCIJ	Permanent Court of International Justice

UDHR	Universal Declaration of Human Rights
UN Doc.	Document of the United Nations
U.N.T.S.	United Nations Treaties Series

TABLE OF LEGAL INSTRUMENTS

International Legal Instruments

International treaties:

- Charter of the International Military Tribunal
- Convention against Torture and other Forms of Cruel, Inhuman or Degrading Treatment or Punishment, 78 U.N.T.S. 277.
- Convention for the Suppression of the Traffic in Persons and of the Exploitation of the Prostitution of Others, 96 U.N.T.S. 271.
- Convention on the Elimination of All Forms of Discrimination against Women, 249 U.N.T.S. 13.
- Convention on the Non-Applicability of Statutory Limitations to War Crimes and Crimes against Humanity, G.A. res. 2391 (XXIII), annex, 23 U.N. GAOR Supp. (No. 18) at 40, U.N. Doc. A/7218 (1968).
- Convention on the Prevention and Punishment of the Crime of Genocide, 78 U.N.T.S. 277.
- Convention on the Rights of the Child, G.A. res. 44/25, annex, 44 U.N. GAOR Supp. (No. 49) at 167, U.N. Doc. A/44/49 (1989).
- Indigenous and Tribal Peoples Convention 1989 (No. 169), 72 ILO Official Bulletin 59.
- International Convention on the Elimination of All Forms of Racial Discrimination, 660 U.N.T.S. 195.
- International Convention on the Protection of the Rights of All Migrant Workers and Members of their Families, adopted by General Assembly resolution 45/158 of 18 December 1990.

- International Convention on the Suppression and Punishment of the Crime of Apartheid, G.A. res. 47/81, 47 U.N. GAOR Supp. (No. 49) at 161, U.N. Doc. A/47/49 (1992).

- International Covenant on Civil and Political Rights, 999 U.N.T.S. 171.

- International Covenant on Economic, Social and Cultural Rights, 993 U.N.T.S. 3.

- International Criminal Court, Rules of Procedure and Evidence, U.N. Doc. PCNICC/2000/1/Add.1 (2000).

- Optional Protocol to the Convention on the Rights of the Child on the Involvement of Children in Armed Conflict, adopted and opened for signature, ratification and accession by General Assembly resolution A/RES/54/263 of 25 May 2000.

- Optional Protocol to the Convention on the Rights of the Child on the Sale of Children, Child Prostitution and Child Pornography. adopted and opened for signature, ratification and accession by General Assembly resolution A/RES/54/263 of 25 May 2000.

- Protocol to Prevent, Suppress and Punish Trafficking in Persons, especially Women and Children, supplementing the United Nations Convention against Transnational Organized Crime, G.A. res. 55/25, annex II, 55 U.N. GAOR Supp. (No. 49) at 60, U.N. Doc. A/45/49 (Vol. I) (2001).

- Rome Statute of the International Criminal Court, U.N. Doc. A/CONF.183/9 (1998).

Declaratory instruments:

- Declaration on the Protection of All Persons from Being Subjected to Torture and Other Cruel, Inhuman or Degrading Treatment or Punishment, adopted by the General Assembly resolution 3452 (XXX) of 9 December 1975.

- Basic Principles on the Independence of the Judiciary, endorsed by General Assembly resolutions 40/32 of 29 November 1985 and 40/146 of 13 December 1985.

- Basic Principles on the Use of Force and Firearms by Law Enforcement Officials, adopted by the Eighth United Nations Congress on the Prevention of Crime and the Treatment of Offenders, Havana, Cuba, 27 August to 7 September 1990.

- Declaration of Basic Principles of Justice for Victims of Crime and Abuse of Power, adopted by General Assembly resolution 40/34 of 29 November 1985.

- Declaration on the Elimination of All Forms of Intolerance and of Discrimination Based on Religion or Belief, proclaimed by General Assembly resolution 36/55 of 25 November 1981.

- Declaration on the Elimination of Violence against Women, proclaimed by General Assembly resolution 48/104 of 20 December 1993.

- Declaration on the Protection of all Persons from Enforced Disappearance, adopted by General Assembly resolution 47/133 of 18 December 1992.

- Declaration on the Right and Responsibility of Individuals, Groups and Organs of Society to Promote and Protect Universally Recognized Human Rights and Fundamental Freedoms, adopted by General Assembly resolution 53/144 (*cited as: Declaration on Human Rights Defenders*).

- Declaration on the Rights of Persons Belonging to National or Ethnic, Religious and Linguistic Minorities, adopted by General Assembly resolution 47/135 of 18 December 1992.

- Principles of International Cooperation in the Detection, Arrest, Extradition and Punishment of Persons Guilty of War Crimes and Crimes against Humanity, adopted by General Assembly resolution 3074 (XXVIII) of 3 December 1973.

- Principles on the Effective Investigation ad Documentation of Torture and Other Cruel Inhuman or Degrading Treatment or Punishment, recommended by General Assembly resolution 55/89 of 4 December 2000 (*cited as UN Principles on the Investigation of Torture*).

- Principles on the Effective Prevention and Investigation of Extra-legal, Arbitrary and Summary Executions, recommended by Economic and Social Council resolution 1989/65 of 24 May 1989 (*cited as: UN Principles on Extra-legal Executions*).

- Programme of Action of the World Conference against Racism, Racial Discrimination, Xenophobia and Related Intolerance, A/CONF.189/ 12 (2001).

- Principles on the right to a remedy and reparation for victims of gross violations of human rights law and serious violations of humanitarian law, adopted by General Assembly resolution 60/147 of 16 december 2005 (*cited as: UN Principles on Reparation*)

- Updated Set of Principles for the protection and promotion of human rights through action to combat impunity (E/CN.4/2005/102/ Add.1, 8 February 2005), recommended by the Commission on Human Rights resolution 2005/81 of 21 April 2005 (*cited as: UN Principles on Impunity*).

- Vienna Declaration and Programme of Action, adopted by the World Conference on Human Rights in Vienna on 25 June 1993.

- UN Principles on Responsibility of States for Internationally Wrongful Acts, elaborated by the International Law Commission in 2001 (Official Records of the General Assembly, Fifty-sixth Session, Supplement No. 10 (A/56/10). Text reproduced as it appears in the annex to General Assembly resolution 56/83 of 12 December 2001).

Regional instruments:

- European Convention on Human Rights, ETS 5.

- Charter of Fundamental Rights of the European Union, Official Journal C 364/01 of 11 December 2000.

- Treaty establishing the European Community, consolidated text, Official Journal C 325 of 24 December 2002.

- European Convention on the Non-Applicability of Statutory Limitation to Crimes Against Humanity and War Crimes, ETS 82.

- American Declaration of the Rights and Duties of Man, approved by the Ninth International Conference of American States, Bogotá, Colombia, 1948.

- American Convention on Human Rights, O.A.S. Treaty Series No. 36.
- Inter-American Convention to Prevent and Punish Torture, O.A.S. Treaty Series No. 67.
- Inter-American Convention on the Prevention, Punishment and Eradication of Violence against Women, 33 I.L.M. 1534 (1994).
- Inter-American Convention on Forced Disappearance of Persons, 33 I.L.M. 1429 (1994).
- African Charter on Human and People's Rights, OAU Doc. CAB/LEG/67/3 rev. 5, 21 I.L.M. 58 (1982).

Humanitarian Law Conventions:

- Geneva Convention for the Amelioration of the Condition of the Wounded and Sick in Armed Forces in the Field, 75 U.N.T.S. 31 (*cited as: First Geneva Convention*).
- Geneva Convention for the Amelioration of the Condition of Wounded, Sick and Shipwrecked Members of Armed Forces at Sea, 75 U.N.T.S. 85 (*cited as: Second Geneva Convention*).
- Geneva Convention relative to the Treatment of Prisoners of War, 75 U.N.T.S. 135 (*cited as: Third Geneva Convention*).
- Geneva Convention relative to the Protection of Civilian Persons in Time of War, 75 U.N.T.S. 287 (*cited as: Fourth Geneva Convention*).
- Protocol Additional to the Geneva Conventions of 12 August 1949, and Relating to the Protection of Victims of International Armed Conflicts (Protocol I), 1125 U.N.T.S. 3 (*cited as: First Additional Protocol to the Geneva Conventions*).
- Protocol Additional to the Geneva Conventions of 12 August 1949, and Relating to the Protection of Victims of Non-International Armed Conflicts (Protocol II) 1125 U.N.T.S. 609 *(cited as Additional Protocol II to the Geneva Conventions)*.

Introduction

'Every human act produces diverse consequences, some proximate and others remote. An old adage puts it as follows: causa causæ est causa causati. Imagine the effect of a stone cast into a lake; it will cause concentric circles to ripple over the water, moving further and further away and becoming ever more imperceptible. Thus it is that all human actions cause remote and distant effects.'[1]

All victims of human rights violations have a right to an effective remedy and to reparation. While this is a recognized consequence of state responsibility for human rights violations, its modalities are often neglected. International legal provisions on this is issue are disparate, frequently vague, and do not follow a uniform terminology. The detailed aspects of states' duty to guarantee reparation have been developed and refined in international jurisprudence. Over time, many principles have been recognized and strengthened by different international bodies. While interpretation and terminology differs from system to system, it is possible to identify a coherent set of principles on the right to a remedy and reparation. On the basis of these acquired legal standards, the Commission on Human Rights has adopted the Basic Principles and Guidelines on the Right to a Remedy and Reparation for Victims of Gross Violations of International Human Rights Law and Serious Violations of International Humanitarian Law (hereinafter: UN Principles on Reparations) at its 61st session in April 2005.[2] At its 60st session, the General Assembly has adopted the UN Principles on Reparations (resolution 60/147 of 16 December 2005).

---

1 Inter-American Court of Human Rights, *Case of Aloeboetoe et al v Suriname*, Judgment of 10 September 1993, Series C No 15, para 48.

2 Commission on Human Rights Resolution E/CN.4/RES/2005/35, of 19 April 2005.

This Practitioners' Guide seeks to outline the international legal principles governing the right to a remedy and reparation of victims of gross human rights violations, by compiling international jurisprudence on the issue of reparations. The main sources for the Guide are the jurisprudence of the United Nations human rights treaty bodies, the Inter-American Court and Commission of Human Rights, the European Court of Human Rights and the African Commission on Human and Peoples' Rights. It also takes account of the practice of the UN Commission on Human Rights and its Special Procedures, the General Assembly and the Security Council.

The Guide is aimed at practitioners who may find it useful to have international sources at hand for their legal, advocacy, social or other work. It is intended for lawyers, magistrates and other members of the legal profession, governments, international and non-governmental organisations and human rights defenders. Following a simple structure, it reviews the practice and jurisprudence of each international body on the addressed subjects. Its purpose is to provide quick guidance on the jurisprudence and practice of international organs.

The Guide first recalls the state's general duty to respect, protect, ensure and promote human rights, particularly the general duty of the state and the general consequences flowing from gross human rights violations **(Chapter I)**. It then defines who is entitled to reparation: victims are, of course, the first beneficiaries of reparations, but other persons also have a right to reparation under certain circumstances **(Chapter II)**. The Guide goes on to address the right to an effective remedy, the right to a prompt, thorough, independent and impartial investigation and the right to truth **(Chapters III-V)**. It then addresses the consequences of gross human rights violations, i.e. the duty of the state to cease the violation if it is ongoing and to guarantee that no further violations will be committed **(Chapter VI)**. It continues by describing the different aspects of the right to reparation, i.e. the right to restitution, compensation, rehabilitation and satisfaction **(Chapter VII)**. While the duty to prosecute and punish perpetrators of human rights violations is not necessarily part of the reparation as such, it is so closely linked to the victim's right to redress and justice that it must be addressed in this Guide **(Chapter VIII)**. Frequent factors of impunity, such as trials in military tribunals, amnesties or comparable measures and statutes of limitations for crimes under international law are also discussed **(Chapter IX)**.

To be complete, a study on remedies and reparations should equally take into account comparative national practice, legislation and jurisprudence. Indeed, it is in the realm of domestic law that the most comprehensive, extensive, and creative forms of reparations have been developed. However, this study cannot address these developments, as it confines itself to international law and practice, so as to provide materials and sources for practitioners who want to use international law to advance national practice and legislation.

CHAPTER I
DUTIES OF STATES ARISING FROM HUMAN RIGHTS

International human rights law not only recognizes the individual human rights of every human being, it also puts an obligation on states to ensure, secure or guarantee the effective enjoyment of human rights with its jurisdiction. It is enshrined in so many international human rights treaties[1] and confirmed in international jurisprudence that it can be considered to be an obligation of customary international law. It is important to present the different aspects of these guarantees, because they are reflected in all of the obligations described in this Practitioners' Guide.

The duty to ensure effective enjoyment of human rights implies, amongst others, that the state must adopt all necessary legislative and other measures to give effect to the rights guaranteed in international law,[2] an obligation confirmed many times by international human rights bodies.[3] Moreover, as

---

1 Article 2 ICCPR; Article 2 CERD; Article 2 CEDAW; Article 2 CRC, Article 1 ACHR, Article 1 American Convention on the Prevention and Punishment of Torture, Article 1 ECHR.

2 Article 2 (2) ICCPR; Article 2 (c) and (d) CERD; Article 2 (a) CEDAW; Article 4 CRC; Article 2 (1) CAT; Article 1 AfrCHPR; Article 2 ACHR; Article 6 Inter-American Convention on the Prevention and Punishment of Torture; Article I (d) Inter-American Convention on Forced Disappearance.

3 Human Rights Committee: *General Comment No 31 on Article 2 of the Covenant: The Nature of the General Legal Obligation Imposed on States Parties to the Covenant*, 21 April 2004, CCPR/C/74/CRP.4

the Inter-American Court and Commission have made clear, the state, in order to comply fully with its duty to give effect to human rights, has to ensure human rights through its entire 'legal, political and institutional system'[4] and to organize 'the governmental apparatus and, in general, all the structures through which public power is exercised, so that they are capable of legally ensuring the free and full enjoyment of human rights.'[5]

The duty to ensure human rights also means that human rights impose a multidimensional obligation on states. In addition to the duty to adopt all necessary legislative and other measures, there are four main components of the state's obligation: the state has a duty to prevent violations and to respect, protect, and promote human rights. The duty to respect entails the obligation to refrain from acts which would violate the rights; the duty to protect can be understood as the duty to protect persons from acts which would impede the enjoyment of their rights; and the duty to promote means the duty to take measures such as dissemination, training and education. Moreover, all human rights always have a procedural component, such as the obligations of states to provide adequate remedies and procedures of protection against human rights violations and investigation of these violations. The Inter-American Court of Human Rights, for instance, held in its first judgment in the case of *Velásquez Rodríguez*:

> 'As a consequence of this obligation, the States must prevent, investigate and punish any violation of the rights recognized by the Convention and, moreover, if possible attempt to restore the right violated and provide compensation as warranted for damages resulting from the violation.'[6]

Rev.6, para 12; Case *Suárez de Guerrero v Colombia*, Communication No. R.11/45 (5 February 1979), U.N. Doc. Supp. No. 40 (A/37/40) at 137 (1982), para 15; Inter-American Commission on Human Rights: Case 10.559, *Chumbivilcas (Peru)*, Report 1/96, 1 March 1996, para V 3; Inter-American Court of Human Rights: *Loayza Tamayo Case (Reparations)*, Judgment of 27 November 1998, Series C No 42, para 164; *Suárez Rosero Case (Reparations)*, Judgment of 20 January 1999, Series C No 44, paras 97-99; European Court of Human Rights: Case *X and Y v the Netherlands*, Judgment of 26 March 1985, Series A 91, para 27; European Court of Human Rights: Case M.C. *v Bulgaria*, Judgment of 4 December 2003, para 153; Recommendation Rec (2004) 5 of the Committee of Ministers of the Council of Europe *on the verification of the compatibility of draft laws, existing laws and administrative practice with the standards laid down in the European Convention on Human Rights* of 12 May 2004 and Recommendation Rec (2004) 6 *on the improvement of domestic remedies*, 12 May 2004; African Commission on Human and Peoples' Rights: Case *Avocats sans Frontières (on behalf of Gaëtan Bwampamye) v Burundi*, Communication 231/ 99 (28th Session, Nov 2000).

4 Case 10.559, *Chumbivilcas (Peru)*, Report 1/96, 1 March 1996, para V 3.

5 Case of *Velásquez-Rodríguez v Honduras*, Judgment of 29 July 1988, Series C No 4, para 166.

6 Case of *Velásquez-Rodríguez v Honduras*, Judgment of 29 July 1988, Series C No 4, para 166; see also

Similarly, it has been held by the Human Rights Committee,[7] the European Court of Human Rights[8] and the African Commission on Human and Peoples' Rights[9] that states have a duty to:

- take legislative and other measures to give effect to rights,
- investigate human rights violations,
- provide effective remedies against violations,
- bring perpetrators of certain violations to justice, and
- provide reparation to victims.

***

The different obligations of the state are **complementary** and **not alternative** and they **cannot be substituted for one another**. As the Special Rapporteur on extrajudicial, summary and arbitrary executions wrote: 'Governments are obliged under international law to carry out exhaustive and impartial investigations into allegations of violations of the right to life, to identify, bring to justice and punish their perpetrators, to grant compensation to the victims or their families, and to take effective measures to avoid future recurrence of such violations. The first two components of this four fold obligation constitute in themselves the most effective deterrent for the prevention of human rights violations. Conversely, if perpetrators may be certain that they will not be held responsible, such violations are most likely to continue unabated. [...] Granting compensation presupposes compliance with the obligation to carry out an investigation into allegations of human rights abuses with a view to identifying and prosecuting their perpe-

Inter-American Commission on Human Rights Case 10.559, *Chumbivilcas (Peru)*, Report 1/96, 1 March 1996, para V 3; Case X *and* Y *v the Netherlands*, Judgment of 26 March 1985, Series A 91, para 27; Case M.C. *v Bulgaria*, Judgment of 4 December 2003, para 153.

7 *General Comment No 31 on Article 2 of the Covenant: The Nature of the General Legal Obligation Imposed on States Parties to the Covenant*, 21 April 2004, CCPR/C/74/CRP.4/Rev.6.

8 Case X *and* Y *v the Netherlands*, Judgment of 26 March 1985, Series A 91, para.27; Case *Aksoy v Turkey*, Judgment of 18 December 1996, Reports 1996-VI, para 98.

9 Case of *The Social and Economic Rights Action Center and the Center for Economic and Social Rights v Nigeria*, Communication 155/96 (30th Ordinary Session, Oct 2001), paras 44-48.

trators. Financial or other compensation provided to the victims or their families before such investigations are initiated or concluded, however, does not exempt Governments from this obligation.'[10] The same has been recalled by the Inter-American Commission on Human Rights and the Inter-American Court of Human Rights.[11]

The obligations of the state are also **unconditional**: they do not depend on one another, nor are they conditional on an individual complaint. They cannot be renounced by victims. While victims may, of course, renounce the individual reparation that is due to them, the state cannot, for instance, forego its obligation to investigate and make public the truth on gross human rights violations and to punish the perpetrators. This is a duty that the state has not only towards victims, but towards society as a whole.[12] In a similar vein, the Human Rights Committee has called human rights obligations of the ICCPR obligations *erga omnes*.[13] The Inter-American Court has also insisted that the obligation to investigate violations and to bring perpetrators to justice is not annulled even if the victims renounce their rights. The Court has held that 'even though the aggrieved party may pardon the author of the violation of his human rights, the State is nonetheless obliged to sanction said author, except when the offence involved is prosecutable by a private party. The State's obligation to investigate the facts and punish those responsible does not erase the consequences of the unlawful act in the affected person. Instead, the purpose of that obligation is that every State party ensure, within its legal system, the rights and freedoms recognized in the Convention.'[14]

Furthermore, the **different forms of reparation are complementary and not alternative**. Article 34 of the Draft Articles on Responsibility of

[10] Report of the Special Rapporteur on Extrajudicial, Summary and Arbitrary Executions, 7 December 1993, E/CN.4/1994/7, paras 688 and 711.

[11] Inter-American Commission on Human Rights: Report No 36/96, Case 10.843 (Chile), 15 October 1996, para 77; Report No 34/96, Cases 11.228 *et al* (Chile), 15 October 1996, para 76; Report No 25/98, Cases 11.505 *et al* (Chile), 7 April 1998, para 50; Inter-American Court of Human Rights, Case *Garrido y Baigorria v Argentina (Reparations)*, Judgment of 27 August 1998, Series C No 39, para 72.

[12] See references in Chapter V on Right to Truth, at II.4.

[13] Human Rights Committee: *General Comment No 31 on Article 2 of the Covenant: The Nature of the General Legal Obligation Imposed on States Parties to the Covenant*, 21 April 2004, CCPR/C/74/CRP.4/Rev.6, para 2.

[14] Case *Garrido y Baigorria v Argentina (Reparations)*, Judgment of 27 August 1998, Series C No 39, para 72.

States for Internationally Wrongful Acts states that full reparation shall take the form of restitution, compensation and satisfaction 'either singly or in combination.' The International Law Commission has noted that this formulation does not leave the form of reparation to the discretion of the state, but rather clarifies that reparation may only be achieved in particular cases by the combination of different forms of reparation.[15] The Independent Expert on impunity of the UN Commission on Human Rights has likewise stressed that an important feature of an effective programme of reparations is its comprehensiveness.[16] The *UN Principles and Guidelines on the Right to a Remedy and Reparation for Victims of Gross Violations of International Human Rights Law and Serious Violations of International Humanitarian Law*[17] (hereinafter: *UN Principles on Reparation*) stipulate that reparation 'includes the following forms: restitution, compensation, rehabilitation, satisfaction and guarantees of non-repetition.'[18] And the *UN Set of Principles for the Protection and Promotion of Human Rights through Action to Combat Impunity*[19] (hereinafter: *UN Principles on Impunity*) state: 'The right to reparation shall cover all injuries suffered by the victim; it shall include individual measures concerning the right to restitution, compensation and rehabilitation, and general measures of satisfaction as provided by international law.'[20] The Inter-American Court of Human Rights has considered that the right to reparation, as a right of customary international law included '*restitutio in integrum*, payment of compensation, satisfaction, guarantees of non-repetitions among others.'[21] As the International Court of Justice has stated in its judgment in the case of *Avena and other Mexican Nationals*, '[w]hat constitutes "reparation in an adequate form" clearly varies depending upon the

15 Commentary of the International Law Commission to Article 34 of the Draft Articles on Responsibility of States for Internationally Wrongful Acts, para 2. (see Official Records of the General Assembly, Fifty-sixth Session, Supplement No. 10 (A/56/10)).

16 Independent Study on Impunity, E/CN.4/2004/88, 27 February 2004, para 60.

17 Adopted by Commission on Human Rights Resolution E/CN.4/RES/2005/35 of 20 April 2005 and by General Assembly resolution 60/147 of 16 december 2005.

18 Principle 18.

19 Recommended by the Commission on Human Rights resolution 2005/81 of 21 April 2005. In its resolutions on impunity, the UN Commission on Human Rights has noted that these Principles have already been applied at regional and national levels: E/CN.4/RES/2004/72, 21 April 2004, para 16; E/CN.4/RES/2003/72, 25 April 2003, para 14; E/CN.4/RES/2005/81, para 21.

20 Principle 34.

21 *Loayza Tamayo Case (Reparations)*, Judgment of 27 November 1998, Series C No 42, para 85.

concrete circumstances surrounding each case and the precise nature and scope of the injury, since the question has to be examined from the viewpoint of what is the "reparation in an adequate form" that corresponds to the injury.'[22] Of course, not all forms of reparations have to always be granted in every case. In particular, when restitution is possible, the other forms of reparation will generally be redundant. Nevertheless, where *restitutio in integrum* is not possible, other forms of reparation must afford relief for the harm suffered.

Sometimes, the duty to ensure human rights implies that the state can have duties that go beyond the individual rights that the victim can invoke. For example, the duty to prosecute and punish does not mean – at least not in every jurisdiction – that the victim has a personal right that the perpetrators be prosecuted and punished. This is the approach, for example, of the Human Rights Committee.[23] Nevertheless, the Committee holds that the state has a duty to prosecute the perpetrators of gross human rights violations.[24]

For victims of gross human rights violations, the above-mentioned different obligations of states - to adopt all necessary legislative and other measures to give effect to rights, to investigate human rights violations, to provide effective remedies against violations, to bring perpetrators of gross human rights violations to justice, and to provide reparation to victims – can be formulated into three main rights that have been asserted by victims of human rights violations: **the right to truth, the right to justice, and the right to reparation**. The right to a remedy gives the victims a possibility to effectively defend themselves against human rights violations; the right to truth puts an obligation on the state to investigate human rights violations and to make the truth public; the right to justice implies a prompt and effective remedy against human rights violations and the obligation of states to combat impunity and to bring perpetrators to justice; the right to reparation comprises the two former, but goes further and entails a right to compensation, restitution, rehabilitation, satisfaction and guarantees of non-repetition.

---

22 Case *Avena and other Mexican Nationals (Mexico v. United States of America)*, Judgment of 31 March 2004, para 119.

23 Case *Nydia Erika Bautista v Colombia*, Views of 13 November 1995, CCPR/C/55/D/563/1993, para 8.6, 10; Case *José Vicente y Amado Villafañe Chaparro v Colombia*, Views of 29 July 1997, CCPR/C/60/D/612/1995, para 8.2; Case *Coronel et al v Colombia*, Views of 13 October 2000, CCPR/C/70/D/778/1997, para 10.

24 *Ibid.*

In this Guide, these rights are divided into several chapters: the right to justice is the widest area and can be divided into the right to an effective remedy (Chapter III), to a prompt, effective, independent and impartial investigation (Chapter IV), but also its corollaries, i.e. the duty of the state to prosecute and punish human rights violations and to combat impunity (Chapters VIII and IX); the right to truth is described in Chapter V; the right to reparation, as well as the closely linked state duty of cessation and non-repetition is addressed in Chapters VI and VII.

***

The duty to provide reparation is a legal consequence for every wrongful act of the state in international law.[25] Conduct of the state that can entail legal responsibility is any act of an organ of that state, 'whether the organ exercises legislative, executive, judicial or any other functions, whatever position it holds in the organization of the State, and whatever its character as an organ of the central government or of a territorial unit of the state'.[26] This means that any conduct, be it lawful or unlawful (*ultra-vires*),[27] be it act or omission, can constitute a violation of human rights.

In terms of human rights, several situations entail the responsibility of the state: (1) The violation is committed by a state agent (be it a lawful, an unlawful or an extra-legal act). (2) The violation is committed by a non-state actor, but under the control or with the authorization, acquiescence, complicity or acknowledgment of state agents.[28] (3) A private party commits an act that affects the enjoyment of human rights, but is not attributable to the state.

In the first two cases, state responsibility always arises. In the third situation, the state has a duty of due diligence to protect all persons from acts of private parties that impair the enjoyment of human rights.[29] In particular, as

[25] Article 28 of the Draft Articles on Responsibility of States for Internationally Wrongful Acts.

[26] Article 4 of the Draft Articles on Responsibility of States for Internationally Wrongful Acts.

[27] Article 7 of the Draft Articles on Responsibility of States for Internationally Wrongful Acts.

[28] These are the situations envisaged in Articles 5, 8, and 11 of the Draft Articles on Responsibility of States for Internationally Wrongful Acts.

[29] See, amongst others, Human Rights Committee: *General Comment No 31 on the Nature of the General Legal Obligation Imposed on States Parties to the Covenant*, 26 May 2004, CCPR/C/21/Rev.1/Add.13, para 8; I/ACtHR: Case *Velásquez Rodríguez v Honduras*, Judgment of 29 July 1988, Series C

will be seen in the chapter on investigations, the state has an obligation to investigate all alleged acts that impair the enjoyment of human rights, be they committed by state actors or private parties.[30]

***

In sum, the duty of the state to ensure human rights has several consequences that are relevant for victims of gross human rights violations:

1. The state has to adopt all necessary legislative and other measures and to organize its entire governmental apparatus in a manner that will enable it to comply with all its human rights obligations. Moreover, it has the duty to provide effective remedies against human rights violations, to investigate and reveal the truth about human rights violations, to bring perpetrators of gross human rights violations to justice, and to provide reparation to victims.

2. The different obligations of the state to ensure human rights are complementary and cannot be substituted for one another. Similarly, the different forms of reparation are generally complementary.

3. States' obligations to ensure the effective enjoyment of human rights can sometimes go beyond the individual rights of victims. They are unconditional and remain in force even if victims renounce them.

4. Victims of gross human rights violations have a right to truth, a right to justice and a right to reparation, to which the above-mentioned obligations are corollaries.

No 4, para 172; I/AComHR: *Pedro Peredo Valderrama* (Mexico), Case N° 11.103, Report 42/00 of 13 April 2000, paras 41 *et seq*; ECtHR: Case *X and Y v the Netherlands*, Judgment of 26 March 1985, Series A No 91, para 27.

30 See Chapter IV.

CHAPTER II
VICTIMS AND PERSONS ENTITLED TO REPARATION

I have a lot of work to do today;
I need to slaughter memory,
Turn my living soul to stone
Then teach myself to live again. . .
But how. The hot summer rustles
Like a carnival outside my window;
I have long had this premonition
Of a bright day and a deserted house.[1]

It is important to briefly address the definition of victims of human rights violations and of persons entitled to reparations. Indeed, the two categories overlap frequently but not always, because sometimes, persons who are not victims can be entitled to reparations because they have suffered harm; they are sometimes referred to as 'indirect victims'.

Certain groups suffer human rights violations collectively; their collective rights, as well as their right to have access to collective procedures, should be recognized. This will also be addressed briefly in this chapter.

In certain cases, there may be doubts as to who is a victim of a human rights violation. Human rights treaties often presuppose the concept of victim and implicitly understand victim as the person whose rights have been violated. This is the case, for instance, of Article 2 (3) ICCPR and Article 1 of its Optional Protocol, Article 6 CERD, Article 2 of the Optional Protocol to CEDAW, Article 13 CAT, Article 13 and Article 34 ECHR, or Definition 31 of the Rules of Procedure of the Inter-American Court of Human Rights.

The notion of victims has been elaborated further in the Declaration of Basic Principles of Justice for Victims of Crime and Abuse of Power. It de-

---

1 Anna Akhmatova, *Requiem*.

fines *victims of crime* as 'persons who, individually or collectively, have suffered harm, including physical or mental injury, emotional suffering, economic loss or substantial impairment of their fundamental rights, through acts or omissions that are in violation of criminal laws operative within Member States, including those laws proscribing criminal abuse of power' (Principle 1). The definition also includes in Principle 2 'where appropriate, the immediate family or dependants of the direct victim and persons who have suffered harm in intervening to assist victims in distress or to prevent victimization.' The principles go on to define *victims of abuse of power* as 'persons who, individually or collectively, have suffered harm, including physical or mental injury, emotional suffering, economic loss or substantial impairment of their fundamental rights, through acts or omissions that do not yet constitute violations of national criminal laws but of internationally recognized norms relating to human rights.'

Principle 8 of the UN Principles on Reparation combines human rights law with the notion of victims in the UN Declaration of Basic Principles of Justice for Victims of Crimes and Abuse of Power. It reads:

> 'For purposes of this document, victims are persons who individually or collectively suffered harm, including physical or mental injury, emotional suffering, economic loss or substantial impairment of their fundamental rights, through acts or omissions that constitute a gross violation of international human rights law, or serious violations of international humanitarian law. Where appropriate, and in accordance with domestic law, the term "victim" also includes, where appropriate, the immediate family or dependants of the direct victim and persons who have suffered harm in intervening to assist victims in distress or to prevent victimization.'

This principle gathers and clarifies several aspects of the notion of victim and links it to the notion of entitlement to reparation. Indeed, the victim definition in this principle does not abstractly define who is a victim of human rights and humanitarian law violations, but seeks to define who is entitled to reparation. It encompasses several aspects: the victim is defined by the fact that he or she has suffered harm, and harm can vary in nature; further, the victim is not only the person who was the direct target of the violation, but any person affected by it directly or indirectly; lastly the victim can be an individual or a group.

These criteria reflect those that appear to have emerged from human rights jurisprudence and practice. Although there is little jurisprudence on the concept of victims since in many cases it is not problematic, international human rights bodies have nevertheless clarified the concept to a certain extent.

***

I. The Notion of Direct and indirect victim and person entitled to reparation

1. International Treaties and Other Legal Instruments

In Principle 8 of the UN Principles on Reparation the term 'victim' comprises not only direct, but also indirect victims: '[w]here appropriate, and in accordance with domestic law, the term "victim" also includes, where appropriate, the immediate family or dependants of the direct victim and persons who have suffered harm in intervening to assist victims in distress or to prevent victimization.' This reflects international jurisprudence, particularly in cases of deaths and disappearances.

However, before recalling this jurisprudence, it should be clarified that not all international or regional human rights systems have exactly equivalent definitions of victim and persons entitled to reparation. Indeed, in some cases, while a person is not considered a victim, he or she may nevertheless have suffered harm and be entitled to reparation. Also, persons who have suffered harm may be considered victims in one system while not in another, but be entitled to reparation in both. In other words: the notion of victim may be narrower than the notion of persons entitled to reparation. This is reflected in Article 41 ECHR and 63 ACHR which regulate the right to reparation and do not speak of 'victims' with regard to this particular obligation of reparation, but of 'injured party'. The differentiation is not reflected in Principle 8 of the UN Principles on Reparation, which defines victims from the angle of reparation, thus adopting a wide definition of victim. The principle should not be understood from this perspective: it does not so much seek to define the notion of 'victims of human rights violations' as to define who is entitled to reparation.

Many international Conventions simply refer to 'victims' of human rights violations without describing more clearly who the victim is.[2] Some trea-

[2] Article 9 (5) ICCPR; Article 14 (1) CAT; Article 75 (1) and 85 Rome Statute of the International Criminal Court; Article 106 of the Statutes of ICTR and ICTY; Article 9 (2) Declaration on Human

ties, however, are more explicit and define more clearly who is entitled to reparation. For instance, Article 16 (4) of the ILO Indigenous and Tribal Peoples Convention 1989 (No. 169) guarantees reparation for 'peoples removed from land' and Article 16 (5) of the same Convention to 'persons relocated.' Article 21 (2) AfrCHPR speaks of 'dispossessed people' whose wealth and natural resources have been spoilt.

2. Jurisprudence

For cases of disappearances, it is clear from international standards and jurisprudence that those entitled to reparation include the relatives of the disappeared. Article 19 of the Declaration on the Protection of all Persons from Enforced Disappearance recognizes reparation for victims, family and dependants. The Working Group on Enforced and Involuntary Disappearances has stated that 'in addition to the victims who survived the disappearance, their families are also entitled to compensation for the suffering during the time of the disappearance, and in the event of the death of the victim, his or her dependants are entitled to compensation.'[3] Equally, the UN Commission on Human Rights has reaffirmed the right to reparation of family members in its resolutions on enforced or involuntary disappearances.[4]

The Human Rights Committee found in the case of *Almeida de Quinteros* that the mother of the disappeared was a victim herself of the of torture or cruel, inhuman or degrading treatment prohibited by in Article 7 ICCPR.[5] It has made similar findings in further cases of disappearances.[6] It has

---

Rights Defenders, Article 5 (5) ECHR, Art. 9 (1) Inter-American Convention to Prevent and Punish Torture.

3 *General Comments on Article 19 of the Declaration on the Protection of All Persons from Enforced Disappearance*, 12 January 1998, E/CN.4 /1998/43, para 72.

4 UN Docs E/CN.4/RES/2003/38 (enforced or involuntary disappearances), 23 April 2003, para 4 (e); E/CN.4/2002/41, 23 April 2002, para 4 (e); E/CN.4/2001/46, 23 April 2001, para 4 (e); E/CN.4/ 2000/47, 20 April 2000, para 4 (e); E/CN.4/1999/38, 26 April 1999, para 4 (e).

5 Case *Almeida de Quinteros et al v Uruguay*, Views of 15 October 1982, 21 July 1983, CCPR/C/OP/ 2, paras 14, 16.

6 Case *Celis Laureano v Peru*, Views of 16 April 1996, CCPR/C/56/D/540/1993, para 10 [victim and family]; Case *Sarma v Sri Lanka*, Views of 31 July 2003, CCPR/C/78/D/950/2000, para 11 [victim and family]; Case *Coronel et al. v Colombia*, Views of 29 November 2002, CCPR/C/76/D/778/1997, para 10 [relatives].

found that other gross human rights violations, such as unlawful killings, may equally cause suffering to direct and indirect victims.[7]

The notion of direct and indirect victims becomes clear in such cases.

The Inter-American Court of Human Rights has granted reparation to relatives, but also partners of victims, not only in cases of disappearances,[8] but also for cases of killings,[9] and other gross human rights violations where the victim did not die or disappear.[10] To award reparation based on the own right of the relatives or other third persons, the Inter-American Court has established certain criteria: first, the payment sought must be based on effective and regular contributions made by the victim to the claimant, regardless of whether or not they were made in fulfilment of a legal obligation to pay support; second, the nature of the relationship between the victim and the claimant should be such that it provides some basis for the assumption that the payments would have continued had the victim not been killed; third, the contributions must be based on a financial need of the recipient.[11] The Inter-American Court considers that it can be presumed that the parents and the children of a direct victim fulfil theses requirements and must be considered as indirect victims.[12] In more recent case law,

7 Case *Suárez de Guerrero v Colombia*, Views of 31 March 1982, CCPR/C/15/D/45/1979, para 15 [compensate husband for death of his wife]; Case *John Khemraadi Baboeram et al. v Suriname*, Communication No. 146/1983 and 148 to 154/1983, 4 April 1985, U.N. Doc. Supp. No. 40 (A/40/40) at 187, para 16 [surviving families]; Case *Nydia Erika Bautista v Colombia*, Views of 13 November 1995, CCPR/C/55/D/563/1993 [family].

8 Case *Velásquez Rodríguez v Honduras (Compensatory damages)*, Judgment of 21 July 1989, Series C No 7, paras 50-52; Case *Garrido and Baigorria v Argentina (Reparations)*, Judgment of 27 August 1998, Series C No 39, paras 62, 63; *Case of Blake v Guatemala*, Judgment of 22 January 1999, para 37; Case *Bámaca Velásquez v Guatemala (Reparations)*, Judgment of 22 February 2002, Series C No 91, paras 33-36.

9 Case *Aloeboetoe v Suriname (Reparations)*, Judgment of 10 September 1993, Series C No 15, para 71; Case *Panel Blanca v Guatemala (Reparations)*, Judgment of 25 May 2001, Series C No 76, para 85, 86; *Case of Street Children v Guatemala (Reparations)*, Judgment of 26 May 2001, Series C No 77, para 68; Case *Juan Humberto Sánchez v Honduras, Series C No 9*, Judgment of 7 June 2003, para 152.

10 Case *Loayza Tamayo v Peru (Reparations)*, Judgment of 27 November 1998, Series C No 42, para 92.

11 Case *Aloeboetoe v Suriname (Reparations)*, Judgment of 10 September 1993, Series C No 15, paras 67, 68.

12 Case *Velásquez Rodríguez v Honduras (Compensatory damages)*, Judgment of 21 July 1989, Series C No 7, paras 50-52 [moral damage] and para 27 [based on the principle of equity]; *Case of Blake v Guatemala (Reparations)*, Judgment of 22 January 1999, para 37 [parents and brothers and sisters of disappeared person, without differentiation in proof]; Case *Garrido and Baigorria v Argentina (Reparations)*, Judgment

the Court has also presumed this for the siblings and partners of the victim.[13]

The European Court of Human Rights has also recognized a right to reparation for members of the family, either as victims in their own right or as injured parties in the sense of Article 41 ECHR. Since the case of *Kurt v Turkey*, the Court has held that the relatives of a disappeared person can themselves be victims of the prohibition of torture and inhuman or degrading treatment guaranteed in Article 3 of the ECHR, if their suffering is distinct from the emotional distress inevitably caused to a relative of a victim of serious human rights violations.[14] To assess the harm done to the relative, the Court takes into account such factors as proximity of the family tie, the particular circumstances of the relationship, the extent to which the family member witnessed the events in question, the involvement of the family members in the attempts to obtain information about the disappeared person and the way in which the authorities responded to those enquiries. The Court pays particular attention to the authorities' reactions and attitudes when the situation is brought to their attention. It considers that it is especially in respect of the latter that a relative may claim to be a direct victim of the authorities' conduct.[15]

Even when the European Court does not qualify a person as a victim, it may consider the person as an injured party in the sense of Article 41 of the Convention. In the case of *Aksoy v Turkey*, the Court awarded just satisfac-

of 27 August 1998, Series C No 39, paras 62, 63 [mother without further proof; brothers did not show that they had very close relation to disappeared, so that moral damage not very grave]; Case *Bámaca Velásquez v Honduras (Reparations)*, Judgment of 22 February 2002, Series C No 91, paras 33-36 [parents, wife and children; other next of kin or third parties if there was a relationship of effective and regular dependence, benefits received by the former would have continued if the victim had not died, and economic need that was covered on a regular basis by the assistance provided by the victim].

13 Case *Blake v Guatemala (Reparations)*, Judgment of 22 January 1999, para 37 [parents and brothers and sisters of disappeared person, without differentiation in proof]; Case *Loayza Tamayo v Peru (Reparations)*, Judgment of 27 November 1998, Series C No 42, para 92 [all persons with a close family link, i.e. children, parents and brothers and sisters]; Case *Juan Humberto Sánchez v Honduras*, Judgment of 7 June 2003, Series C No 99, para 152 [family members for victim and in their own right; siblings; non biological father; wife and other partner]; *Case of 19 Merchants v Colombia*, Judgment of 5 July 2004, Series C No 109, para 249 [children, partner, parents and siblings].

14 Case *Kurt v Turkey*, Judgment of 25 May 1998, Reports 1998-III, para 174.

15 Case *Kiliç v Turkey*, Judgment of 18 June 2002, para 358; Case *Çakici v Turkey*, Judgment of 8 July 1999, Reports 1999-IV, para 98.

tion to the father of the victim, not only for the suffering of his son, but also on account of his own suffering, even though it found no violation in his regard.[16] The possible difference between the notion of 'victim' and the notion of 'person entitled to reparation' becomes clear in the cases of *Çakici v Turkey* and *Aktas v Turkey*. The Court held that, although it had not found a violation of the Convention with respect to the applicant whose relative had disappeared, 'he was undoubtedly affected by the violations found by the Court and may be regarded as an "injured party" for the purposes of Article 41.'[17] 'Having regard to the gravity of the violations and to equitable considerations', the Court awarded non-pecuniary damages to the applicants. The notion of a relative of the victim who is considered as an injured party can be likened to the notion of indirect victims.

The African Commission on Human and Peoples' Rights also recommended that 'compensatory benefit' be paid to the widows and beneficiaries of victims of disappearances and killings.[18]

In sum, persons entitled to reparation are both direct and indirect victims:

- the direct victims of the violation themselves, and
- other persons who are not victims as such but have suffered harm as a result of the violation, be it physical, mental or economic harm, such as members of the family of the victim.

***

II. The Notion of Harm Suffered

Reparation presupposes harm suffered. However, the notion of harm is rather vague and may be misleading.[19] Given the fundamental nature of

16 Case *Aksoy v Turkey*, Judgment of 18 December 1996, Reports 1996-VI, para 113.

17 Case *Çakici v Turkey*, Judgment of 8 July 1999, Reports 1999-IV, para 130; Case *Aktas v Turkey*, Judgment of 24 April 2004, para 364.

18 Case *Malawi African Association et al v Mauritania*, Communications 54/91, 61/91, 98/93, 164/97, 196/97, 210/98 (27th Ordinary Session, May 2000), Recommendations.

19 The notion of harm is also embedded in Rule 85 Rules of Procedure and Evidence of the ICC:

"For the purposes of the Statute and the Rules of Procedure and Evidence:

(a) 'Victims' means natural persons who have suffered harm as a result of the commission of any crime human rights, and the fact that they protect the most basic rights and needs and constitute but a minimum standard of protection for the well-being of the person, any violation of a human right involves harm for the person, at least in so far as the person suffers injustice. This is made clear by the formulation of Principle 8 of the UN Principles on Reparation, as it comprises the violation of human rights as a sort of fallback clause, speaking about 'harm, including physical or mental injury, emotional suffering, economic loss, *or substantial impairment of their fundamental legal rights*.'[20] Indeed, the obligation of reparation arising out of the breach of an international obligation flows from the mere fact of the existing violation, and not from the consequence of the violation. Indeed, state responsibility follows directly from a breach of international law, which may be a breach of an obligation under international human rights law. This is the general principle of law codified in Article 1 of the Draft Articles on Responsibility of States for Internationally Wrongful Acts, which reads: 'Every internationally wrongful act of a state entails the international responsibility of that State.' The question of harm will be critical for the entitlement to and the modalities of reparation, since reparation has to be proportionate and provide redress for the harm suffered. Harm should be presumed in cases of gross human rights violations.

Persons entitled to reparation are those who suffer harm as a consequence of a violation. Harm can be of physical, mental or economic nature. Harm should be presumed in cases of gross human rights violations.

***

III. The Notion of 'Collective Victim'

1. International Treaties and Other Legal Instruments

The Declaration of Basic Principles of Justice for Victims of Crime and Abuse of Power contains several references to collective rights: it recognizes that persons may suffer harm and impairment of their fundamental rights collectively (Prin-

within the jurisdiction of the Court;

(b) Victims may include organizations or institutions that have sustained direct harm to any of their property which is dedicated to religion, education, art or science or charitable purposes, and to their historic monuments, hospitals and other places and objects for humanitarian purposes."

ciple 1). It also recognizes that in cases of harm to the environment, restitution may benefit a 'community' if the community is affected (Principle 10). These formulations have informed the drafting of the UN Principles on Reparation, which refer to collective rights on several occasions.[21]

The complex concept of collective victim will be covered only briefly in this Guide. Some international treaties and declarations contain rights of groups as opposed to individuals. The two main groups to be found in these instruments are 'peoples' and 'indigenous peoples.'

The rights of peoples are recognized in Articles 1 ICCPR and ICESCR, which state that 'all peoples have the right to self-determination.' This right is also recognized in many other texts, such as the Declaration on the Granting of Independence to Colonial Countries and Peoples[22] and the General Assembly resolution on 'Permanent sovereignty over natural resources.'[23] It is also a fundamental notion at the root of the African Charter on Human and Peoples' Rights. Article 21 (2) AfrCHPR states that '[i]n case of spoliation the dispossessed people shall have the right to the lawful recovery of its property as well as to an adequate compensation.' The jurisprudence of the African Commission on Human Rights has made clear that this right could be invoked in a complaint before it and 'made effective.'[24]

As far as indigenous peoples are concerned, the Indigenous and Tribal People's Convention 1989 (No. 169) of the International Labour Organization contains an innovative provision in Article 15 which regulates the issue of natural resources. It provides that if the state exploits resources pertaining to the lands of indigenous or tribal peoples, '[t]he peoples concerned shall wherever possible participate in the benefits of such activities, and shall receive fair compensation for any damages which they may sustain as a result of such activities.' This Article clearly recognizes a right to compensation for a 'people.'

---

[20] Emphasis added.

[21] See Principles 8 and 13.

[22] General Assembly resolution 1514 (XV) of 14 December 1960.

[23] General Assembly resolution 1803 (XVII) of 14 December 1962.

[24] Case *The Social and Economic Rights Action Center and the Center for Economic and Social Rights v Nigeria*, Communication 155/96 (30th Ordinary Session, Oct 2001), para 68.

A different concept from that of rights of groups as collective entities are the rights of groups of individuals. This latter formulation is indeed misleading as it does not refer to group rights, but rather to the rights of every individual in a group. This formulation is chosen, for instance, in Article 2 of the Optional Protocol to CEDAW. Similar formulations exist in international treaties and declarations concerning minorities. Article 27 ICCPR speaks of the right of persons belonging to minorities to exercise their rights 'in community with the other members of their group.' Article 3 (1) of the Declaration on the Rights of Persons Belonging to National or Ethnic, Religious and Linguistic Minorities equally states that '[p]ersons belonging to minorities may exercise their rights, including those set forth in the present Declaration, individually as well as in community with other members of their group, without any discrimination." Article 3 (2) of the European Framework Convention for the Protection of Minorities uses a similar wording.

2. Jurisprudence

International jurisprudence has had to address the question of human rights violations committed against groups.

The Inter-American Court and Commission of Human Rights have been confronted to cases involving indigenous communities. In the case of the *Caloto massacre*, in which numerous persons from an indigenous community were massacred, the Inter-American Commission recommended 'social reparations' for the whole community.[25] In the *Mayagna (Sumo) Awas Tingni Community Case*, the petitioners were a 'community' consistent of an undefined number of persons, who claimed a violation of their right to communal property and judicial protection. The Court, after finding violations of these rights, ordered that the state must adopt in its domestic law the necessary measures 'to create an effective mechanism for delimitation, demarcation, and titling of the property of indigenous communities, in accordance with their customary law, values, customs and mores' and 'carry out the delimitation, demarcation, and titling of the corresponding lands of the members of the Mayagna (Sumo) Awas Tingni Community' and 'invest, as reparation for immaterial damages, in the course of 12 months, the total sum of US$ 50,000 in works or services of collective interest for the benefit of the Mayagna (Sumo) Awas Tingni Community, by common agreement

[25] Report No. 36/00, Case 11.101, "*Caloto Massacre*" (Colombia), 13 April 2000, paras 23, 28, 75 (3).

with the Community and under supervision by the Inter-American Commission of Human Rights.'[26] Thus, the Inter-American Court accepted that the rights of a group (the community) could be violated, and that reparation could consist of works or services of collective interest.

The African Commission on Human and Peoples' Rights has also addressed the question on collective rights. After the destruction of land of the Ogoni communities in Nigeria by oil companies, these communities complained to the African Commission about violations of their rights and asked for reparation. The Commission considered that collective rights were an essential element of human rights in Africa.[27] After finding multiple violations of the rights of the communities as well as of their members, it appealed to the government of Nigeria 'to ensure the protection of the environment, health and livelihood of the people of Ogoniland' by adopting various measures, such as investigations, environmental impact assessment, information, and 'compensation to victims of the human rights violations, including relief and resettlement assistance to victims of government sponsored raids, and undertaking a comprehensive cleanup of lands and rivers damaged by oil operations.'[28] In other words, the African Commission recommended both collective reparation to benefit the wider community and individual reparation.

> To summarize, some international treaties recognize substantive group rights, such as rights of peoples, particularly indigenous peoples. International law, moreover, recognizes the rights of individuals to exercise their rights in community with others.

***

Another different concept to that of rights of groups is the question of collective enforcement of individual rights. When a violation occurs that affects many people, collective enforcement procedures are important to obtain redress in simplified procedures that can have a real impact for a great number of persons. While the former is a substantive right of the group, the latter is a procedural right, a right of standing. It allows certain

[26] Case *The Mayagna (Sumo) Awas Tingni Community*, Judgment of 31 August 2001, Series C No 79, para 173 (3), (4) and (6).

[27] Case *The Social and Economic Rights Action Center and the Center for Economic and Social Rights v Nigeria*, Communication 155/96, paras 57, 61 (30th Ordinary Session, Oct 2001), para 68.

[28] *Ibid.*

individuals, groups or organizations to bring a claim on behalf of a number of individuals. This may be a defined or undefined number of individuals. Such procedural rights exist in many national jurisdictions. While international treaties are silent on these procedures, they have been recognized by the Inter-American Commission and Court of Human Rights and the African Commission on Human and Peoples' Rights who accepted complaints presented on behalf of an undefined number of persons. However, all persons affected by a violation of their human rights also have an individual right to reparation, which cannot be circumvented by collective reparation.

***

Summary

- While the notion of victim is not always clearly defined in international treaties, it has been interpreted and clarified by international jurisprudence. International law thus recognizes not only direct victims of violations, but also indirect victims, when they suffer physical, mental, material or moral harm from the violation. Relatives, but also other persons close to the victim may suffer from violations that are not 'targeted' at them, but nevertheless affect them, such as enforced disappearances.

- The notion of 'victim' does not necessarily coincide with the notion of 'person entitled to reparation.' Indeed, a person may not be considered a direct victim but may nevertheless be entitled to reparation, if this person suffers physical, mental, material or moral harm as a consequence of the violation. This person may be considered as an indirect victim.

- International law also recognizes in principle that certain groups may have rights, such as indigenous peoples. In these cases, they may also claim reparation collectively. When a great number of persons has suffered from human rights violations, there should also be collective procedures to enforce their rights, a practice accepted by some international human rights bodies.

CHAPTER III
THE RIGHT TO A REMEDY

'It is a general rule of both the civil and the common law that every invasion of a private right imports an injury and that for every injury the law gives a remedy.'[1]

The right to a remedy guarantees, first of all, the right to vindicate one's right before an independent and impartial body, with a view to obtaining a recognition of the violation, cessation of the violation if it is continuing, and adequate reparation. The right to a remedy is also linked in several ways to the right to reparation: an independent assessment constitutes the first step in obtaining reparation, and indeed the term remedy is sometimes understood as comprising reparation, for example by the Human Rights Committee.

The English term 'remedy' also sometimes causes confusion. It can mean both a procedural remedy as well as a substantive remedy such as reparation. In French or Spanish, the term 'recours' or 'recurso' is commonly used to refer only to a procedural remedy. This is quite clearly reflected in the ACHR and the ECHR, where the procedural right to a remedy and the right to reparation are guaranteed in different provisions.[2] In the ICCPR, however, Article 2 only refers to a remedy, and its wording, particularly in

---

1 *Opinion in the Lusitania Case*, 1 November 1923, Recueil def sentences arbitrales, Volume VII, p 32, at 35.

2 Articles 13, 41 ECHR; Articles 25, 63 ACHR.

the French and Spanish would not encompass a substantive right to reparation. Yet, the Human Rights Committee has stated that the right to an effective remedy necessarily entails the right to reparation.[3] In this Guide, remedy is used to refer to a procedural remedy, while reparation refers to the obligation to provide compensation, satisfaction, restitution and rehabilitation.

Universal and regional conventions guarantee the right to an effective remedy to all persons who allege that their human rights have been violated.[4] It has frequently been qualified as one of the most fundamental and essential rights for the effective protection of all other human rights.[5] The Human Rights Committee has indeed underlined in its *General Comment No 29 on derogations during a state of emergency* that the right to a remedy constitutes 'a treaty obligation inherent in the Covenant as a whole' and that even in times of emergency, 'the State party must comply with the fundamental obligation, under article 2, paragraph 3, of the Covenant to provide a remedy that is effective.'[6]

***

A special category of remedies guaranteed and protected under international law are remedies against unlawful detention, such as the right to be brought promptly before a judge or other officer authorized by law to exer-

[3] See *General Comment No 31 on the Nature of the General Legal Obligation Imposed on States Parties to the Covenant*, 26 May 2004, CCPR/C/21/Rev.1/Add.13, para 16.

[4] Article 2 (3) ICCPR; Article 13 CAT; Article 6 CERD; Article 8 UDHR; Articles 9 and 13 Declaration on the Protection of All Persons from Enforced Disappearance; Principles 4 and 16 of the UN Principles on Extra-legal Executions; Principles 4-7 of the Declaration of Basic Principles of Justice for Victims of Crime and Abuse of Power; Article 27 of the Vienna Declaration and Programme of Action; Articles 13, 160-162, 165 of the Programme of Action of the World Conference against Racism, Racial Discrimination, Xenophobia and Related Intolerance; Article 9 of the Declaration on Human Rights Defenders; Article 13 ECHR; Article 47 of the Charter of Fundamental Rights of the European Union; Articles 7 (1) (a) and 25 ACHR; Article XVIII of the American Declaration of the Rights and Duties of Man; Article III (1) of the Inter-American Convention on Forced Disappearance of Persons; Article 8 (1) of the Inter-American Convention to Prevent and Punish Torture; Article 7 (1) (a) AfrCHPR; and Article 9 Arab Charter on Human Rights.

[5] *Report of the Special Representative on Human Rights Defenders*, A/56/341, 10 September 2001, para 9; *Report of the Special Rapporteur on violence against women, its causes and consequences*, E/CN.4/2002/83, 31 January 2002, para 116.

[6] *General Comment No 29 on derogations during a state of emergency*, 31 August 2001, CCPR/C/21/Rev.1/Add.11, para 14.

cise judicial power[7] and the right to *habeas corpus* or similar remedies (*recours en référé, amparo, etc*) to challenge the legality of a deprivation of liberty before a court of law.[8] This right is essential as it not only shields individuals from unlawful detention but also constitutes an important safeguard against torture and other forms of ill-treatment or abuse in detention and enforced disappearance.[9] The importance of this right has been re-affirmed by the General Assembly of the United Nations.[10]

It should be noted that these remedies are fundamental and apply in times of peace as well as of public emergency or conflict. Indeed, the Human Rights Committee has held that the remedy of *habeas corpus* is *per se* non-derogable.[11] The UN Commission on Human Rights has held that the recourse of *habeas corpus* must be maintained even during states of exception.[12] The European Court of Human Rights has held that even in times of emergency, a state may only derogate from the requirements of Article 5 ECHR to the extent strictly required by the situation. States always have to comply with their obligations, including safeguards against abuse in detention, access to a lawyer and a doctor, the guarantee of *habeas corpus* proceedings and the right to contact family members.[13] The Inter-American Court of Human Rights has expressly held that 'the writs of habeas corpus and of "amparo" are among those judicial guarantees that are essential for the protection of various rights whose derogation is prohibited by Article 27 (2) and that serve, moreover, to preserve legality in a democratic society',[14] and that

---

7 Article 9 (3) ICCPR; Article 5 (3) ECHR; Article 7 (5) ACHR.

8 Article 9 (4) ICCPR; Article 37 (d) CRC; Article 5 (4) ECHR; Article 7 (6) ACHR; Article X of the Inter-American Convention on Forced Disappearance of Persons; Principle 32 of the Body of Principles for the Protection of All Persons under Any Form of Detention or Imprisonment,; Article 9 of the Declaration on the Protection of All Persons from Enforced Disappearance.

9 See *Report of the Special Rapporteur on torture*, E/CN.4/2003/68, 17 December 2002, para 26 (i).

10 Resolution on the right of amparo, habeas corpus or other legal remedies to the same effect, A/RES/34/178, 17 December 1979.

11 *General Comment No 29 on derogations during a state of emergency*, 31 August 2001, CCPR/C/21/Rev.1/Add.11, para 16.

12 Resolution on habeas corpus, E/CN.4/RES/1992/35, 28 February 1992, para 2.

13 Case *Aksoy v Turkey*, Judgment of 18 December 1996, Reports 1996-VI, para 83.

14 Advisory Opinion OC-8/87, *Habeas Corpus in Emergency Situations*, 30 January 1987, Series A No. 8, para 42; Advisory Opinion OC-9/87, *Judicial Guarantees in States of Emergency*, 6 October 1987, operative para 2.

these guarantees 'should be exercised within the framework and the principles of due process of law.'[15]

***

I. Requirements of the Right to a Remedy, Especially Right to a Judicial Remedy

The content of the notion of an effective remedy has been gradually interpreted and developed by international human rights bodies. It is a form of access to an independent authority which has the power to decide whether a human rights violation has taken place or is taking place and the power to offer a remedy in the sense of ordering cessation or reparation.

1. Promptness and Effectiveness

The first requirement for a remedy is that it should be prompt and effective, i.e. provide meaningful access to justice for a victim of a human rights violation. This has been the jurisprudence of all international human rights bodies.[16] Effectiveness means that the remedy must not be theoretical and illusory, but provide practical and real access to justice.[17] It must be capable of finding whether a violation took place and be able to remedy it.[18] As the Inter-American Court of Human Rights wrote in the *Caracazo Case*:

> 'any person who considers himself or herself to be a victim of such violations has the right to resort to the system of justice to attain compliance with the duty by the State, for his or her benefit and that of society as a whole.'[19]

---

[15] Advisory Opinion OC-9/87, *supra*, operative para 3.

[16] HRC: *General Comment No 31 on the Nature of the General Legal Obligation Imposed on States Parties to the Covenant*, 26 May 2004, CCPR/C/21/Rev.1/Add.13, para 15; I/ACtHR: Advisory Opinion OC-9/87, *Judicial Guarantees in States of Emergency*, 6 October 1987, Series A No 9, para 24; AfrCmHPR, *Principles and Guidelines on the Right to a Fair Trial and Legal Assistance in Africa*, Principle C, African Union Doc. DOC/OS (XXX) 247; Case *The Social and Economic Rights Action Center and the Center for Economic and Social Rights v Nigeria*, Communication 155/96 (30th Ordinary Session, Oct 2001), para 61, in which the Commission considered that the State had to ensure 'legal remedies'; ECtHR: Case *Airey v Ireland*, Judgment of 9 October 1979, Series A No. 32, para 33.

[17] EctHR: Case *Airey v Ireland*, Judgment of 9 October 1979, Series A No 32, para 24.

[18] I/ACtHR: Advisory Opinion OC-9/87, *Judicial Guarantees in States of Emergency*, 6 October 1987, Series A No 9, para 24; Case *Silver v the United Kingdom*, Judgment of 25 March 1983m Series A No 61, para 113.

[19] *Case of Caracazo v Venezuela (Reparation)*, Judgment of 29 August 2002, Series C No 95, para 115.

2. Independent Authority

The authority which reviews the remedy must be independent.[20] This means that the remedy must not be subject to interference by the authorities against which the complaint is brought.[21]

3. Accessibility, including Legal Assistance

A practical and effective remedy means that it must be simple and accessible. The Human Rights Committee has stressed that this requires that the special vulnerability of certain categories of persons be taken into account,[22] and that persons should obtain legal aid.[23] The Inter-American Court has stressed that the remedy must be simple and rapid.[24] The European Court of Human Rights and the African Commission on Human and Peoples' Rights consider that the remedy must be expeditious and that the person concerned must have access to legal representation and free legal aid if required.[25] Legal aid is also guaranteed in Article 47 of the Charter of Fundamental Rights of the European Union. There is thus a tendency towards recognition in international law, already consolidated in the European region, that an effective remedy implies a positive obligation of the state to assist those persons who do not have the means to access justice: this assistance can take the form of free legal aid (usually a monetary support to an

[20] In some international instruments, this is explicitly recognized, such as in Article 13 of the Declaration on the Protection of All Persons from Enforced Disappearance or Article 27 of the Vienna Declaration and Programme of Action.

[21] *General Comment No 31 on the Nature of the General Legal Obligation Imposed on States Parties to the Covenant*, 26 May 2004, CCPR/C/21/Rev.1/Add.13, para 15; ECtHR: Case *Keenan v the United Kingdom*, Judgment of 3 April 2001, Reports 2001-III, para 122; I/ACtHR: Advisory Opinion OC-9/87, *Judicial Guarantees in States of Emergency*, 6 October 1987, Series A No 9, para 24.

[22] *General Comment No 31 on the Nature of the General Legal Obligation Imposed on States Parties to the Covenant*, 26 May 2004, CCPR/C/21/Rev.1/Add.13, para 15; see also UN Commission on Human Rights Resolution on the Situation of human rights in parts of south-eastern Europe (E/CN.4/RES/2002/13), in which the Commission '*calls upon* the authorities of the region to consolidate the rule of law by providing effective judicial mechanisms which protect the rights and fundamental freedoms of all citizens, regardless of their ethnic origin.'

[23] *Concluding observations on Poland*, 2 December 2004, CCPR/CO/82/POL, para 14.

[24] Case *Castillo Páez v Peru*, Judgment of 3 November 1997, Series C No 34, para 82; Case *Mayagna (Sumo) Awas Tigni Community v Nicaragua*, Judgment of 31 August 2001, Series C No 79, para 112.

[25] Case *Airey v Ireland*, Judgment of 9 October 1979, Series A No. 32, para 33; *Principles and Guidelines on the Right to a Fair Trial and Legal Assistance in Africa*, Principle H.

access to justice and be represented in the justice system), or the guarantee of representation by a lawyer.

4. Leading to Cessation and Reparation

The Human Rights Committee has stressed that effective remedies include cessation, reparation, and the prevention of recurring violations.[26] The Inter-American Court, the African Commission on Human and Peoples' Rights, and the European Court of Human Rights have similarly held that an effective remedy must be capable of providing redress.[27]

The Committee on the Elimination of Discrimination against Women has considered that civil remedies and compensatory remedies are part of effective remedies.[28]

The Committee on the Elimination of Racial Discrimination has found that 'the victim's claim for compensation has to be considered in every case, including those cases where no bodily harm has been inflicted but where the victim has suffered humiliation, defamation or other attack against his/her reputation and self-esteem.'[29]

The European Court has considered that remedy must be able to lead to the quashing of the challenged decision.[30] In the case of punishment, the Court held that the remedy had to provide a possibility to quash the punishment even before it was executed.[31]

---

[26] *General Comment No 31 on the Nature of the General Legal Obligation Imposed on States Parties to the Covenant*, 26 May 2004, CCPR/C/21/Rev.1/Add.13, para 15.

[27] I/ACtHR: Advisory Opinion OC-9/87, *Judicial Guarantees in States of Emergency (Arts. 27.2, 25 and 8 American Convention on Human Rights)*, 6 October 1987, Series A No 9, para 24; ECtHR: Case *Silver v the United Kingdom*, Judgment of 25 March 1983m Series A No 61, para 113; AfrCmHPR: *Principles and Guidelines on the Right to a Fair Trial and Legal Assistance in Africa*, Principle C (a).

[28] *General Recommendation No 19 on Violence against Women*, 29 January 1992, A/47/38, para 24 (t).

[29] Case *B.J. v Denmark*, Views of 17 March 2000, CERD/C/57/D/17/1999, para 6.2.

[30] Case *Keenan v the United Kingdom*, Judgment of 3 April 2001, Reports 2001-III, para 126.

[31] *Ibid*, para 127.

5. Leading to an Investigation

International human rights bodies have considered that the right to an effective remedy encompasses the right to a prompt, thorough, independent and impartial effective investigation.[32] Indeed, effective justice, but also reparation, presupposes that the facts are thoroughly and exhaustively investigated. The right to a prompt, thorough, independent and impartial investigation is discussed in Chapter IV.

6. Nature of the Remedy – Judicial Remedy in Case of Gross Human Rights Violations

a) UN Treaty Bodies

The Human Rights Committee has held that the remedy could be assured by the judiciary, but also involve administrative mechanisms, particularly to investigate allegations of violations.[33] In its jurisprudence on individual cases, the Committee has frequently insisted on judicial remedies in cases of serious violations of the Covenant. In the case of *F. Birindwa ci Bithashwiwa and E. Tshisekedi wa Mulumba* it considered that the state had to provide the applicants with an effective remedy under Article 2 (3) of the Covenant, and 'in particular to ensure that they can effectively challenge these violations before a court of law.'[34] The cases against Colombia are ambiguous in this regard, as they do not deal with the remedy of access of the victims to a court to vindicate their rights, but a remedy including investigation and

[32] HRC: *General Comment No 31 on the Nature of the General Legal Obligation Imposed on States Parties to the Covenant,* 26 May 2004, CCPR/C/21/Rev.1/Add.13, para 15; CERD Committee: Case *L.K. v the Netherlands*, Views of 16 March 1993, CERD/C/42/D/4/1991, para 6.9; Case *Habassi v Denmark*, Views of 6 April 1999, CERD/C/54/D/10/1997, paras 9.3-10; I/ACtHR: Case *Blake v Guatemala*, Judgment of January 24, 1998, Series C No 36, para 97; *Villagrán Morales et al v Guatemala (The "Street Children" Case)*, Judgment of 19 November 1999, para 225; Case *Castillo Páez v Peru*, Judgment of 3 November 1997, Series C No 34, para 90; I/ACmHR: Case 10.247 *et al.*, *Extrajudicial Executions and Forced Disappearances of Persons* (Peru), Report of 11 October 2001, para 243; see also Report No. 62/01, Case 11.654, *Riofrío Massacre* (Colombia), 6 April 2001, para 74; ECtHR: Case *Aksoy v Turkey*, Judgment of 18 December 1996, Reports 1996-VII, paras 95-100. On the right to investigation see below Chapter IV.

[33] *General Comment No 31 on the Nature of the General Legal Obligation Imposed on States Parties to the Covenant,* 26 May 2004, CCPR/C/21/Rev.1/Add.13, para 15.

[34] Case *F. Birindwa ci Bithashwiwa and E. Tshisekedi wa Mulumba v Zaire*, Views of 29 November 1989, CCPR/C/37/D/241/1987, para 14.

sanction of those responsible for the violations. In these cases, the Committee held that mere disciplinary or administrative sanctions were not sufficient in case of serious violations and that the remedy under Article 2 (3) had to be judicial in nature.[35]

The Committee on the Elimination of Discrimination against Women held that effective protection included effective legal measures, including penal sanctions, civil remedies and compensatory remedies, preventive measures and protective measures.[36]

The Committee on Economic, Social and Cultural Rights has held that the right to an effective remedy may be of judicial or administrative nature; administrative remedies had to be 'accessible, affordable, timely and effective'; some remedies would require a judicial remedy and 'whenever a Covenant right cannot be made fully effective without some role of the judiciary, judicial remedies are necessary.'[37]

b) Regional Systems

In the Inter-American human rights system, the right to a judicial remedy is enshrined in Article XVIII of the American Declaration of the Rights and Duties of Man and Article 25 of the American Convention on Human Rights. In the light of these clear provisions, the Inter-American Court has held since its very first judgment that victims must have a right to judicial remedies, 'remedies that must be substantiated in accordance with the rules of due process of law (Art. 8 (1).'[38] Thus, it applies the fair trial requirements of Article 8 to the judicial remedy in Article 25.[39] As far as the re-

[35] Case *Nydia Erika Bautista v. Colombia*, Views of 13 November 1993, CCPR/C/55/D/563/1993, para 8.2; Case *José Vicente y Amado Villafañe Chaparro et al v Colombia*, Views of 29 July 1997, CCPR/C/60/D/612/1995, para 8.2.

[36] *General Recommendation No 19 on Violence against Women*, 29 January 1992, A/47/38, para 24 (t).

[37] *General Comment No 9 on the domestic application of the Covenant*, 3 December 1998, E/C.12/1998/24, para 9.

[38] Case *Velásquez Rodríguez v Honduras*, Preliminary Objections, Judgment of 26 June 26 1987, Series C No 1, para 91; Advisory Opinion OC-9/87, *Judicial Guarantees in States of Emergency (Arts. 27.2, 25 and 8 American Convention on Human Rights)*, 6 October 1987, Series A No 9, para 24.

[39] Case *Bámaca Velásquez v Guatemala*, Judgment of 25 November 2000, Series C No 79, paras 184-196; Case *Juan Humberto Sánchez v Honduras*, Judgment of 7 June 2003, Series C No 99, paras 114-136; Case *Myrna Mack Chang v Guatemala*, Judgment of 25 November 2003, Series C No 101, paras 159-218; Case *Maritza Urrutia v Guatemala*, Judgment of 27 November 2003, Series C No 103, para 111.

quirements for the remedy are concerned, the Inter-American Court has considered that a remedy is ineffective 'when the Judicial Power lacks the necessary independence to render impartial decisions or the means to carry out its judgments; or in any other situation that constitutes a denial of justice, as when there is an unjustified delay in the decision; or when, for any reason, the alleged victim is denied access to a judicial remedy.'[40]

The African Commission on Human and Peoples' Rights has interpreted the right to an effective remedy in its Principles and Guidelines on the Rights to a Fair Trial and Legal Assistance in Africa. It considers that '[e]veryone has the right to an effective remedy by *competent national tribunals* for acts violating the rights granted by the constitution, by law or by the Charter, notwithstanding that the acts were committed by persons in an official capacity.'[41] Thus, the African Commission considers that an effective remedy means a judicial remedy.

The European Court has held that the right to a remedy in Article 13 did not require in all instances a judicial remedy.[42] It considers however, that the scope of the remedy varies with the nature of the right.[43] It can be concluded that where gross violations such as torture or executions are committed, the remedy should be of judicial nature. Article 13 also requires that orders of the court must be implemented by the authorities.[44] It can be seen from this case law that the remedy demanded by the Court comes close to a judicial remedy. Beyond this, it should be noted that the Court considers that Article 6 ECHR does not only grant individuals a right to a fair trial, but also a right of *access to court* 'in the determination of his civil rights and obligations

40 Advisory Opinion OC-9/87, *Judicial Guarantees in States of Emergency*, 6 October 1987, Series A No 9, para 24.

41 *Principles and Guidelines on the Right to a Fair Trial and Legal Assistance in Africa*, Principle C (a), emphasis added; see also the case of *The Social and Economic Rights Action Center and the Center for Economic and Social Rights v Nigeria*, Communication 155/96 (30th Ordinary Session, Oct 2001), para 61, in which the Commission considered that the State had to ensure 'legal remedies'.

42 Case *Silver v the United Kingdom*, Judgment of 25 March 1983, Series A No 61, para 113.

43 Case *Chahal v the United Kingdom*, Judgment of 15 November 1996, Reports 1996-V, paras 150-51; Case *Aksoy v Turkey*, Judgment of 18 December 1996, Reports 1996-VI, para 95; Case *Aydin v Turkey*, Judgment of 25 September 1997, Reports 1997-VI, para 103; Case *Kaya v Turkey*, Judgment of 19 February 1998, Reports 1998-I, para 106; Case *Keenan v the United Kingdom*, Judgment of 3 April 2001, Reports 2001-III, para 123.

44 Case *Iatridis v Greece*, Judgment of 15 March 1999, Reports 1999-II, para 66.

or of any criminal charge against him.'[45] This means that if there exists a remedy under national law in form of a civil right, then Article 6 applies.

Within the realm of the European Union, Article 47 of the Charter of Fundamental Rights of the European Union makes clear that the right to a judicial remedy forms part of the general principles of European law. It crystallizes the practice found in primary[46] and secondary EU legislation[47] as well as the jurisprudence of the Court of Justice of the European Communities (ECJ).[48] The Court's qualification of the principle of access to court as a general principle of Community Law is significant, since it then constitutes a binding source of law, comparable to the 'general principles of law recognized by civilised nations' in Article 38 (1) (c) of the Statute of the International Court of Justice. This acceptance of the right to a judicial remedy has lead to the formulation of Article 47 of the Charter of Fundamental Rights of the European Union, which reads:

> 'Everyone whose rights and freedoms guaranteed by the law of the Union are violated has the right to an effective remedy before a tribunal in compliance with the conditions laid down in this Article.'

---

[45] Case *Golder v the United Kingdom*, Judgment of 21 February 1975, Series A No. 18, para 36 [right to a court for civil rights and obligations]; Case *Holy Monasteries v Greece*, Judgment of 9 December 1994, Series A no. 301-A, pp. 36-37, para 80 [right to a court for interference with property right]; Case *Tomasi v France*, Judgment of 27 August 1992, Series A No. 241-A, paras 121-22 [right to a court under Art. 6 (1) ECHR to claim compensation for ill-treatment by agents of the state].

[46] See Article 230 of the EC Treaty.

[47] Article 2 of Council Directive 75/117/EEC of 10 February 1975 *on the approximation of the laws of the Member States relating to the application of the principle of equal pay for men and women*; Article 6 of Council Directive 76/207/EEC of 9 February 1976 *on the implementation of the principle of equal treatment for men and women as regards access to employment, vocational training and promotion, and working conditions*; Article 6 of Council Directive 79/7/EEC of 19 December 1978 *on the progressive implementation of the principle of equal treatment for men and women in matters of social security*; Article 10 of Council Directive 86/378/EEC of 24 July 1986 *on the implementation of the principle of equal treatment for men and women in occupational social security schemes*; Article 9 of Council Directive 86/613/EEC of 11 December 1986 *on the application of the principle of equal treatment between men and women engaged in an activity, including agriculture, in a self-employed capacity, and on the protection of self-employed women during pregnancy and motherhood*.

[48] *Johnston v Chief Constable of the Royal Ulster Constabulary*, Case 222/84, Judgment of 15 May 1986, European Court Reports 1986, p 01651, para 18; *Union nationale des entraîneurs et cadres techniques professionnels du football (Unectef) v Georges Heylens and others*, Case 222/86, Judgment of the Court of 15 October 1987, European Court Reports 1987, p 04097, para 14 (citation omitted); *Oleificio Borelli SpA v Commission of the European Communities*, Case C-97/91, Judgment of the Court (Fifth Chamber) of 3 December 1992, European Court Reports 1992, p I-06313, para 14.

While the Charter is not, as yet, binding for Member States, it 'reaffirms [...] the rights as they result, in particular, from the constitutional traditions and international obligations common to the Member States [....].'

c) International Court of Justice

Lastly, the jurisprudence of the International Court of Justice should be mentioned, as it has an impact on the right to a judicial remedy. Relevant decisions in this respect are the *LaGrand Case* and the *Avena and other Mexican Nationals Case*. In these judgments, the International Court of Justice found that the United States had violated the right to consular protection of foreign nationals who later faced capital punishment. The International Court of Justice emphasised that in such cases an apology was not sufficient, but that the state had to review and reconsider both the sentence and the conviction.[49] The review and reconsideration had to take into account the violations, which included 'the question of the legal consequences of the violation upon the criminal proceedings that have followed the violation.'[50] The Court held that 'it is the judicial process that is suited to this task.'[51] It held that clemency proceedings did not meet these requirements as they did not fully examine and take into account the violation.[52] Thus, although the ICJ did not examine a case of human rights violations, it follows from its judgment that in cases of violations of international law leading to unlawful criminal proceedings, both the sentence and the conviction must be subject to judicial review and reconsideration. A *fortiori* it follows that in cases of gross human rights violations with similarly severe consequences, the individual must have a right to have the consequences of such violations reviewed in a judicial procedure.

The nature of the remedy varies depending on the right that is at stake. From the mentioned treaties and jurisprudence it follows clearly the in case of gross human rights violations, states have an obligation to guarantee a remedy of a judicial nature.

---

[49] Case *Avena and other Mexican Nationals (Mexico v. United States of America)*, Judgment of 31 March 2004, paras 131, 138; this judgment clarifies the previous judgment in the *LaGrand Case (Germany v the United States)*, Judgment of 27 June 2001, I.C.J. Reports 2001, p 514, para 125.

[50] *Ibid*, para 131.

[51] *Ibid*, para 140.

[52] *Ibid*, paras 138, 143.

7. Compliance and Enforcement by the Authorities

Finally, it should be stressed that an effective remedy requires its enforceability against other public authorities. If the judicial power lacks the means to carry out its judgments, the remedy cannot be considered to be effective.[53] The African Commission on Human and Peoples' Rights considers that 'any remedy granted shall be enforced by competent authorities', and that 'any state body against which a judicial order or other remedy has been granted shall comply fully with such an order or remedy.'[54] The European Court of Human Rights has also required that judgments must be enforceable.[55]

***

II. Right to a Remedy to Claim Reparation

A sub-category of remedies guaranteed in international law is the right to a remedy to claim compensation. To ensure fair and adequate reparation, this remedy is essential: not only does international human rights law provide a right to substantive (monetary) compensation, it also puts a duty on states to provide in their internal law the procedural remedy to obtain it. This is the case for compensation for unlawful detention. Indeed, Article 9 (5) ICCPR provides that 'anyone who has been the victim of unlawful arrest or detention shall have an *enforceable* right to compensation.'[56] The Committee on the Elimination of Racial Discrimination held in the case of *B.J. v Denmark* that the right to an effective remedy against racial discrimination (Article 6) entails an obligation of states to afford a remedy in which a claim for compensation has to be considered.[57] In the same vein, the right to a remedy to claim compensation in the European Convention on Human Rights is not only enshrined in Article 5 (5) ECHR for unlawful detention, but also in Article 13 which guarantees the right to an effective remedy.[58] The Court

---

[53] I/ACtHR, Advisory Opinion OC-9/87, *Habeas Corpus in Emergency Situations*, 6 October 1987, Serie A No 9, para 24.

[54] *Principles and Guidelines on the Right to a Fair Trial and Legal Assistance in Africa*, Principle C.

[55] Case *Hornsby v Greece*, Judgment of 19 March 1997, Reports 1997-II, para 40.

[56] Emphasis added; the same formulation is found in Article 5 (5) ECHR, Article 85 (1) Rome Statute of the International Criminal Court.

[57] Case *B.J. v Denmark*, Views of 10 May 2000, CERD/C/56/D/17/1999, para 6.2.

[58] Case *Aksoy v Turkey*, Judgment of 18 December 1996, Reports 1996-VI, para 98.

also made clear that where there exists a remedy in national law to claim compensation, this remedy constitutes a civil right in the sense of Article 6 ECHR so that the procedure must comply with the exigencies of a fair trial as set out in this provision.[59]

***

Summary

International law prescribes that states must provide an effective remedy for everyone who alleges a violation of his or her human rights. The remedy must be made known, so that all persons can avail themselves of it, without discrimination. In order to be effective, the authority competent to investigate and decide on the case must be independent and impartial. In the realm of the American Convention on Human Rights and the Charter of Fundamental Rights of the European Union, the remedy guaranteed is an explicitly judicial remedy, which corresponds to Article 8 of the Universal Declaration of Human Rights. The African Commission on Human and Peoples' Rights has also clearly stated that individuals must have access to tribunals for alleged human rights violations. As far as United Nations treaties and the European Convention on Human Rights are concerned, the remedy need not necessarily consist of access to courts. However, the Human Rights Committee and the European Court of Human Rights agree in demanding that the remedy should be commensurate to the alleged violation. In this sense, the Human Rights Committee has required judicial remedies for gross human rights violations. The European Court of Human Rights has in practice developed requirements which correspond to a judicial remedy.

In all cases, the remedy must be **practical** and **effective** and not illusory:

- It must be effective, prompt and accessible.
- It must be a remedy before an independent authority.
- The victim should have access to legal counsel and if necessary to free legal assistance.
- The remedy must be capable of leading to relief, including reparation and compensation.

59 Case *Tomasi v France*, Judgment of 27 August 1992, Series A No. 241-A, paras 121-22.

- The right to a prompt, effective and impartial investigation is part of the right to a remedy.
- The remedy must be expeditious and enforceable by the competent authorities.
- The remedy must be judicial in case of gross human rights violations.

CHAPTER IV
THE RIGHT TO AN INVESTIGATION

The right to a remedy cannot be effectively guaranteed when state authorities do not investigate human rights violations seriously, deliberately skew investigations or conceal the facts. Investigation, the right to have active part in the investigation, and the right to know the truth about all the facts surrounding a human rights violation are critical elements of the right to a remedy. This has been recognized by international practice and jurisprudence and criteria have been developed to assess the effectiveness of an investigation.

More specific principles have been developed within the UN system clarifying standards on investigations of torture, ill-treatment and killings. These in turn provide guidelines for international bodies in their interpretation. In the following, the criteria, which recur in the practice and case law of different international organs, will be described, as they constitute a fundamental basis to achieve not only investigations, but also truth and eventually the prosecution and punishment of those responsible.

***

It should be noted that it is frequently not clear who committed the violation, which is one of the reasons to conduct an investigation. It can be committed by *de jure* or *de facto* state agents, with the authorization, acquiescence or complicity of the state, or arise from acts of private parties. Frequently, public authorities deny their involvement. International jurisprudence, however, has found that the right to an investigation applies also in cases of killings or other acts which affect the enjoyment of human rights that are not imputable to the state. The obligation to investigate in these cases arises from the duty of the state to protect all individuals under its jurisdiction from acts committed by private persons which may impede the enjoyment of their human rights.[1]

I. Legal Sources of the Right to an Investigation

The right to a prompt, thorough, independent and impartial investigation can be found in many international legal instruments and has been further developed in international jurisprudence.

1. International Treaties and Declaratory Instruments

The most frequent explicit references to the right to a prompt, effective, independent and impartial investigation arise in treaties and instruments concerning the prohibition of torture and ill-treatment, such as in Article 12 CAT, which reads: 'Each State Party shall ensure that its competent authorities proceed to a prompt and impartial investigation, wherever there is reasonable ground to believe that an act of torture has been committed in any territory under its jurisdiction.'[2] The duty to investigate torture has been developed and its modalities and requirements set out in the UN Principles on Investigation of Torture, recommended by the General Assembly in December 2000.[3]

---

[1] Human Rights Committee: *General Comment No 31 on the Nature of the General Legal Obligation Imposed on States Parties to the Covenant*, 26 May 2004, CCPR/C/21/Rev.1/Add.13, para 8; I/ACtHR: Case *Velásquez Rodríguez v Honduras*, Judgment of 29 July 1988, Series C No 4, para 172; I/ACmHR: Case *Pedro Peredo Valderrama* (Mexico), Report of 13 April 2000, paras 41 *et seq*; Report No. 54/01, Case 12.051, *Maria Da Penha Maia Fernandes* (Brazil), 16 April 2001, paras 37 *et seq*; *Report on the Situation of the Rights of Women in Ciudad Juárez, Mexico: The Right to be Free from Violence and Discrimination*, OEA/Ser.L/V/II.117 Doc. 44, 7 March 2003, paras 131 *et seq*; ECtHR: Case *Ergi v Turkey*, Judgment of 28 July 1998, Reports 1998-IV, para 82; see also Case *Tanrikulu v Turkey*, Judgment of 8 July 1999, Reports 1999-IV, para 103; Case *Demiray v Turkey*, Judgment of 21 November 2000, Reports 2000-XII, para 50.

[2] See also Article 9 of the Declaration on the Protection of All Persons from Being Subjected to Torture and Other Cruel, Inhuman or Degrading Treatment or Punishment; Article 8 of the Inter-American Convention to Prevent and Punish Torture.

[3] A/RES/55/89 of 4 December 2000.

The right to an investigation also explicitly appears in instruments concerning enforced disappearances. In particular, Article 13 of the Declaration on the Protection of All Persons from Enforced Disappearance stipulates that '[e]ach State shall ensure that any person having knowledge of or legitimate interest who alleges that a person has been subjected to enforced disappearance has the right to complain to a competent and independent state authority and to have that complaint promptly, thoroughly and impartially investigated by that authority.' Equally Art. 62 of the Vienna Declaration and Programme of Action of 1993 affirms 'that there is a duty of all States, under any circumstances, to make investigations whenever there is reason to believe that an enforced disappearance has taken place on a territory under their jurisdiction [...].'

The duty to investigate also exists with regard to violations of the right to life and of the right to liberty and security of the person. Principle 9 of the UN Principles on Extra-legal Executions postulates that '[t]here shall be thorough, prompt and impartial investigation of all suspected cases of extra-legal, arbitrary and summary executions [...].'[4]

Other United Nations declaratory instruments make clear that the duty to investigate is not necessarily linked to a specific cause or violation, but applies to all violations. For example, Article 9 (5) of the Declaration on Human Rights Defenders states that '[t]he State shall conduct a prompt and impartial investigation or ensure that an inquiry takes place whenever there is reasonable ground to believe that a violation of human rights and fundamental freedoms has occurred in any territory under its jurisdiction.'

2. Practice and Jurisprudence

Although not all human rights instruments have explicit references to the obligation to investigate violations, it is clear from the unanimous interpretation of all human rights bodies that there is a right to a prompt, effective, impartial and independent investigation for all human rights violations, in the same manner as there is a right to an effective remedy for all violations of human rights. It is obvious, moreover, that a thorough investigation is the

[4] See also Principles 7 and 34 of the Body of Principles for the Protection of All Persons under Any Form of Detention or Imprisonment; Principle 57 of the United Nations Rules for the Protection of Juveniles Deprived of their Liberty; Principle 23 of the UN Basic Principles on the use of force and firearms by Law Enforcement Officials.

first component of an effective remedy, because, as explained above, an effective remedy implies a thorough investigation of the facts. This has been stressed by the Special Rapporteur of the Sub-Commission on the question of impunity, who describes the obligation of states to investigate as part of the right to a fair and effective remedy.[5]

a) UN Commission on Human Rights and Special Procedures of the Commission

The United Nations Commission on Human Rights has repeatedly affirmed the duty of states to conduct effective, thorough and impartial investigations into allegations of gross human rights violations, particularly extra-judicial, arbitrary or summary executions, disappearances and torture.[6] Similar recommendations are made by the Special procedures of the Commission, such as the Special Rapporteur on torture,[7] the Special Rapporteur on violence against women,[8] the Special Rapporteur on the independence of judges and lawyers,[9] the Special Rapporteur on extrajudicial, summary and arbitrary executions,[10] and the Working Group on Enforced or Involuntary Disappearances.[11]

---

5 *Report of the Special Rapporteur on the question of impunity of perpetrators of human rights violations (civil and political)*, E/CN.4/Sub.2/1997/20/Rev1, para 27.

6 See the Resolutions E/CN.4/2003/72, 25 April 2003, para 8; E/CN.4/RES/2003/32 (torture), 23 April 2003, para 8; E/CN.4/RES/2003/53 (extrajudicial, summary and arbitrary executions), 24 April 2003, paras 4, 5; E/CN.4/RES/2003/72 (impunity), 25 April 2003, para 8.; E/CN.4/RES/2003/38 (enforced or involuntary disappearances), 23 April 2003, para 5 (c) restating former resolutions with the same requirements.

7 *Report of the Special Rapporteur on torture*, 17 December 2002, E/CN.4/2003/68, recommendation (k).

8 *Report of the Special Rapporteur on violence against women on cultural practices in the family that are violent towards women*, E/CN.4/2002/83, 31 January 2002, para 124.

9 *Report of the Special Rapporteur on the independence of judges and lawyers on its mission to Guatemala*, 21 December 2001, E/CN.4/2002/72/Add.2, recommendation a); *Report of the Special Rapporteur on the independence of judges and lawyers on the mission to Peru*, 19 February 1998, E/CN.4/1998/39/Add.1, para 131; *Report of the Special Rapporteur on the independence of judges and lawyers on the mission to Mexico*, 24 January 2000, E/CN.4/2002/72/Add.1, recommendations b), j), k), p).

10 *Report of the Special Rapporteur on Extrajudicial, summary and arbitrary executions*, 24 December 1996, E/CN.4/1997/60, para 46; *Report of the Special Rapporteur on extrajudicial, summary and arbitrary executions on the mission to Brazil*, 28 January 2004, E/CN.4/2004/7/Add.3, paras 55-64.

11 See, *inter alia*, Report of the Working Group on Enforced and Involuntary Disappearances, 21 January 2003, E/CN.4/2003/70 and Corr.1, para 27.

b) UN Treaty Bodies

In 1982, the Human Rights Committee, in its *General Comment No 6 on Article 6 ICCPR*, held that 'States should establish effective facilities and procedures to investigate thoroughly cases of missing and disappeared persons in circumstances which may involve a violation of the right to life.'[12] A year later, it held in the case of *Almeida de Quinteros* that the state must 'establish what has happened' to a person who disappeared and secure her release.[13] It later subsumed this obligation under the right to an effective remedy, guaranteed in Article 2 (3) of the Covenant.[14] Similarly it has established a duty to investigate allegations of torture and ill-treatment,[15] and stated that "[c]omplaints must be investigated promptly and impartially by competent authorities so as to make the remedy effective".[16] Allegations of excessive use of force by the police must also be investigated.[17] The Human Rights Committee regularly recalls the duty of states to investigate human rights violations in its concluding observations on state reports.[18]

---

12 *General Comment No 6 on Article 6*, 30 April 1982, HRI/GEN/1/Rev7, para 4.

13 Case *Almeida de Quinteros et al v Uruguay*, Views of 21 July 1983, CCPR/C/19/D/107/1981, para 138.

14 See, amongst others, the cases *Nydia Erika Bautista v Colombia*, Views of 13 November 1995, CCPR/C/55/D/563/1993, para 8.6; *Celis Laureano v Peru*, Views of 16 April 1996, CCPR/C/56/D/540/1993, para 10; *Sarma v Sri Lanka*, Views of 31 July 2003, CCPR/C/78/D/950/2000, para 11.

15 Case *Hugo Rodríguez v Uruguay*, Views of 19 July 1994, CCPR/C/51/D/322/1988, para 12(3). See also Case *José Vicente and Amado Villafañe Chaparro et al v Colombia*, Views of 29 July 1997, CCPR/C/60/D/612/1995, para 8.8; Case *Blanco v Nicaragua*, Views of 18 August 1994, CCPR/C/51/D/328/1988, para 11.

16 *General Comment No 20 on Article 7*, 13 March 1992, HRI/GEN/1/Rev7, para 14.

17 *Concluding Observations on Peru*, 25 July 1995, CCPR/C/79/Add.67, para 22; *Concluding Observations on Ukraine*, 12 November 2001, CCPR/CO/73/UKR, para 13.

18 *Concluding Observations on Colombia*, 25 March 2004, CCPR/CO/80/COL, paras 10, 15; *Concluding Observations on Germany*, CCPR/CO/80/GER, 30 March 2004, para 15, 16; *Concluding Observations on Lithuania*, CCPR/CO/80/LTU, 1 April 2004, para 10; *Concluding Observations on Suriname*, 30 March 2004, para 11; *Concluding Observations on Kuwait*, 27 July 2000, CCPR/CO/KWT, para 13; *Concluding Observations on Sri Lanka*, 23 July 1995, CCPR/C/79/Add.56, para 30; *Concluding Observations on Yemen*, 3 October 1995, A/50/40, section N° 5; *Concluding Observations on Guyana*, 25 April 2000, CCPR/C/79/Add.121, para 10; *Concluding Observations on Algeria*, 18 August 1998, CCPR/C/79/Add.95, paras 6, 7 and 9; *Concluding Observations on Peru*, 25 July 1995, CCPR/C/79/Add.67, para 22 [investigate excessive use of force]; *Concluding Observations on Mexico*, 27 July 1999, CCPR/C/79/Add.109, paras 6, 9, 16; *Concluding Observations on Argentina*, 3 November 2000, CCPR/CO/70/ARG, para 9, 13; *Concluding Observations on Guatemala*, 27 August 2001, CCPR/CO/72/GTM, para 12; *Concluding Observations on Hungary*, 19 April 2002, CCPR/CO/74/HUN, para 12; *Concluding Observations on Ukraine*, 12 November 2001, CCPR/CO/73/UKR, para 13.

The Committee against Torture also considers that all allegations of torture must be promptly and impartially investigated in accordance with Article 12 CAT.[19]

The Committee on the Elimination of Racial Discrimination has held that states have a duty to promptly, effectively and impartially investigate acts of racial discrimination.[20] It stressed the importance of the role of the police in the case of *M.B. v Denmark*, in which it stated that it 'wishes to emphasize the importance it attaches to the duty of the state party and, for that matter, of all states parties, to remain vigilant, in particular by prompt and effective police investigations of complaints, that the right established under article 5, paragraph f, is enjoyed without discrimination by all persons, national or foreigners, under the jurisdiction of the state party.'[21]

c) Inter-American Commission and Court of Human Rights

The Inter-American Court first held in its Judgment in the Case of *Velásquez Rodríguez* that '[t]he State has a legal duty to take reasonable steps to prevent human rights violations and to use the means at its disposal to carry out a serious investigation of violations committed within its jurisdiction'[22] and has upheld this in its case-law.[23] A lack of investigation or an

[19] *Conclusions and recommendations on Saudi Arabia*, 28 May 2002, CAT/C/CR/28/5, para 8 f); *Indonesia*, 22 November 2001, CAT/C/XXVII/Concl.3, (Indonesia); para 10 f); *Conclusions and recommendations on Brazil*, 16 May 2001, A/56/44, paras 115-120, para 120 b); *Conclusions and recommendations on USA*, 15 May 2000, A/55/44, paras 175-180, para 180 b); *Conclusions and recommendations on Turkey*, 27 May 2003, CAT/C/CR/30/5, para 7 (b); *Conclusions and recommendations on Slovenia*, 27 May 2003, CAT/C/CR/30/4, para 6 (c); *Conclusions and recommendations on Cambodia*, 27 May 2003, CAT/C/CR/30/2, para 7 (c), (d); Case *Encarnación Blanco Abad v Spain*, Views of 14 May 1998, CAT/C/20/D/59/1996, para 8.6; Case *Ristic v Yugoslavia*, Views of 11 May 2001, Communication N° 113/1998, para 9.9; Case *Hajrizi Dzemajl et al. v Yugoslavia*, Views of 2 December 2002, CAT/C/29/D/161/2000, paras 9.4, 11.

[20] CERD Committee: Case *L.K. v the Netherlands*, Views of 16 March 1993, CERD/C/42/D/4/1991, para 6.9; *Habassi v Denmark*, 6 April 1999, CERD/C/54/D/10/1997, para 9.3-10 [investigation as part of the remedy pursuant to Art. 6]; Case *Kashif Ahmad v Denmark*, Views of 8 May 2000, CERD/C/56/D/16/1999, para 6.4.

[21] Case *M.B. v Denmark*, Views of 15 March 2002, CERD/C/60/D/20/2000, para 10.

[22] Case *Velásquez Rodríguez v Honduras*, Judgment of July 29, 1988, Series C No. 4, para 174.

[23] Case *Neira Alegría et al v Peru*, Judgment of 19 January 1995, Series C No. 20, para 69 and operative paragraph 4; Case *Caballero Delgado and Santana v Colombia*, Judgment of 8 December 1995, Series C No 22, paras 58 and 59; Case *El Amparo v Venezuela (Reparations)*, Judgment of September 14, 1996. Series C No. 28, para 61, and operative paragraph 4.

ineffective investigation constitute violations of the right to judicial protection under Article 25 and to a fair trial under Article 8, both in conjunction with Article 1(1) of the Convention.[24] The Court made clear that the duty to investigate and punish are part of the obligations of the state to counter impunity,[25] understanding impunity as 'the total lack of investigation, prosecution, capture, trial and conviction of those responsible for violations of the rights protected by the American Convention, in view of the fact that the state has the obligation to use all the legal means at its disposal to combat that situation, since impunity fosters chronic recidivism of human rights violations, and total defenselessness of victims and their relatives.'[26] In almost all of its cases, the Inter-American Court of Human Rights has found a violation of the Convention for lack of investigation.[27]

The Inter-American Commission has similarly held that the state has a duty to investigate human rights violations. Like the Inter-American Court, the Commission sees the obligation to investigate as a way of combating impunity. The obligation to investigate - and correlatively to combat impunity - flows from Articles 25, 8 and 1(1) of the American Convention.[28]

d) European Court of Human Rights

In the case of *McCann v the United Kingdom*, the European Court of Human Rights held that whenever there was an allegation of unlawful killing by state agents, there had to be an investigation into the facts, because investi-

[24] Case *Blake v Guatemala*, Judgment of January 24, 1998, Series C No 36, para 97; *Villagrán Morales et al v Guatemala (The "Street Children" Case)*, Judgment of 19 November 1999, para 225; Case *Castillo Páez v Peru*, Judgment of 3 November 1997, Series C No 34, para 90; Case *Durand and Ugarte v Peru*, Judgment of 16 August 2000, Series C No 68, para 130; Case *Bámaca Velásquez v Guatemala*, Judgment of 25 November 2000, Series C No 70, para 197; *Case of Las Palmeras v Colombia*, Judgment of 6 December 2001, Series C No 90, para 65; *Juan Humberto Sánchez Case*, Judgment of 7 June 2003, Series C No 99, para 121-136.

[25] Case *Bulacio v Argentina*, Judgment of 18 September 2003, Series C No 100, para 110-120; Case *Myrna Mack Chang v Guatemala*, Judgment of 25 November 2003, Series C No 101, para 272-277.

[26] Case of *"Panel Blanca" (Paniagua Morales et al) v Guatemala*, Judgment of 8 March 1998, Series C No 37, para 173.

[27] Case *Blake v Guatemala*, Judgment of 24 January 1998, Series C No 36, para 97;

[28] Case 10.247 *et al.*, *Extrajudicial Executions and Forced Disappearances of Persons* (Peru), 11 October 2001, para 243; see also Report No. 62/01, Case 11.654, *Riofrío Massacre* (Colombia), 6 April 2001, para 74.

gations were a procedural obligation of states under the right to life.[29] It later found that the right to an effective remedy of the victim or relatives could be violated if there was no effective investigation.[30] It has also held that whenever there are allegations of torture or ill-treatment, the right to be free from torture or ill-treatment requires that the allegations should be investigated.[31]

e) African Commission on Human and Peoples' Rights

In a disappearance case, the African Commission on Human and Peoples' Rights has ordered the state to 'arrange for the commencement of an independent enquiry in order to clarify the fate of the persons considered as disappeared, identify and bring to book the authors of the violations perpetrated at the time of the facts arraigned.'[32] In another case, it ordered that the perpetrators of human rights violations should be identified and taken to court.[33] The case concerning oil exploitation in Ogoniland in Northern Nigeria is of particular interest, because it concerns the obligation to investigate violations of economic, social and cultural rights, including group rights. The African Commission found that the state had violated the rights of local communities by granting concessions to foreign oil companies. The Commission, after having found multiple violations of the rights of the Ogoni people, appealed to the government to ensure the protection of the environment, health, and livelihood of the victims by '[...] permitting independent investigators free access to the territory; conducting an investigation into the human rights violations [...] and prosecuting officials of the security forces [...] and relevant agencies involved in the human rights violations; [...] ensuring that appropriate environmental and social impact assessments are prepared for any future oil development and that the safe operation of any further oil development is guaranteed through effective and independent oversight bodies for the petroleum industry [...].'[34]

[29] Case *McCann v the United Kingdom*, Judgment of 27 September 1995, Series A No 324, para 161.

[30] Case *Aksoy v Turkey*, Judgment of 18 December 1996, Reports 1996-VII, paras 95-100.

[31] Case *Assenov v Bulgaria*, Judgment of 28 October 1998, Reports 1998-VIII, para 102.

[32] Case *Malawi African Association et al. v Mauritania*, Communications 54/91 *et al.* (27th Ordinary Session, May 2000), recommendations, lit. 1.

[33] *Mouvement Burkinabé des Droits de l'Homme et des Peuples v Burkina Faso*, Communication 204/97 (29th Ordinary Session, May 2001), recommendations, lit 1.

[34] Case *The Social and Economic Rights Action Center and the Center for Economic and Social Rights v Nigeria*, Communication 155/96 (30th Ordinary Session, Oct 2001), recommendations lit. 1, 2, 4.

Thus, it may be said that the African Commission recognizes the duty to investigate both violations of civil and political as well as economic, social and cultural rights as an obligation under the African Charter.

***

II. Requirements of the Investigation

The duty to investigate is a duty of conduct and not a duty of result.[35] This means that it is not necessarily violated if it does not lead to the complete elucidation of the facts and legal consequences surrounding a violation, as long as the authorities carry out the investigation according to international standards. International jurisprudence has established a number of requirements which the inquiry has to comply with.

Increasingly, criteria are being developed by the United Nations and in the regional systems to achieve a meaningful investigation. The modalities of the investigation have been developed in particular in the UN Principles on Extra-legal Executions and the UN Principles on the Investigation of Torture (the so called Istanbul Protocol). The UN Principles on Extra-legal Executions are supplemented by the *United Nations Manual on the Effective Prevention and Investigation of Extra-legal, Arbitrary or Summary Executions*, which further specifies the duties of states.[36] It has, for example, been used by the Inter-American Commission on Human Rights to set its standards for investigations.[37]

1. Prompt, Impartial, Thorough and Independent Official Investigation

It is important to mention the cornerstones of the right to an investigation, which are its promptness,[38] thoroughness,[39] independence[40] and impartial-

[35] I/ActHR, Case *Velásquez Rodríguez v Honduras*, Judgment of 29 July 1988, Series C No. 4, para 166; see also para 174; EctHR, Case *Finucane v the United Kingdom*, Judgment of 1 July 2003, para 69.

[36] E/ST/CSDHA/12 (1991).

[37] Report No. 136/99, Case 10.488, *Ignacio Ellacuría S.J. et al* (El Salvador), 22 December 1999, para 175.

[38] UN Principles on the Investigation of Torture, Principle 2; Article 12 CAT; Principle 9 of the UN Principles on Extra-legal Executions; Human Rights Committee: *General Comment No 31 on Article 2 of the Covenant: The Nature of the General Legal Obligation Imposed on States Parties to the Covenant*, 21 April 2004, CCPR/C/74/CRP.4/Rev.6, para 15; Committee against Torture: *Conclusions and recom-*

ity.[41] The investigation must be carried out *ex officio*, i.e. without the victims or their relatives having to launch a complaint.[42]

a) Independence

An independent inquiry requires that it be carried out by an independent authority, i.e. an authority not involved in the alleged violations. Thus, the

---

mendations on Colombia, 4 February 2004, CAT/C/CR/31/1, para 9 (a); see also *Conclusions and recommendations on Yemen*, 5 February 2004, CAT/C/CR/31/4, para 6 (e); *Conclusions and recommendations on Morocco*, 5 February 2004, CAT/C/CR/31/2, para 6 (f); *Conclusions and recommendations on Cambodia*, 27 May 2003, CAT/C/CR/30/2, para 7 (c); I/ACtHR: Case *Tibi v Ecuador*, Judgment of 7 September 2004, Series C No 114 para 159; ECtHR: Case *Finucane v the United Kingdom*, Judgment of 1 July 2003, para 70; Case *Yasa v Turkey*, Judgment of 2 September 1998, Reports 1998-VI, para 102-04; Case *Çakici v Turkey* [GC], Judgment of 8 July 1999, Reports 1999-IV, para 80, 87 and 106; Case *Tanrikulu v Turkey*, Judgment of 8 July 1999, Reports 1999-IV, para 109; Case *Mahmut Kaya v Turkey*, Judgment of 28 March 2000, Reports 2000-III, para 106-07.

39 ECtHR: Case *Kaya v Turkey*, Judgment of 19 February 1998, Reports 1998-I, para 107; Human Rights Committee: *General Comment No 31 on Article 2 of the Covenant*, Doc. Cit., para 15; Case *José Vicente and Amado Villafañe Chaparro et al v Colombia*, 19 August 1997, CCPR/C/60/D/612/1995, para 8.8; UN Principles on Extra-legal Executions, Principle 9; CAT Committee: *Conclusions and recommendations on Colombia*, 4 February 2004, CAT/C/CR/31/1, para 9 (a); see also *Conclusions and recommendations on Yemen*, 5 February 2004, CAT/C/CR/31/4, para 6 (e); *Conclusions and recommendations on Morocco*, 5 February 2004, CAT/C/CR/31/2, para 6 (f); *Conclusions and recommendations on Cambodia*, 27 May 2003, CAT/C/CR/30/2, para 7 (c); UN Principles on the Investigation of Torture, Principle 2.

40 Committee against Torture: *Conclusions and recommendations on Egypt*, 23 December 2002, CAT/C/CR/29/4, para 6 (c); *Conclusions and recommendations on Cambodia*, 27 May 2003, CAT/C/CR/30/2, para 7 (d); Human Rights Committee: *General Comment No 31 on Article 2 of the Covenant*, Doc.cit, para 15; ECtHR, Case *Finucane v the United Kingdom*, Judgment of 1 July 2003, para 69; Case *Hugh Jordan v the United Kingdom*, Judgment of 4 May 2001, para 120; Case *Gülec v Turkey*, Judgment of 27 July 1998, Reports 1998-IV, para 80; Case *Ogur v Turkey*, Judgment of 20 May 1999, Reports 1999-III, para 91; AfrCmHPR: Case *Amnesty International et al v Sudan*, (26th and 27th Ordinary Sessions, May 2000), para 51; UN Principles on the Investigation of Torture, Principle 2.

41 Human Rights Committee, *General Comment No 31 on Article 2 of the Covenant: The Nature of the General Legal Obligation Imposed on States Parties to the Covenant*, 21 April 2004, CCPR/C/74/CRP.4/Rev.6, para 15; *General Comment No 20 on Article 7 of the Covenant*, 10 March 1992, para 14; UN Principles on Extra-legal Executions, Principle 9; UN Principles on the Investigation of Torture, Principle 2; Committee against Torture: *Conclusions and recommendations on Colombia*, 4 February 2004, CAT/C/CR/31/1, para 9 (a); see also *Conclusions and recommendations on Yemen*, 5 February 2004, CAT/C/CR/31/4, para 6 (e); *Conclusions and recommendations on Morocco*, 5 February 2004, CAT/C/CR/31/2, para 6 (f); *Conclusions and recommendations on Cambodia*, 27 May 2003, CAT/C/CR/30/2, para 7 (c); Article 12 CAT.

42 I/ACtHR: Case *Velázquez Rodríguez v Honduras*, Judgment of 29 July 1988, Series C No 4, para 176; Case *Tibi v Ecuador*, Judgment of 7 September 2004, Series C No 114 para 159; ECtHR, Case *Aksoy v Turkey*, Judgment of 18 December 1996, Reports 1996-VII, para 99; Case *Hugh Jordan v the United Kingdom*, Judgment of 4 May 2001, Reports 2001-III, para 141.

UN Principles on the Investigation of Torture state that '[t]he investigators, who shall be independent of the suspected perpetrators and the agency they serve, shall be competent and impartial.'[43] The UN Principles on Extra-legal Executions require that if investigations are inadequate, 'Governments shall pursue investigations through an independent commission of inquiry or similar procedure. Members of such a commission shall be chosen for their recognized impartiality, competence and independence as individuals. In particular, they shall be independent of any institution, agency or person that may be the subject of the inquiry.'[44] The European Court considers that 'it may generally be regarded as necessary for the persons responsible for and carrying out the investigation to be independent from those implicated in the events. This means not only that there should be no hierarchical or institutional connection but also clear independence.'[45]

Independence can be compromised if investigations into alleged violations by members of the armed forces are carried out by the armed forces themselves. The Inter-American Court and Commission have considered that in those cases, the investigation will not comply with the requirements of the American Convention on Human Rights.[46] The Human Rights Committee has stressed that at least in cases of human rights violations by the military or armed forces, the investigations should be carried out by civilian authorities.[47] Similarly, the Committee against Torture has expressed concern at the fact that the military courts were 'investigating offences that are totally excluded from their competence, such as torture, genocide and forced disappearance in which members of the police or armed forces are suspected of

43 Principle 2.

44 Principle 11.

45 Case *McKerr v the United Kingdom*, Judgment of 4 May 2001, Reports 2001-III, para 112; Case *Finucane v the United Kingdom*, Judgment of 1 July 2003, para 68.

46 I/ACtHR: Case *Velázquez Rodríguez v Honduras*, Judgment of 29 July 1988, Series C No 4, para 180; *Second Report on the Situation of Human Rights in Peru*, 2 June 2000, OEA/Ser.L/V/II.106, Doc 59 rev, para 210.

47 See, *e.g.*, *Concluding Observations on Colombia*, CCPR/C/79/Add.76, 5 May 1997, para 19, 23, 32, 34; *Concluding Observations on Venezuela*, 26 April 2001, CCPR/CO/71/VEN, para 8; *Concluding Observations on Kyrgyzstan*, 24 July 2000, CCPR/CO/69/KGZ, para 7; *Concluding Observations on Chile*, 30 March 1999, CCPR/C/79/Add.104, para 10; *Concluding Observations on Belarus*, 19 November 1997, CCPR/C/79/Add.86, para 9; *Concluding Observations on Macedonia*, 18 August 1998, CCPR/C/79/Add.96, para 10; *Concluding Observations on France*, 4 August 1997, CCPR/C/79/Add.80, para 16 *et seq*; Report of the Human Rights Committee to the General Assembly, 35th period of session, UN Doc A/35/40 (1980), para 249 *et seq*.

having been involved.'[48] It has encouraged the state to undertake legislative reforms 'to place the criminal justice system (from the investigation of offences to the serving of sentences) under the direct supervision of independent members of the judiciary and ensure that they can quickly investigate reported or suspected cases of torture or ill-treatment.'[49] The European Court of Human Rights has equally found that investigations by military courts did not meet the required standards of independence in cases of human rights violations committed by the armed forces.[50]

b) Impartiality

Impartiality presupposes a lack of pre-conceived ideas and prejudice by those who carry out the investigation.

A particular issue of impartiality can arise in cases where the alleged violations concern members of racial, ethnic, religious or other groups. In this respect, the Committee on the Elimination of Racial Discrimination has held that the enactment of legislation making racial discrimination a criminal offence does not in itself represent full compliance with the obligations of states parties under the Convention. It is incumbent upon states to investigate with due diligence and expedition.[51]

In a recent case, the European Court developed criteria to investigate violent acts that may be racially or ethnically motivated. It is of significant importance for all human rights violations that occur in the context of ethnically or racially discriminatory practices of governments, security forces, police forces, or others. It held that in cases where there is suspicion that racial attitudes induced a violent act, it was particularly important that the official investigation be pursued with vigour and impartiality:

> 'The Court considers that when investigating violent incidents and, in particular, deaths at the hands of State agents, State authorities have the additional duty to take all reasonable steps to unmask any racist motive and to establish whether or not ethnic hatred or prejudice may have played a role in the

[48] *Conclusions and recommendations on Colombia*, 4 February 2004, CAT/C/CR/31/1, para 9 (d) (iii).

[49] *Conclusions and recommendations on Ecuador*, 15 November 1993, A/49/44, paras 97-105, at 105.

[50] Case *Incal v Turkey*, Judgment of 9 June 1998, Reports 1998-IV, paras 65-73.

[51] Case *L.K. v the Netherlands*, CERD/C/42/D/4/1991, 16 March 1993, paras 6.4 and 6.6.

events. Failing to do so and treating racially induced violence and brutality on an equal footing with cases that have no racist overtones would be to turn a blind eye to the specific nature of acts that are particularly destructive of fundamental rights.'[52]

2. Capable of Leading to the Identification and, if Appropriate, the Punishment of the Authors

The European Court of Human Rights and the Inter-American Court of Human Rights have stressed that the investigation should be capable of identifying those responsible for the violations.[53]

The Working Group on Enforced or Involuntary Disappearances has stressed that '[t]he identity of the victims, the identity of those responsible for devising policies and practices leading to disappearances, as well as the identity of persons who commit the disappearances and those who have aided or encouraged (abbeted) them, should be made known to the public".[54]

The Inter-American Commission has clearly stated that where a Truth Commission only partially investigates violations, where it is not a judicial body and lacks the power to establish the identity of the perpetrators, to bring them to justice and to award compensation to the victims, such a Commission does not fulfil the obligation of the state under Article 1 (1) of the American Convention on Human Rights.[55]

---

[52] Case *Nachova and others v Bulgaria*, 26 February 2004, (in French); see also the earlier case of *Menson and Others v the United Kingdom* (Decision), no. 47916/99, ECHR 2003-V.

[53] ECtHR: Case *Finucane v the United Kingdom*, Judgment of 1 July 2003, para 69; Case *McCann and other v the United Kingdom*, Judgment of 27 September 1995, Series A no 324, para 161; Case *Kaya v Turkey*, Judgment of 19 February 1998, Reports 1998-I, para 86; Case *Assenov v Bulgaria*, Judgment of 28 October 1998, Reports 1998-VIII, para 102; Case *Ogur v Turkey*, Judgment of 20 May 1999, Reports 1999-III, para 88; I/ACtHR: Case *Juan Humberto Sánchez v Honduras*, Judgment of 7 June 2003, Series C No. 99, para 186; Case *Tibi v Ecuador*, Judgment of 7 September 2004, Series C No 114 para 159.

[54] *Report of the Working Group on Enforced or Involuntary Disappearances*, 22 December 1993, E/CN.4/1994/26, para 45 f).

[55] Report No. 36/96, Case 10.843, *Héctor Marcial Garay Hermosilla (Chile)*, 15 October 1996, paras 74-77. It is significant to notice that the Government of Chile, whose amnesty law was criticized in the mentioned report, fully accepted the legal criticism emitted by the Commission. See also Report 34/96, Cases 11.228 *et al* (Chile), 15 October 1996, paras 72 *et seq*; Report No. 25/98, Cases 11.505 *et al.* (Chile), 7 April 1998, paras 66 *et seq*.

The fact that the investigation must lead, if appropriate, to the prosecution and punishment of the authors also means that the investigation report must be disclosed to the judicial authorities without manipulation.[56] The Inter-American Court and Commission have considered, moreover, that in cases of human rights violations, the State authorities cannot resort to mechanisms such as 'official secret' or confidentiality of the information, or reasons of public interest or national security, to refuse to supply the information required by the judicial or administrative authorities in charge of the ongoing investigation or proceeding.[57]

The African Commission on Human and Peoples' Rights held in the case *Amnesty International et al v Sudan* that '[i]nvestigations must be carried out by entirely independent individuals, provided with necessary resources, and their findings should be made public and prosecutions initiated in accordance with the information uncovered.'[58]

The UN Principles on Extra-legal Executions stipulate that the purpose of the investigation shall be to determine the cause, manner and time of death, the person responsible, and any pattern or practice which may have brought about that death.[59] The UN Principles on the Investigation of Torture states that the investigation must bring '[c]larification of the facts and establishment and acknowledgment of individual and State responsibility for victims and their families.'[60]

3. Powers of the Investigatory Authorities

The investigation authorities must have the resources and powers necessary to carry out an effective investigation, which includes, in particular, the power to oblige all involved actors and witnesses to appear and testify.[61]

---

56 Case *Myrna Mack-Chang v Guatemala*, Judgment of 25 November 2003, Series C No 101, paras 171-174.

57 Case *Myrna Mack-Chang v Guatemala*, Judgment of 25 November 2003, Series C No 101, para 180 and footnote 258 with reference to the Commission's opinion.

58 Case *Amnesty International and Others v. Sudan*, Communications No. 48/90, 50/91, 52/91, 89/93 (1999), African Commission on Human and Peoples' Rights, 26th and 27th Ordinary Sessions, May 2000, para 51.

59 Principle 9.

60 Principle 1 (a).

61 Article 13 (2) of the Declaration on the Protection of All Persons against Enforced Disappearance; Principle 10 of the UN Principles on Extra-legal Executions; UN Principles on the Investigation of

4. Participation of Victims and their Relatives

The investigation must be public and victims and their families must have access to them.

In this sense, the European Court of Human Rights has insisted that victims and their families must be 'involved in the procedure to the extent necessary to safeguard his or her legitimate interests.'[62] Their testimony must be heard and they must have access to relevant information.[63] Decisions not to prosecute must be publicly reasoned and notice must be given to the families.[64]

In the *Caracazo Case* (Reparations), the Inter-American Court of Human Rights noted that '[a]ll the States party to the American Convention have the duty to investigate human rights violations and to punish the perpetrators and accessories after the fact in said violations. And any person who considers himself or herself to be a victim of such violations has the right to resort to the system of justice to attain compliance with this duty by the state, for his or her benefit and that of society as a whole.'[65] The Court criticized the 'lack of access by the victims, their next of kin or their representatives to the criminal investigations and proceedings due to the so called "secrecy of the preliminary investigations".'[66] In the case of *Juan Humberto Sánchez*, the Inter-American Court held that '[t]he next of kin of the victim must have full access and the capacity to act, at all stages and levels of said investigations, in accordance with domestic laws and the provi-

Torture, Principle 3 (a); AfrCmHPR, Case *Amnesty International et al v Sudan*, (26th and 27th Ordinary Sessions, May 2000), para 51; Case *Hugh Jordan v the United Kingdom*, Judgment of 4 May 2001, Reports 2001-III, para 127; EcrHR, Case *McKerr v the United Kingdom*, Judgment of 4 May 2001, Reports 2001-III, para 124.

62 ECtHR: Case *Finucane v the United Kingdom*, Judgment of 1 July 2003, para 71; Case *Güleç v Turkey*, Judgment of 27 July 1998, Reports 1998-IV, para 82; Case *Ogur v Turkey*, Judgment of 20 May 1999, Reports 1999-III, para 92.

63 ECtHR: Case *Hugh Jordan v the United Kingdom*, Judgment of 4 May 2001, Reports 2001-III, para 133; Case *McKerr v the United Kingdom*, Judgment of 4 May 2001, Reports 2001-III, para 147; Case *Kelly v the United Kingdom*, Judgment of 4 May 2001, Reports 2001-III, para 127.

64 ECtHR: Case *Hugh Jordan v the United Kingdom*, Judgment of 4 May 2001, Reports 2001-III, para 122 *et seq*; Case *McKerr v the United Kingdom*, Judgment of 4 May 2001, Reports 2001-III, para 145; Case *Kelly v the United Kingdom*, Judgment of 4 May 2001, Reports 2001-III, paras 116 *et seq*.

65 *Case of Caracazo v Venezuela* (Reparation), Judgment of 29 August 2002, Series C No 95, para 115.

66 *Ibid*, para 116.

sions of the American Convention. The results of those investigations must be made known to the public, for Honduran society to know the truth.'[67]

The UN Principles on Extra-legal Executions state that families of the deceased and their legal representatives shall be informed of, and have access to any hearing as well as to all information relevant to the investigation, and shall be entitled to present other evidence. The family of the deceased shall have the right to insist that a medical or other qualified representative be present at the autopsy. When the identity of a deceased person has been determined, a notification of death shall be posted, and the family or relatives of the deceased shall be informed immediately. The body of the deceased shall be returned to them upon completion of the investigation.[68]

An effective participation also implies assistance, including assistance by social workers and mental health-care practitioners, and the reimbursement of expenses.[69] In particular, victims and their families should have access to legal and psychological counselling and advice, and to legal aid and translation where necessary.[70]

It should be noted that certain norms acknowledge that the publication of certain aspects of the investigation might compromise the prosecution and punishment of the perpetrators. In this sense, Article 13 (4) of the Declaration on the Protection of All Persons from Enforced Disappearance states that the findings of the investigation must be disclosed to the persons concerned, 'unless doing so would jeopardize an ongoing criminal investigation.'[71] On the other hand, the Draft International Convention on the Protection of All Persons from Forced Disappearance prepared by the UN Sub-Commission states that even if the

---

[67] *Juan Humberto Sánchez Case*, Judgment of 7 June 2003, Series C No 99, para 186.

[68] Principle 16 of the UN Principles on Extra-legal Executions; see also Principle 4 of the UN Principles on the Investigation of Torture.

[69] Principle 10 of the UN Principles on Impunity; Case *Airey v Ireland*, Judgment of 9 October 1979, Series A No. 32, para 33; *Principles and Guidelines on the Right to a Fair Trial and Legal Assistance in Africa*, Principle H.

[70] Principle 14-17 of the UN Declaration of Basic Principles of Justice for Victims of Crime and Abuse of Power; Articles 6 and 7 of the Council Framework Decision of 15 March 2001 on the standing of victims in criminal proceedings, Official Journal L 082, 22 March 2001 P. 0001 – 0004; Recommendation No. R (85) 11 on the position of victim in criminal law and criminal procedure, IA2.

[71] See also Principle 34 of the Body of Principles for the Protection of All Persons under Any Form of Detention or Imprisonment.

findings are not revealed because of an ongoing investigation, the competent authority shall nevertheless 'communicate regularly and without delay to the relatives of the disappeared person the results of the inquiry into the fate and whereabouts of that person.'[72] In other words, while some finding might have to remain undisclosed for the purpose of criminal proceedings, information about the fate and whereabouts of the victim should always be given to the family.

In sum, victims and their relatives have a right to effective participation in the investigation, which includes the right to challenge and present evidence, and to be informed of and have access the proceedings. It also implies assistance, in particular counselling, advice, and legal aid and translation if necessary.

5. Protection of Victims, their Relatives and Witnesses against Threats and Intimidation

Since its first resolution on enforced or involuntary disappearances, the General Assembly has expressed that it is deeply moved by the anguish and sorrow which disappearances cause to relatives.[73] Since Resolution 42/142 of 1987, it also appeals to governments to take steps 'to protect the families of disappeared persons against any intimidation or any ill-treatment of which they may be the target.'[74] The duty to protect victims and their families is also enshrined in Article 13 (3) of the Declaration of the Protection of All Persons from Enforced Disappearance.

[72] E/CN.4/Sub.2/1998/19, 19 August 1998, Annex, Article 11 (6).

[73] UN Docs A/RES/33/173 of 20 December 1978; A/RES/35/193 of 15 December 1980; A/RES/36/163 of 16 December 1981; A/RES/37/180 of 17 December 1982; A/RES/38/94 of 16 December 1983; A/RES/39/111 of 14 December 1984; A/RES/40/147 of 13 December 1985; A/RES/41/145 of 4 December 1986; A/RES/42/142 of 7 December 1987; A/RES/43/159 of 8 December 1988; A/RES/44/160 of 15 December 1989; A/RES/45/165 of 18 December 1990; A/RES/46/125 of 17 December 1991; A/RES/47/132 of 18 December 1992; A/RES/49/193 of 23 December 1994; A/RES/51/94 of 12 December 1994; A/RES/53/150 of 9 December 1998, A/RES/55/103 of 4 December 2000; A/RES/57/215 of 18 December 2002; see also Article 13 (3) of the Declaration on the Protection of All Persons against Enforced Disappearance.

[74] A/RES/42/142 of 7 December 1987, para 6; see also A/RES/43/159 of 8 December 1988; A/RES/44/160 of 15 December 1989; A/RES/45/165 of 18 December 1990; A/RES/46/125 of 17 December 1991; A/RES/47/132 of 18 December 1992; A/RES/49/193 of 23 December 1994; A/RES/51/94 of 12 December 1994; A/RES/53/150 of 9 December 1998, A/RES/55/103 of 4 December 2000; A/RES/57/215 of 18 December 2002.

The UN Principles on Extra-legal Executions, and the UN Principles on the Investigation of Torture both require that complainants, witnesses, those conducting the investigation and their families must be protected from violence, threats of violence or any other form of intimidation. Families of the deceased and their legal representatives shall have access to information and be entitled to present evidence. The body of the deceased must be returned to them upon completion of the investigation.[75] The Inter-American Court of Human Rights has also insisted that the state must take all necessary measures of protection for legal operators, investigators, witnesses and next of kin of the victims.[76]

6. Documentation of all Relevant Evidence

An effective investigation requires that all evidence be gathered and documented. The Committee against Torture has recommended that 'in cases of violation of the right to life any signs of torture, especially sexual violence, that the victim may show be documented. That evidence should be included in forensic reports so that the investigation may cover not only the homicide but also the torture. The Committee also recommend[ed] that the state party provide medical staff with the training necessary to determine when torture or ill-treatment of any kind has occurred.'[77]

The Inter-American Court has held that '[t]he State must, therefore, locate, exhume, identify by means of undoubtedly suitable techniques and instruments, the remains of the victims [...].'[78] It has considered that the protection of the scene of crime, the preservation of fingerprints, the taking of blood samples and carrying out of respective laboratory tests, the examination of clothes and the photographing of the victim's wounds are essential parts of the investigations.[79]

Similarly, the European Court of Human Rights has held that '[t]he authorities must have taken the reasonable steps available to them to secure

[75] Principle 15 of the UN Principles on Extra-legal Executions; Principle 3 (b) of the UN Principles on the Investigation of Torture.

[76] Case *Myrna Mack-Chang v Guatemala*, Judgment of 25 November 2003, Series C No 101, para 199.

[77] *Conclusions and recommendations on Colombia*, 4 February 2004, CAT/C/CR/31/1, para 10 (f).

[78] Case of *Caracazo v Venezuela* (Reparation), Judgment of 29 August 2002, Series C No 95, paras 115, 124.

[79] Case *Myrna Mack-Chang v Guatemala*, Judgment of 25 November 2003, Series C No 101, para 167.

the evidence concerning the incident, including *inter alia* eye witness testimony, forensic evidence and, where appropriate, an autopsy which provides a complete and accurate record of injury and an objective analysis of clinical findings, including the cause of death. Any deficiency in the investigation which undermines its ability to establish the cause of death or the person or persons responsible will risk falling foul of this standard.'[80] Persons who have taken part in the killings must give testimony in an oral hearing, written submissions are insufficient.[81] The authorities cannot exclude in advance that the violations were committed by agents of the state.[82] It must investigate possible perpetrators.[83] The Court has criticized shortcomings in forensic examinations,[84] in the identification of weapons and their use,[85] in the conduct of autopsies,[86] in the lack of explanation given for injuries.[87] The court has also criticized reports of investigations when they were superficial and not 'effective'.[88]

The UN Principles Extra-legal Executions state that the inquiry must include and analyse all physical and documentary evidence and statements from witnesses.[89] To this end, the investigation authority must have the

80 Case *Finucane v the United Kingdom*, Judgment of 1 July 2003, para 69.

81 Case *Hugh Jordan v the United Kingdom*, Judgment of 4 May 2001, Reports 2001-III, para 127; Case *McKerr v the United Kingdom*, Judgment of 4 May 2001, Reports 2001-III, para 144; Case *Kelly v the United Kingdom*, Judgment of 4 May 2001, Reports 2001-III, para 124.

82 Case *Yasa v Turkey*, Judgment of 2 September 1998, Reports 1998-VI, para 105; Case *Ergi v Turkey*, Judgment of 28 July 1998, Reports 1998-IV, para 83; Case *Assenov v Bulgaria*, Judgment of 28 October 1998, Reports 1998-VIII, paras 103, 105; Case *Mahmut Kaya v Turkey*, Judgment of 28 March 2000, Reports 2000-III, para 96.

83 *Mahmut Kaya v Turkey*, Judgment of 28 March 2000, Reports 2000-III, para 105; *Kiliç v Turkey*, Judgment of 28 March 2000, Reports 2000-III, para 80.

84 Case *Mahmut Kaya v Turkey*, Judgment of 28 March 2000, Reports 2000-III, para 104.

85 Case *Kaya v Turkey*, Judgment of 19 February 1998, Reports 1998-I, para 89; Case *Ogur v Turkey*, Judgment of 20 May 1999, Reports 1999-III, para 89.

86 Case *Kaya v Turkey*, Judgment of 19 February 1998, Reports 1998-I, para 89; Case *Ogur v Turkey*, Judgment of 20 May 1999, Reports 1999-III, para 89; Case *Salman v Turkey*, Judgment of 27 June 2000, Reports 2000-V, para 106.

87 Case *Mahmut Kaya v Turkey*, Judgment of 28 March 2000, Reports 2000-III, para 104.

88 Case *Ergi v Turkey*, Judgment of 28 July 1998, Reports 1998-IV, para 84; Case *Assenov v Bulgaria*, Judgment of 28 October 1998, Reports 1998-VIII, para 103; Case *Ogur v Turkey*, Judgment of 20 May 1999, Reports 1999-III, para 89.

89 Principle 9 of the Principles on Extra-legal Executions.

power to oblige all persons to testify and present evidence, and have the power to summon witnesses, including officials.[90] It must have at its disposal all the necessary budgetary and technical resources for effective investigation.[91] Where the investigation is inadequate, governments have to set up a new, independent and impartial inquiry.[92]

The Principles also have very detailed requirements for the autopsy, which must be conducted by an impartial expert, who must have access to all relevant data. The body shall not be disposed of until an adequate autopsy is conducted.[93] If the body has been buried and it later appears that an investigation is required, the body shall be promptly and competently exhumed for an autopsy. If skeletal remains are discovered, they should be carefully exhumed and studied according to systematic anthropological techniques.[94] The autopsy must identify the deceased and the cause of death and all other relevant circumstances and describe all injuries including evidence of torture.[95]

The UN Principles on the Investigation of Torture contain detailed requirements for the medical examination, which must be carried out with the highest ethical standards.[96] The Special Rapporteur on torture has recommended that public forensic medical services should not have a monopoly on expert forensic evidence for judicial purposes.[97]

7. Suspension of Officials during Investigation

The need to suspend officials during investigation is enshrined in some international instruments and is increasingly recognized by human rights bodies.

---

90 Principle 10.

91 Principle 10.

92 Principle 11.

93 Principle 12.

94 Principle 12.

95 Principle 13.

96 Principle 6.

97 *Report of the Special Rapporteur on torture*, 17 December 2002, UN Doc E/CN.4/2003/68, recommendation 26 (k); see also *Consolidated Recommendations of the Special Rapporteur on torture*, UN Doc A/56/156 of 3 July 2001, para 39 (j).

The Declaration on the Protection of All Persons from Enforced Disappearance,[98] the UN Principles on Extra-legal Executions,[99] and the UN Principles on the Investigation of Torture[100] require that those potentially implicated in the violations shall be removed from any position of control or power, whether direct or indirect over complainants, witnesses and their families, as well as over those conducting investigations.

While these instruments require suspension of officials who are in positions of control or power over the complainants, witnesses and their families, the Human Rights Committee and the Committee against Torture have gone further. The Human Rights Committee has insisted that '[p]ersons alleged to have committed serious violations should be suspended from official duties during the investigation of allegations.'[101] The Committee against Torture and the Special Rapporteur on torture have recommended similar measures.[102]

8. Disclosure of Investigation to Public

The inquiry will only fulfil its purpose if the report is made public immediately and discloses the methods and findings of such investigations.[103] The report must describe in detail specific events that were found to have occurred and the evidence upon which such findings were based, and list the names of witnesses who testified, with the exception of those whose identities have been withheld for their own protection.[104] The Inter-American Court and Commission, the European Court of Human Rights and the

98 Article 16.

99 Principle 15.

100 Principle 3 (b).

101 *Concluding Observations on Serbia and Montenegro*, CCPR/CO/81/SEMO, 12 August 2004, para 9; see also *Concluding Observations on Brazil*, CCPR/C/79/Add.66, para 20; *Concluding Observations on Colombia*, CCPR/C/79/Add. 76, 5 May 1997, paras 32 and 34.

102 *Concluding Observations on Bolivia*, 10 May 2001, A/56/44, paras 89-98, para 97; *Recommendations of the Special Rapporteur on torture*, E/CN.4/2003/68, 17 December 2002, Recommendation 26 (k).

103 See Article 13 (4) of the Declaration on the Protection of All Persons against Enforced Disappearance.

104 Principle 17 of the UN Principles on Extra-legal Executions; Principle 5 (b) of the UN Principles on the Investigation of Torture; I/ACtHR, Case *Juan Humberto Sánchez v Honduras*, Judgment of 7 June 2003, Series C No. 99, para 186.

African Commission on Human and Peoples' Rights have also asked that the findings of investigations should be made public.[105]

* * *

Summary

International law has developed and elaborated a significant range of requirements for investigations to be conducted promptly, effectively, independently and impartially. They pertain to the institutional structure of the investigating authority, to the modalities of the investigation, the rights of victims and witnesses and the measures of compensation. Case law has also made clear that the investigation should be conducted by a judicial or quasi-judicial body.

- Victims and their relatives of human rights violations have a right to a prompt, impartial, thorough and independent official investigation, which implies a personal and institutional independence of the investigating authority. In cases of violations implicating the military forces, the investigation should be carried out by civilian authorities.
- The investigation must be capable of leading to the identification and, if appropriate, the punishment of the authors.
- The investigating authorities must be vested with the necessary powers and resources to conduct meaningful investigations, in particular to order the appearance of all witnesses.
- Victims and their relatives have a right to effective participation in the investigation, which includes the right to challenge and present evidence, and to be informed of and have access to the proceedings. It also implies assistance, in particular counselling, advice, and legal aid and translation if necessary. Victims, their relatives and witnesses must be protected against threats and intimidation.
- The investigation must collect and document all evidence, disclose the facts of the violation and the causes, and disclose the methods, evidence

[105] I/ACtHR: Case *Juan Humberto Sánchez v Honduras*, Judgment of 7 June 2003, Series C No. 99, para 186; ECtHR: Case *McKerr v the United Kingdom*, Judgment of 4 may 2001, Reports 2001-III, para 141; AfrCHPR, Case *Amnesty International et al v Sudan*, (26th and 27th Ordinary Sessions, May 2000), para 51.

and results of the investigation to victims, their relatives and to the public.

- Officials who are under investigation should be suspended during the time of the investigation.
- In cases of investigations involving acts of racial violence, the authorities have an additional duty to take all reasonable steps to unmask any racist motive and to establish whether or not ethnic hatred or prejudice has played a role in the events.

CHAPTER V

THE RIGHT TO TRUTH

Life can be buried forever,
but truth will always be found.[1]

The right to truth is the right of family members and other close relatives and society to know the truth about serious human rights violations. It lies both at the root and at the outcome of a right to a remedy and to investigation. But the failure of authorities to investigate disappearances sometimes causes such suffering to the family that a denial of the right to truth constitutes cruel, inhuman or degrading treatment.

The right to truth is also an autonomous right, independent of other claims of the victims and their relatives, that is owed to society as a whole, as an objective state obligation flowing from the duty to ensure human rights to all.

***

I. Humanitarian Law

The concept of a right to truth has evolved from humanitarian law into human rights law, where it was first developed in the context of enforced or involuntary disappearances. Indeed, Articles 15 *et seq* and 18 *et seq* of the

1 F.M. Dostoyevski, *Crime and Punishment*, Part 3, Chapter 1.

First and Second Geneva Conventions state the obligation to search for, care for, and identify the wounded, sick and dead of the adverse party to the conflict and set out requirements for the forwarding of information and the burial of the dead. Similarly Articles 122 *et seq* of the Third Geneva Convention and *136 et seq* of the Fourth Geneva Convention regulate the recollection and forwarding of information on prisoners of war and civilian persons. Most importantly, Article 32 of the First Additional Protocol to the Geneva Conventions, regulating the protection of victims in international armed conflicts, expressly mentions the 'right of families to know the fate of their relatives'. Article 33 paragraph 1 of the same Protocol enshrines an obligation of each party to the conflict to 'search for the persons who have been reported missing by an adverse Party'. Both of these obligations - to inform families of the fate of their relatives and to search for missing persons - are at the heart of the right to truth as it was later developed in international human rights law.

To strengthen these obligations, the International Conference of the Red Cross and Red Crescent has urged parties to a conflict 'to help locate the graves of the dead and cooperate with the ICRC and the National Societies in their work of accounting for the missing and the dead'[2] and has urged the state 'to take any appropriate action that might help in ascertaining the fate of missing persons' and asked 'governments to try and prevent disappearances and to undertake thorough inquiries into every case of disappearance occurring on their territory.'[3] It has 'emphasize[d] that family reunification must begin with the tracing of separated family members at the request of one of them and end with their coming together as a family', 'call[ed] upon States to facilitate the tracing activities of their respective National Red Cross or Red Crescent Societies by granting them access to the relevant data' and 'stresse[d] the need and the *right* of families to obtain information on missing persons, including missing prisoners of war and those missing in action, and strongly urge[d] States and parties to armed conflict to provide families with information on the fate of their missing relatives.'[4]

---

2 22nd International Conference of the Red Cross and Red Crescent, Tehran 1973, Resolution V.

3 24th International Conference of the Red Cross and Red Crescent, Manila 1981, Resolution II.

4 Resolution 2 on the *Protection of the civilian population in period of armed conflict* adopted at the 26th International Conference of the Red Cross and Red Crescent, December 1995, paras D (c), (g) and (k), emphasis added.

The Agenda for Humanitarian Action adopted by the 28th International Conference of the Red Cross and Red Crescent defines the issue of missing persons as one of its four humanitarian concerns. It recalls Article 32 of the 1977 Additional Protocol I and states that '[i]n this spirit, families are to be informed of the fate, including the whereabouts, and, if dead, the cause of death of their family members who are missing as a result of armed conflict or other situations of armed violence. Families and communities receive acknowledgment of the events leading to persons becoming missing, and the perpetrators of violations leading to such situations must be held accountable.'[5] It further gives details for efficiency in the process of managing information and processing files on missing persons, for informing families and putting an end to their uncertainty and anxiety, and taking specific measures to protect and assist the family members, with particular regard to the needs of women and children.[6]

***

It was on the basis of the First Protocol to the Geneva Conventions that the United Nations Working Group on Enforced or Involuntary Disappearances recognized the right of the members of the family to know the truth about the disappeared.[7]

In its resolutions on missing persons, the General Assembly has reaffirmed the 'right of families to know the fate of their relatives reported missing in connection with armed conflicts', the right enshrined in Article 32 of the Additional Protocol I to the Geneva Conventions.[8] It has affirmed that 'each party to an armed conflict, as soon as circumstances permit and, at the latest, from the end of active hostilities, shall search for the persons who have been reported missing by an adverse party', as enshrined in Article 33 of the First Additional Protocol, and 'calls upon States which are parties to an armed conflict to take immediate steps to determine the identity and fate of persons reported missing in connection with the armed conflict.'[9] It also

5 Agenda for Humanitarian Action adopted by the 28th International Conference of the Red Cross and Red Crescent, 6 December 2003, Final Goal 1.2.

6 *Ibid*, Goals 1.3-1.5 and actions proposed.

7 E/CN.4/1435, 22 January 1981, paras 186 *et seq*; E/CN.4/1983/14, 21 January 1983, para 134.

8 A/RES/57/207, 14 February 2003, para 2.

9 A/RES/57/207, 14 February 2003, para 4.

'[r]equests States to pay the utmost attention to cases of children reported missing in connection with armed conflicts and to take appropriate measures to search for and identify those children.'[10]

Similarly, the Secretary General promulgated some principles and rules on the *Observance by United Nations forces of international humanitarian law*, which contain the rule that '[t]he United Nations force shall respect the right of the families to know about the fate of their sick, wounded and deceased relatives.'[11]

The UN Commission on Human Rights has equally recognized that 'for victims of human rights violations, public knowledge of their suffering and the truth about perpetrators, including their accomplices, of these violations are essential steps towards rehabilitation and reconciliation.'[12] In its Resolution on Missing Persons, the Commission urges states to strictly observe, respect and ensure respect for the rules of international humanitarian law and reaffirms the right of families to know the fate of their relatives reported missing in connection with armed conflicts.[13]

***

II. Human Rights Law

In the realm of international human rights law, the right to truth is a legal concept developed through the jurisprudence of international human rights bodies.

1. United Nations System

In the area of international human rights law, the right to truth is mentioned in the jurisprudence of the Human Rights Committee. In 1981, the Committee held in the case of *Almeida de Quinteros* that it 'understands the anguish and stress caused to the mother by the disappearance of her daughter and by the continuing uncertainty concerning her fate and whereabouts. The author has *the right to know* what has happened to her daughter. In these

10 A/RES/57/207, 14 February 2003, para 5.

11 ST/SGB/1999/13, 6 August 1999, para 9.8.

12 Resolution E/CN.4/RES/2003/72, para 8; see also the resolutions E/CN.4/RES/2002/79, para 9; E/CN.4/RES/2001/70, para 8; E/CN.4/RES/2000/68, para 2.

13 E/CN.4/RES/2002/60, 25 April 2002, paras 1 and 2.

respects, she too is a victim of the violations of the Covenant suffered by her daughter, in particular of article 7.'[14] It is important to notice that in this case, the Committee considered the right to know the truth as a substantive and not merely a procedural right, whose violation amounts to a breach of the right to be free from torture or other cruel, inhuman and degrading treatment and punishment.[15]

While the right to truth was, in the beginning, associated with enforced disappearances, the Human Rights Committee has made it clear that it applies to human rights violations in general.[16]

Other mechanisms of the United Nations have emphasized the right to truth. Beyond, the above-mentioned recognition of the right to truth by the UN Working Group on Enforced or Involuntary Disappearances, the UN Principles on Impunity recommended by the Commission on Human Rights in April 2005, establish as fundamental rights the 'inalienable right to the truth', 'the duty to remember', the 'victim's right to know', and 'guarantees to give effect to the right to know.'[17]

In its study on the *Question of Human Rights and States of Emergency*, the Special Rapporteur of the Sub-Commission considered that the 'right to know' or 'right to truth' should be recognized as non-derogable. This right is, in his opinion, 'closely linked to rights of the family and the right to a remedy' and 'the existence of concurring jurisprudence in these systems [*viz* the UN and Inter-American] in the opinions of the pertinent United Nations rapporteurs evidences the existence of a rule of customary international law.'[18]

The Special Rapporteur on the question of impunity of the Sub-Commission on the Promotion and Protection of Human Rights proposed two measures that states should adopt in order to uphold and guarantee the right to

[14] Case *Almeida de Quinteros et al v Uruguay*, 21 July 1983, CCPR/C/19/D/107/1981, para 14, emphasis added.

[15] See also Case *Sarma v Sri Lanka*, 31 July 2003, CCPR/C/78/D/950/2000, para 9.5.

[16] *Concluding Observations on Guatemala*, 3 April 1996, CCPR/C/79/Add.63, para 25; Case *Hugo Rodríguez v Uruguay*, 19 July 1994, CCPR/C/51/D/322/1988, paras 12 (3) and 14.

[17] Principles 2-5 of the UN Principles on Impunity.

[18] *Report of the United Nations Special Rapporteur on the Question of human rights and states of emergency*, 26 June 1995, E/CN.4/Sub.2/1995/20, Annex I, para 39.

truth. The first is the establishment of 'extrajudicial commissions of inquiry', in order to dismantle the previous machinery that allowed criminal behaviour, to ensure that such practices do not recur, to preserve evidence for the courts, and also to rehabilitate those who were discredited for denouncing grave violations.[19] He underlined, however, that such commissions must not be a pretext for not going before the courts,[20] confirming the basic principle that the right to truth and the right to justice are complementary and cannot be substituted for one another. The second component of the right to truth is, in the eyes of the Special Rapporteur, the need to preserve archives.[21] These components of the right to truth are reflected in the UN Principles on Impunity prepared by the Special Rapporteur of the Sub-Commission and updated by the independent expert of the Commission.[22]

2. Inter-American Commission and Court of Human Rights

The Inter-American Commission on Human Rights stated in its Annual Report 1985-1986:

> 'Every society has the inalienable right to know the truth about past events, as well as the motives and circumstances in which aberrant crimes came to be committed, in order to prevent repetition of such acts in the future. Moreover, the family members of the victims are entitled to information as to what happened to their relatives. Such access to the truth presupposes freedom of speech, which of course should be exercised responsibly; the establishment of investigating committees whose membership and authority must be determined in accordance with the internal legislation of each country, or the provision of the necessary resources, so that the judiciary itself may undertake whatever investigations may be necessary. The Commission considers that the observance of the principles cited above will bring about justice rather than vengeance, and thus neither the urgent need for national reconciliation nor the consolidation of democratic government will be jeopardized.'[23]

---

[19] *Revised final report of the Special Rapporteur on the question of impunity of perpetrators of human rights violations (civil and political)*, 2 October 1997, E/CN.4/Sub.2/1997/20/Rev.1, para 19.

[20] *Ibidem*.

[21] *Ibid*, para 25.

[22] *Ibid*, Annex II and Updated Principles, E/CN.4/2005/102/Add.1, 8 February 2005, Principles 2-5.

[23] Annual Report 1985-1986, OEA/Ser.L/V/II.68, Doc. 8, rev 1, 28 September 1986, Chapter V; see also Annual Report 1987-1988, OEA/Ser.L/V/II.74, Doc. 10, rev. 1, p. 359 [right to know the whereabouts of children of the disappeared].

The Commission has derived the right to truth from the right to access to a fair trial and judicial protection (Articles 8 and 15 ACHR) and the right to information (Article 13 ACHR).[24] It has subsumed the right to truth under 'the right of the victim or his next of kin to obtain clarification of the facts relating to the violation and the corresponding responsibilities from the competent State organs, through the investigation and prosecution established in Articles 8 and 25 of the Convention.'[25] It has also recognized the right 'to know the full, complete, and public truth as to the events that transpired, their specific circumstances, and who participated in them' as 'part of the right to reparation for human rights violations.'[26]

The right to truth, in the interpretation of the Inter-American Commission, is the right to a judicial search for truth and investigation, and to judicial sanctions of the perpetrators. A non-judicial body, such as a truth commission cannot substitute this right. The Commission held:

> 'The IACHR considers that, despite the important contribution that the Truth Commission made in establishing the facts surrounding the most serious violations, and in promoting national reconciliation, the role that it played, although highly relevant, cannot be considered as a suitable substitute for proper judicial procedures as a method for arriving at the truth. The value of truth commissions is that they are created, not with the presumption that there will be no trials, but to constitute a step towards knowing the truth and, ultimately, making justice prevail. Nor can the institution of a Truth Commission be accepted as a substitute for the State's obligation, which cannot be delegated, to investigate violations committed within its jurisdiction, and to identify those responsible, punish them, and ensure adequate compensation for the victim (Article 1.1 of the American Convention), all within the overriding need to combat impunity.'[27]

After the case of *Carmen Aguiar de Lapacó*[28] was brought before the Inter-American Commission on Human Rights and a friendly settlement was

[24] Case 10.480, Report Nº 1/99, *Lucio Parada Cea and others*, 27 January 1999, paragraph 148 *et seq.*

[25] Case *Bámaca Velásquez v Guatemala*, Judgment of 25 November 2000, Series C No 70, para 201; *Barrios Altos Case (Chumbipuma Aguirre et al. v Peru)*, Judgment of 14 March 2001, Series C No 75, para 48.

[26] Report No. 37/00, Case 11.481, *Monsignor Oscar Arnulfo Romero y Galdámez* (El Salvador), 13 April 2000, para 148; Report Nº 1/99, Case 10.480, *Lucio Parada Cea and others*, 27 January 1999, para 155.

[27] Report No. 136/99, Case 10.488, *Ignacio Ellacuría S.J. et al* (El Salvador), 22 December 1999, para 229 *et seq.*

[28] Report No 70/99, Case 12.059, *Carmen Aguiar de Lapacó* (Argentina), 4 May 1999.

reached between the parties, the Government of Argentina undertook to guarantee, despite the Amnesty Laws which prevented the prosecution of perpetrators of gross human rights violations, 'the right to truth, which involves the exhaustion of all means to obtain information on the whereabouts of the disappeared persons.'[29] As a result, Argentinian courts are allowed to carry on 'truth trials' and an *ad hoc* Prosecutor's Commission on truth proceedings was established to investigate cases. In July 2001, approximately 3,570 human rights cases were being investigated.[30]

The Inter-American Court has, until now, avoided the question of the right to truth, but found violations of the right to access justice and a fair trial when states have failed to carry the necessary judicial proceedings to find and identify relatives of complainants.[31]

3. European System

Although the European Court of Human Rights has not explicitly spoken of a 'right to truth', it has nevertheless recognized the suffering of relatives of victims of disappearances and held that a state's failure to investigate such a gross violation and to inform the relatives of the results constitutes a violation of their own right not to be subjected to cruel and inhuman treatment. In the case of *Kurt v Turkey*, the European Court of Human Rights recognized that failure of the authorities to provide information about the whereabouts of the disappeared amounted to a violation of the prohibition of torture and cruel and inhuman treatment in Article 3 ECHR.[32] It has upheld this finding in subsequent decisions.[33]

The Human Rights Chamber of Bosnia and Herzegovina, which also bases its judgments on the European Convention on Human Rights, has held in

---

[29] Report 21/00, Case 12.059, *Carmen Aguiar de Lapacó* (Argentina), 29 February 2000.

[30] Independent Study on Impunity, E/CN.4/2004/88, 27 February 2004, para 16.

[31] Case *Bámaca-Velásquez v Guatemala*, Judgment of 25 November 2000, paras 182-196; Case *Serrano Cruz sisters v El Salvador*, Judgment of 1 March 2005, Series C No 10, paras 58-107.

[32] Case *Kurt v Turkey*, Judgment of 25 May 1998, Report 1998-III, para 174.

[33] Case *Tanrikulu v Turkey*, Judgment of 8 September 1999, Reports 1999-IV, para 138; Case *Timurtas v Turkey*, 13 June 2000, Reports 2000-VI, para 128; Case *Ipek v Turkey*, 2 February 2004, para 238; Case *Orhan v Turkey*, Judgment of 18 June 2002, para 358; Case *Cyprus v Turkey*, Judgment of 21 May 2001, Reports 2001-IV, paras 156f.

the case concerning the 1995 massacre in Srebrenica, that the failure of the authorities of the Republika Srpska 'to inform the applicants about the truth of the fate and whereabouts of their missing loved ones' (about 7,500 missing men) and their failure to conduct a 'meaningful and effective investigation into the massacre' amounted to a violation of Article 3 ECHR with regard to the family members[34] and to a violation of their right to respect for their private and family life, protected under Article 8 ECHR. Like the Inter-American Commission, the Human Rights Chamber regarded the right to an investigation as beneficial not only for the victims, but for society as a whole, in that it ordered the Republika Srpska 'to conduct a full, meaningful, thorough, and detailed investigation' into the events surrounding the Srebrenica massacre with a view to making known to 'the applicants, all other family members, *and the public*'[35] its role in the massacre, its subsequent efforts to cover up the facts and the fate and whereabouts of the victims.

***

- The right to truth is a right of victims and families to obtain knowledge and clarification of the facts leading to gross human rights violations. A denial of this right amounts not only to a denial of the right to a remedy, to investigation and to reparation; it can also constitute in itself cruel, inhuman and degrading treatment because it causes new suffering to victims and their relatives.
- The right to truth also entails the duty of the states to collect and preserve archives of gross human rights violations.
- The right to truth and the right to justice are complementary and cannot be substituted for one another.

4. The Right to Truth as an Individual and Collective Right

The circle of persons entitled to the right to truth is not limited to the direct victims of the violation. This is particularly obvious in the case of disap-

[34] *The Srebrenica Cases (49 applications)*, Decision admissibility and merits, Cases Nos CH/01/8397 *et al*, 3 March 2003, paras 191, 220 (4).

[35] *The Srebrenica Cases (49 applications)*, Decision admissibility and merits, Cases Nos CH/01/8397 *et al*, 3 March 2003, para 212, emphasis added.

pearance, where the members of the family or persons close to the victim are themselves victims of the uncertainty surrounding the disappearance. In this sense, the UN Working Group on Enforced or Involuntary Disappearances has spoken of a 'wide circle of victims.'[36]

The right to truth may also be a right of a wider circle of persons, particularly in the case of gross and systematic human rights violations, which occurred over a long period of time and affected the society at large or a specific community. Here, the holders of the right to truth may not only be individuals, but also groups and communities, such as was described by the Special Rapporteur on the right to reparation, particularly with regard to indigenous peoples.[37] This was confirmed by the Special Rapporteur on the question of impunity, who stated that '[t]he right to know is also a collective right, drawing upon history to prevent violations from recurring in the future.'[38]

For the Inter-American Commission on Human Rights, the right to truth has an even wider reach, and is characterized not only as an individual claim, but as a right of society as a whole. In this sense, it found:

> 'The right to know the truth is a collective right that ensures society access to information that is essential for the workings of democratic systems, and it is also a private right for relatives of the victims, which affords a form of compensation, in particular, in cases where amnesty laws are adopted. Article 13 of the American Convention protects the right of access to information'.[39]

The Inter-American Court has equally stressed the wider dimension of the right to truth. It has stated that 'preventive measures and measures of non-repetition begin with the revelation and recognition of the atrocities of the past, as the Court has ordered it in its judgment on the merits. The society

[36] Report of the Working Group on Enforced or Involuntary Disappearances, E/CN.4/1990/13, 20 January 1990, para 339.

[37] *Final report by the Special Rapporteur on the right to restitution, compensation and rehabilitation*, 2 July 1993, E/CN.4/Sub.2/1993/8, para 14.

[38] *Revised final report of the Special Rapporteur on the question of impunity of perpetrators of human rights violations (civil and political)*, 2 October 1997, E/CN.4/Sub.2/1997/20/Rev.1, para 17.

[39] Report No. 136/99, Case 10.488, *Ignacio Ellacuría S.J et al* (El Salvador), 22 December 1999, para 224; see also Report No. 1/99, Case 10.480, *Lucio Parada Cea et al* (El Salvador), 27 January 1999, para 148; see also the submission of the Commission to the Inter-American Court in the *Bámaca Velásquez Case*, Judgment of 25 November 2000, Series C No. 70, para 197.

has a right to know the truth with regard to those crimes, 'so as to be capable of preventing them in the future.'[40] It has also ordered in its judgments that the results of investigations should be publicly disclosed, so that society learns the truth.[41] The recent decisions make clear that the right to truth is not confined to the next of kin of disappeared persons, but also of other indirect victims of gross human rights violations.[42]

The right to truth entails a duty of the state to clarify and disclose the truth on gross human rights violations not only to victims and their relatives, but also to society as a whole.

5. Content of the Right to Truth

The UN Principles on Impunity stipulate that victims and their relatives have the right to know the truth about 'past events and about the circumstances and reasons which lead, through systematic, gross violations of human rights, to the perpetration of heinous crimes'.[43] This extends beyond a mere 'humanitarian' information and includes knowledge as to how, when, why and by whom the violations were committed. The Principles also require that extrajudicial commissions of inquiry shall establish the facts[44] and "shall endeavour to safeguard evidence for later use in the administration of justice".[45] The Principles on Impunity stated also that "'Investigations undertaken by a commission of inquiry may relate to all persons alleged to have been responsible for violations of human rights and/or humanitarian law, whether they ordered them or actually committed them, acting as perpetrators or accomplices, and whether they are public officials or members of quasi-governmental or private armed groups with any kind of

[40] Case *Bámaca Velásquez v Guatemala (Reparations)*, Judgment of 22 February 2002, Series C No 91, para 77; Case of *Caracazo v Venezuela (Reparation)*, Judgment of 29 August 2002, Series C No 95, para 115, 118; Case *Juan Humberto Sánchez v Honduras*, Judgment of 7 June 2003, Series C No 99, para 185.

[41] Case of *Caracazo v Venezuela (Reparation)*, Judgment of 29 August 2002, Series C No 95, para 118.

[42] *Ibidem*; see also Case *Caballero Delgado and Santana v Colombia*, Judgment of 8 December, 1995, Series C No 22, para 58; Case *Trujillo Oroza v Bolivia (Reparations)*, Judgment of 27 February 2002, Series C No 92, para 99-111.

[43] Principle 2.

[44] Principle 5.

[45] Principle 8, e).

link to the State, or of non-governmental armed movements. Commissions of inquiry may also consider the role of other actors in facilitating violations of human rights and humanitarian law".[46] The Principles on Impunity also suggest that the right to the truth includes knowing the identity of perpetrators.[47]

The UN Principles on Reparation establish that victims shall obtain satisfaction, 'including verification of the facts and full and public disclosure of the truth'.[48] The Inter-American Commission has recognized that the right to truth entails the right 'to know the full, complete, and public truth as to the events transpired, their specific circumstances, and who participated in them.'[49]

The right to truth entails the right to know the truth not only about the facts and circumstances surrounding human rights violation, but also the reasons that led to them and the implicated authors. This knowledge must be disclosed and made public.

***

Summary

The right to truth is intrinsically linked to the right to a remedy and investigation and to the right to reparation for human rights violations. It is not, however, confined to being a mere aspect of those. Indeed, while investigations presuppose that there are facts that remain unclear or unresolved, the right to the truth goes beyond this, in that it demands revelation of facts that may simply be concealed. Also, the right to truth is not merely a right of the victim, but, because of the importance of truth as the basis to prevent further violations, a right that transcends the claim of victims and pertains to society as a whole.

46 Principle 8, c)

47 Principle 9.

48 Principle 22 (b).

49 Report No. 37/00, Case 11.481, *Monsignor Oscar Arnulfo Romero y Galdámez* (El Salvador), 13 April 2000, para 148; Report Nº 1/99, Case 10.480, *Lucio Parada Cea and others*, 27 January 1999, para 147; Report No. 136/99, Case 10.488, *Ignacio Ellacuría S.J. et al* (El Salvador), 22 December 1999, para 221.

Truth is not an alternative for a judicial remedy in case of gross human rights violations. Truth commissions or other extra-judicial bodies of inquiry cannot substitute the obligation of the state to conduct investigations into the violations and to bring perpetrators to justice.

CHAPTER VI
CESSATION AND GUARANTEES OF NON-REPETITION

Both are aspects of the restoration and repair of the legal relationship affected by the breach.[1]

The obligation of cessation and to give guarantees of non-repetition for breaches of international obligations derives from general international law. The International Law Commission has retained them in the Draft Articles on Responsibility of States for Internationally Wrongful Acts as one of the legal consequences of an internationally wrongful act.[2] Cessation, according to the commentary to the Draft Articles, 'is the first requirement in eliminating the consequences of wrongful conduct.'[3] As the arbitration tribunal in the *Rainbow Warrior arbitration* stressed, two essential conditions exist for the obligation of cessation to arise, 'namely that the wrongful act has a continuing character and that the violated rule is still in force at the time in which the order is issued.'[4]

[1] International Law Commission, Commentary to the Article 30 of the Draft Articles on Responsibility of States for Internationally Wrongful Acts, para 1.

[2] Article 30 of the Draft Articles on Responsibility of States for Internationally Wrongful Acts.

[3] Commentary to Article 30, para 4.

[4] *Case concerning the Difference between New Zealand and France concerning the Interpretation or Application of two Agreements, concluded on 9 July 1986 between the two States and which related to the Problems arising from the Rainbow Warrior Affair*, award of 30 April 1990, Recueil de sentences arbitrales, Volume XX, p 217, at para 114.

***

I. Terminology

In the UN Principles on Reparation, guarantees of non-repetition and prevention are one form of reparation.[5] Cessation, in the Principles, is part of satisfaction.[6] While this is not the case in the Draft Articles on Responsibility of States for Internationally Wrongful Acts, where they are a separate category from reparation,[7] the International Law Commission nevertheless explains in its Commentary that cessation of the violation of an international obligation and guarantees of non-repetition are 'aspects of the restoration and repair of the legal relationship affected by the breach.'[8] Similarly, the Commentary to the Draft Articles on Responsibility of States for Internationally Wrongful Acts justifies the mention of cessation as part of the Articles because 'cessation is more than simply a function of the duty to comply with the primary obligation [...]. The question of cessation only arises in the event of a breach. What must then occur depends not only on the interpretation of the primary obligation, but also on the secondary rules relating to remedies [...].'[9] Cessation also often overlaps with restitution, particularly in cases of detention or deprivation of property. But unlike restitution, cessation is not subject to limitations relating to proportionality: whereas restitution must only be provided if it is not impossible or creates an unreasonable burden on the state who has to provide reparation, no such limitations apply to the duty of cessation, which must always be complied with.[10] Similarly, the Commentary notes that assurances or guarantees of non-repetition may be sought by way of satisfaction and that there is overlap between the two in practice.[11]

In the words of the International Law Commission, '[a]ssurances and guarantees are concerned with the restoration of confidence in a continuing

[5] Principle 23.

[6] Principle 22 (a).

[7] Article 30.

[8] Commentary to Article 30, para 1.

[9] Commentary to Article 30, para 6.

[10] Commentary to Article 30, para 7.

[11] Commentary to Article 30, para 11.

relationship.'[12] As held by the International Court of Justice in the *LaGrand Case*, in which foreign nationals were 'subjected to prolonged detention or sentenced to severe penalties' following a failure of consular notification, a mere apology would not be sufficient. Rather, the state had to give guarantees of non-repetition.[13] This obligation was met by the commitment to follow through with efforts to achieve compliance with its obligations.[14]

In international human rights law, guarantees of non-repetition may be indistinguishable from the duty to prevent violations. Indeed, under international human rights law, states have a duty to prevent human rights violations. This primary obligation overlaps with the secondary obligation to guarantee non-repetition, which essentially means to prevent further violations. Both obligations may involve the adoption of general measures in order to avoid recurring violations. These measures may be of legislative or other nature. Guarantees of non-repetition may also be sought by way of satisfaction, so that there is some overlap between the two in practice.[15]

While the obligation of cessation appears to be assumed by international human rights bodies in a rather self-evident and implicit manner,[16] guarantees of non-repetition have been required expressly by these bodies as legal consequences of their decisions or judgments. This is the case for the UN Commission on Human Rights,[17] the Human Rights Committee,[18] the In-

[12] Commentary to Article 30 para 9.

[13] *LaGrand Case (Germany v the United States)*, Judgment of 27 June 2001, I.C.J. Reports 2001, p 514, para 123.

[14] *Ibid*, para 124; see also Case *Avena and other Mexican Nationals (Mexico v United States of America)*, Judgment of 31 March 2004, para 150.

[15] Commentary to Article 30 para 11.

[16] See *General Comment No 31 on the Nature of the General Legal Obligation Imposed on States Parties to the Covenant*, 26 May 2004, CCPR/C/21/Rev.1/Add.13, para 15: 'Cessation of an ongoing violation is an essential element of the right to an effective remedy.'

[17] Resolution E/CN.4/RES/2003/53 (extrajudicial, summary and arbitrary executions), 24 April 2003, para 4.

[18] Case *Bleier v Uruguay*, Views of 23 May 1978, CCPR/C/15/D/30/1978, para 5; Case *Dermit Barbato v Uruguay*, Views of 21 October 1982, CCPR/C/17/D/84/1981, para 11; Case *Almeida de Quinteros et al v Uruguay*, Views of 21 July 1983, CCPR/C/19/D/107/1981, para 138; Case *Raul Sendic Antonaccio v Uruguay*, Views of 28 October 1981, CCPR/C/14/D/63/1979, para 21; Case *Elena Beatriz Vasilskis v Uruguay*, Views of 31 March 1983, CCPR/C/18/D/80/1980, para 12; Case *Sterling v Jamaica*, Views of 18 October 1994, CCPR/C/57/D/598/1994, para 10; Case *Blanco v Nicaragua*, Views of 18 August

ter-American Court and Commission on Human Rights,[19] the Committee of Ministers and Parliamentary Assembly of the Council of Europe,[20] and the African Commission on Human and Peoples' Rights[21].

***

II. Guarantees of Non-Repetition

Whereas the obligation of cessation requires little interpretation, guarantees of non-repetition may take such diverse forms that there is a considerable body of jurisprudence indicating the different measures to be taken by states in order to ensure that similar violations to those found will not occur in the future, including the duty to adopt legislative measures to prevent further violations. The jurisprudence and practice have been classified in the UN Principles on Reparation as encompassing, amongst others, measures such as ensuring civilian control over military and security forces, strengthening the independence of the judiciary, protection of legal, medical, media and related personnel and human rights defenders, and human rights training.[22]

Note that these are only some of the possible guarantees of non-repetition. Many other types of measures could be warranted in different situations. An important measure of non-repetition that is not addressed in the Guide

1994, CCPR/C/51/D/328/1988, para 11; *General Comment No 6 on Article 6*, 20 April 1982, HRI/GEN/1/Rev.7, para 3; *General Comment No 20 on Article 7*, 10 March 1992, *ibid*, para 8-10.

[19] Case *Velásquez Rodríguez v Honduras (Compensatory damages)*, Judgment of 21 July 1989, Series C No 7, paras 34, 35 [duty to prevent further forced disappearances]; Case *Castillo Páez v Peru*, Judgment of 3 November 1997, Series C No 34, para 90 [duty to prevent further forced disappearances]; Case *Trujillo Oroza v Bolivia (Reparations)*, Judgment of 27 February 2002, Series C No 92, para 110; I/ACmHR: Report No. 63/99, Case 11.427, *Víctor Rosario Congo* (Ecuador), 13 April 1999, para 103 (3, 4) [ensure that trained medical staff and specialist are assigned to penitentiaries].

[20] Committee of Ministers of the Council of Europe: Interim Resolution DH (2000) 135, 25 October 2000, *Excessive length of judicial proceedings in Italy: General measures* [states are required to adopt general measures preventing new violations of the Convention similar to those already found]; Parliamentary Assembly Recommendation 1477 (2000) on the execution of judgments of the European Court of Human Rights, para iv (b).

[21] AfrCmHR: Case *The Social and Economic Rights Action Center and the Center for Economic and Social Rights v Nigeria*, Communication 155/96 (30th Ordinary Session, October 2001), paras 57, 61.

[22] Article 23 of the UN Principles on Reparation.

is, for example, the necessity to remove officials implicated in gross human rights violations from office.[23] Another measure of importance in the context of armed conflicts is the demobilisation and rehabilitation of child soldiers.

1. Duty to Adopt Legislative Measures to Prevent Further Violations

Guarantees of non-repetition involve structural changes and these can frequently be achieved through legislative measures. Thus, international jurisprudence has insisted on the obligation to adopt legislative changes as a consequence of its views, reports or judgments, even when it only decided on individual cases. Guarantees of non-repetition indeed constitute the wider legal consequence based on individual findings of a violation of international law. While the decisions and judgments of international bodies in principle are only binding *inter partes*, international case law has gone far beyond this narrow view and underlined the legal consequences of a wider, structural nature of its findings.

Before the jurisprudence in this area is outlined, it should be recalled that many human rights instruments contain obligations for states to adopt legislative measures as primary obligations.[24] The Human Rights Committee has reiterated this obligation in its *General Comment No 31 on Article 2*.[25] The obligation to adopt legislative measures as guarantees of non-repetition overlaps to a certain extent with the primary duty to adopt legislative measures. In this sense, the UN treaty bodies frequently recommend that states adopt certain legislative measures to bring their domestic laws into conformity with the respective treaty.

The Human Rights Committee underlined in the case of *Suárez de Guerrero* that domestic law should be amended to provide an effective protection for the right to life, as the applicable law at the time made justifiable certain actions by the police that were contrary to Article 6 of the Covenant.[26] In

[23] See Principle 36 a) of the UN Principles on Impunity.

[24] See the description of the duty to ensure human rights in Chapter I.

[25] See *General Comment No 31 on the Nature of the General Legal Obligation Imposed on States Parties to the Covenant*, 26 May 2004, CCPR/C/21/Rev.1/Add.13, para 7.

[26] Case *Suárez de Guerrero v Colombia*, Views of 30 March 1982, CCPR/C/15/D/45/1979, para 15; see also *Concluding Observations on Venezuela*, 26 April 2001, CCPR/CO/71/VEN, para 8.

the case of *Young v Australia*, the Committee held that the state should reconsider the applicant's pension claim, if necessary through an amendment of the law.[27] In the case of *Cesario Gómez Vázquez v Spain* the Committee found that the applicant had not had a right to review of his criminal conviction in violation of the Covenant. It held that the conviction had to be set aside unless it was reviewed, which implicitly required an amendment of the domestic law.[28] Pursuant to this decision, the state reformed its national legislation, expressly mentioning the decision of the Committee.[29] In its *General Comment No 31 on Article 2*, it insisted that 'the purposes of the Covenant would be defeated without an obligation integral to article 2 to take measures to prevent a recurrence of a violation of the Covenant.'[30]

The Inter-American Commission on Human Rights has sometimes given rather precise instructions for states to adopt legislation. It has, for example, recommended that states should accede to the Inter-American Convention on Enforced Disappearances;[31] that they review their domestic laws to ensure the right to consular assistance;[32] that they adapt their national laws so that they comply with international obligations concerning the fair trial and the death penalty;[33] or that they adopt laws to ensure that property rights of indigenous persons are determined in compliance with the American Declaration of the Rights and Duties of Man.[34]

The Inter-American Court follows a similar approach and orders the adoption of legislative measures to comply with the American Convention on Human Rights, when the violation is a direct consequence of legislation contravening

27 Case *Young v Australia*, Views of 29 August 2003, CCPR/C/78/D/941/2000, para 12.

28 Case *Cesario Gómez Vázquez v Spain*, Views of 11 August 2000, CCPR/C/69/D/701/1996, para 13.

29 Ley Orgánica 19/2003 of 23 December 2003, motives II.

30 *General Comment No 31 on the Nature of the General Legal Obligation Imposed on States Parties to the Covenant*, 26 May 2004, CCPR/C/21/Rev.1/Add.13, para 17.

31 Report No 51/99, Cases 10.471, *Anetro Castillo Pero et al* (Peru), 13 April 1999, para 151 (4); Report No. 101/01, Case 10.247 *et al, Extrajudicial Executions and Forced Disappearances of Persons* (Peru), 11 October 2001, para 253 (4).

32 Report No. 52/02, Merits, Case 11.753, *Ramón Martínez Villareal* (United States), 10 October 2002, para 101 (2)

33 Report No. 55/02, Merits, Case 11.765, *Paul Lallion* (Grenada), 21 October 2002, para 119 (2-4); Report No. 58/02, Merits, Case 12.275, *Denton Aitken*, 21 October 2002, para 161 (2-5).

34 Report No. 75/02, Case 11.140, *Mary and Carrie Dann* (United States), 27 December 2002, para 173.

the American Convention.[35] In the '*Last Temptation of Christ*' *Case*, it ordered that Chile should change its laws on censorship.[36] In the case concerning capital punishment it ordered that Trinidad and Tobago should change its laws on homicide.[37] In the case of *Trujillo Oroza*, it directed the state to introduce the crime of enforced disappearance in its criminal law.[38] In the case of *Castillo-Petruzzi*, the Court found that the scope of the military jurisdiction was incompatible with the American Convention on Human Rights because it allowed the trial of civilians by military tribunals. It consequently ordered that the state amend its legislation to bring it into conformity with the Convention.[39]

The most notable judgment of the Inter-American Court in this regard may be the case of *Barrios Altos (Peru)*. After the Court had adopted a judgment stating that the amnesty laws of Peru prevented the effective investigation and prosecution of gross human rights violations in the particular case brought before it, the government asked for an interpretation of the judgment on the merits. The Court answered in its interpretative judgment that the judgment on the merits on the incompatibility of amnesty laws had a general effect. This implied that Peru had to disregard or repeal its amnesty laws for all cases of gross human rights violations.[40]

The African Commission on Human and Peoples' Rights does not hesitate to recommend legislative changes when it finds that violations of the African Charter result directly from domestic laws in contravention of the Charter. In those cases, it recommends that the state 'bring its legislation in conformity to the Charter', be it criminal legislation, other laws or the constitution.[41]

---

35 Case *Loayza Tamayo v Peru (Reparations)*, Judgment of 27 November 1998, Series C No 42, para 164; Case *Suárez Rosero v Ecuador (Reparations)*, Judgment of 20 January 1999, Series C No 44, paras 97-99.

36 *Case of "The Last Temptation of Christ" v Chile*, Judgment of 5 February 2001, Series C No 73, para 88

37 Case *Hilaire, Constantine and Benjamin et al v Trinidad and Tobago*, Judgment of 21 June 2002, Series C No. 94, para 212.

38 Case *Trujillo Oroza v Bolivia (Reparations)*, Judgment of 27 February 2002, Series C No 92, para 122.

39 Case *Castillo-Petruzzi et al v Peru*, Judgment of 30 May 1999, Series C No 52, operative para 14.

40 *Case of Barrios Altos v Peru, Interpretation of the Judgment on the Merits*, Judgment of 3 September 2001, Series C No 83, para 18 and operative para 2.

41 Case *Avocats sans Frontières (on behalf of Gaëtan Bwampamye) v Burundi*, Communication 231/99 (28th Session, Nov 2000); Case *Civil Liberties Organisation, Legal Defence Centre, Legal Defence and Assistance Project v Nigeria*, Communication 218/98 (29th Ordinary Session, May 2001); Case *Legal resources foundation v Zambia*, Communication 211/98 (29th Ordinary Session, May 2001).

The European Court of Human Rights has recently adopted a radical change in its jurisprudence and, like other international human rights bodies, recommends legislative change. For a long time before this change, the Committee of Ministers of the Council of Europe, however, has made clear that states have an obligation to adopt legislative measures to comply with the judgments. Many states have changed their legislation pursuant to judgments of the European Court. For example, Belgium changed its laws on adoption pursuant to the cases of *Marckx v Belgium* and *Vermeire v Belgium*.[42] The United Kingdom is revising its military justice system after a series of judgments of the Court.[43] In the case of *Çiraklar v Turkey*, in which the Court had found a violation of the right to trial by an independent and impartial tribunal, the Committee of Ministers considered that the state had to amend its constitution to regulate national security courts in conformity with the Convention.[44] In resolutions concerning the implementation of several judgments against Turkey, the Committee of Ministers urged the state to reform the Turkish criminal procedure to enable an independent criminal investigation and to establish minimum prison sentences for torture and ill-treatment,[45] as well as to reform the system of criminal proceedings against members of security forces and the prosecutor's office.[46] In other resolutions it considered as measures of implementation a change in the act on criminal evidence[47] or in the legislation on data protection.[48]

In the judgement of *Broniowski v Poland* of 22 June 2004, the European Court decided to give directions to the state whose legislation led to a systemic violation of the European Convention to adopt legislative and other measures to address the systemic situation.[49]

[42] Case *Marckx v Belgium*, Judgment of 30 June 1979, Series A No 31; Case *Vermeire v Belgium*, Judgment of 29 November 1991, Series A No 214-C.

[43] Case *Findlay v the United Kingdom*, Judgment of 25 February 1997, Reports 1997-I; Case *Coyne v the United Kingdom*, 24 September 1997, Reports 1997-V; Case *Hood v the United Kingdom*, Judgment of 18 February 1999, Reports 1999-I.

[44] Resolution DH (99) 555, 28 October 1998 in the case of *Çiraklar v Turkey*.

[45] Interim Resolution ResDH (2002)98, Action of the security forces in turkey: Progress achieved and outstanding problems.

[46] Interim resolution DH (99) 434, *Action f the Security Forces in Turkey: Measures of a General Character*, 9 June 1999.

[47] Interim resolution DH (2000) 26, on the case of *John Murray v the United Kingdom*.

[48] Resolution DH (2000) 106, 24 July 2000, on the case of *Gaskin v the United Kingdom*.

[49] Case *Broniowski v Poland*, 22 June 2004, para 194; the Court uphald this jurisprudence in the case of *Hutten-Czapska v Poland*, 22 February 2005, para 192.

2. Protection of Human Rights Defenders, Medical, Legal, Media and Other Personnel

To prevent further violations, persons particularly at risk of human rights violations must receive special protection. This has been recognized within the United Nations systems with regard to human rights defenders, through the Declaration on Human Rights Defenders and in the mandate of the Special Representative of the Secretary General on Human Rights Defenders.[50]

The Human Rights Committee pays particular attention to human rights defenders or other groups likely to suffer human rights violation in the course of the exercise of their profession. In its Concluding Observations to Kyrgyzstan it expressed concern about 'the intimidation and harassment, in particular by government officials, of journalists and human rights activists, including members of human rights non-governmental organizations, who have been subjected to prosecution, fines and imprisonment' and especially about 'the use of libel suits against journalists who criticize the Government.'[51] In its Observations to Guatemala it recommended that '[t]he state party should take all necessary preventive and protective measures to ensure that the members of various sectors of society, particularly members of the judiciary, lawyers, human rights activists and trade unionists, can carry out their functions without intimidation of any kind.'[52] It expressed similar concerns in its Observations to Argentina and Colombia.[53]

The Committee against Torture has also taken into account the risks for such persons. The Committee recommended that human rights defenders should be protected from harassments, threats, and other attacks;[54] that human rights defenders and non-governmental organizations should be respected, together with their premises and archives;[55] and that the state should '[a]dopt adequate measures to permit the creation of independent

---

[50] UN Commission on Human Rights Resolution E/CN.4/RES/2000/61, 26 April 2000, para 3.

[51] *Concluding Observations: Kyrgyz Republic*, 24 July 2000, CCPR/CO/69/KGZ, para 20.

[52] *Concluding Observations: Guatemala*, 27 August 2001, CCPR/CO/72/GTM, para 21.

[53] *Concluding Observations: Argentina*, 03 November 2000, CCPR/CO/70/ARG, para 13; *Concluding Observations: Colombia*, 26 May 2004, CCPR/CO/80/COL, para 11.

[54] *Conclusions and recommendations: Indonesia*, CAT/C/XXVII/Concl.3, 22 November 2001, para 10 j).

[55] *Conclusions and recommendations: Turkey*, 27 May 2003, CAT/C/CR/30/5, para 7 (i).

non-governmental organizations and the development of their activities in the area of the defence of human rights.'[56]

Medical personnel must be subject to special protection, particularly when it is involved in the examination of cases of torture or killings.[57] In its Resolutions on the question of torture, the UN Commission on Human Rights '[u]rges Governments to protect medical and other personnel for their role in documenting torture or any other form of cruel, inhuman or degrading treatment or punishment and in treating victims of such acts.'[58]

Other professional groups can also come under particular threat. The Inter-American Commission has particularly noted the danger to which representatives of rural workers were exposed in Brazil and recommended their protection as well as that of human rights defenders.[59] In its Observations to Colombia, the Human Rights Committee expressed concern that human rights defenders, political and trade union leaders, judges and journalists were targets of arbitrary detention, forced disappearance, extrajudicial executions and murder.[60] These groups must be particularly protected to avoid further human rights violations.

3. Human Rights Training

Training in human rights to police and military forces, to persons working in the legal profession or prisons, and other actors concerned with human rights issues is a recurring recommendation to prevent human rights violations. It is recommended in some legal instruments such as in Article 25 AfrCHPR, Article 15 of the Declaration on Human Rights Defenders, Principle 16 of the Declaration of Basic Principles of Justice for Victims of Crime and Abuse of Power, and Article 10 (2) of the Protocol to Prevent, Suppress and Punish Trafficking in Persons, especially Women and Chil-

[56] *Conclusions and recommendations: Saudi Arabia*, CAT/C/CR/28/5, 28 May 2002, para 8 k).

[57] Medical Personnel is explicitly protected in Articles 12- 31 of the First Additional Protocol to the Geneva Conventions.

[58] Resolution E/CN.4/RES/2003/32 (torture), 23 April 2003, para 11; E/CN.4/RES/2002/38, 22 April 2002, para 38.

[59] Report No. 59/99, Case 11.405, *Newton Countinho Mendes* (Brazil), 13 April 1999, para 120 (2).

[60] *Concluding Observations on Colombia*, 26 May 2004, CCPR/CO/80/COL, para 11.

dren, supplementing the United Nations Convention against Transnational Organized Crime, Article 10 of the Convention against Torture and Other Cruel, Inhuman or Degrading Treatment or Punishment, Article 6 (3) of the Declaration on the Protection of All Persons from Enforced Disappearance, and Principle 3 of the UN Principles Extra-legal Executions.

Training on human rights has also been recommended by the UN Commission on Human Rights[61] and its special procedures,[62] the Human Rights Committee,[63] the Committee against Torture,[64] the Inter-American Court of Human Rights,[65] the Inter-American Commission on Human Rights,[66] and the Committee of Ministers of the Council of Europe.[67]

[61] Resolution E/CN.4/RES/2003/32 (torture), 23 April 2003, para 20; Resolution E/CN.4/RES/2003/53 (extrajudicial, summary and arbitrary executions), 24 April 2003, para 9.

[62] *Consolidated Recommendations of the Special Rapporteur on torture*, A/56/156, 3 July 2001, para 39 (i), (k), (l); *Report of the Special Rapporteur on violence against women on cultural practices in the family that are violent towards women*, 31 January 2002, E/CN.4/2002/83, paras 126, 128, 129.

[63] *Concluding Observations: Colombia*, 5 May 1997, CCPR/C/79/Add.76, para 35; *Concluding Observations: Libyan Arab Jamahiriya*, 6 November 98, CCPR/C/79/Add.101, para 10; *Concluding Observations: Kyrgyz Republic*, 24 July 2000, CCPR/CO/69/KGZ, para 6; *Concluding Observations: Hungary*, 19 April 2002, CCPR/CO/74/HUN, para 12.

[64] *Conclusions and recommendations: Zambia*, CAT/C/XXVII/Concl.4, 23 November 2001, para 8 f); *Conclusions and recommendations: Indonesia*, CAT/C/XXVII/Concl.3, 22 November 2001, para 10 k); *Conclusions and recommendations: Saudi Arabia*, CAT/C/CR/28/5, 28 May 2002, para 8 j); *Conclusions and recommendations: Brazil*, A/56/44, paras 115-120, 16 May 2001, para 120 e); *Conclusions and recommendations*: Turkey, 27 May 2003, CAT/C/CR/30/5, para 7 (j), (k); *Conclusions and recommendations: Cambodia*, 27 May 2003, CAT/C/CR/30/2, para 7 (j).

[65] Case *Trujillo Oroza v Bolivia (Reparations)*, Judgment of February 27, 2002, Series C No 92, para 121; *Case of Caracazo v Venezuela (Reparation)*, Judgment of August 29, 2002, Series C No 95, para 127.

[66] Report 34/00, Case 11.291, *Carandiru* (Brazil), 13 April 2000, Recommendation 3 [training of prison personnel]; Report No. 54/01, Case 12.051, *Maria Da Penha Maia Fernandes* (Brazil), 16 April 2001, para 61 (4, a, e) [training on domestic violence]; Report No. 78/02, Merits, Case 11.335, *Guy Malary* (Haiti), 27 December 2002, para 101 (c) [training of judicial authorities to carry out investigations].

[67] Interim resolution DH (99) 434, *Action of the Security Forces in Turkey: Measures of a General Character*, 9 June 1999. The Committee of Ministers of the Council of Europe has encouraged the training of judges as measures of implementation of the judgment of the European Court of Human Rights: Interim Resolution ResDH(2004)14 *concerning the judgment of the European Court of Human Rights* of 25 July 2002 (final on 6 November 2002) in the case of *Sovtransavto Holding against Ukraine*; Interim Resolution ResDH(2002)98, *Action of the security forces in Turkey, Progress achieved and outstanding problems, General measures to ensure compliance with the judgments of the European Court of Human Rights in the cases against Turkey* listed in Appendix II (Follow-up to Interim Resolution DH(99/434), 10 July 2002.

4. Civilian Control over Military and Security Forces

As mentioned above,[68] international case law has found that the trial of military personnel by military courts in cases of gross human rights violations may perpetuate impunity for these violations. They should be tried in civilian courts. Beyond this specific aspect of control of the military, there is a wider aspect to the embedding of the military in the democratic structures of a state.

Gross human rights violations and violations of humanitarian law are frequently committed by members of the armed forces where these have a close link to the government such as in military regimes. On the background of this experience, human rights norms and practice have sometimes recommended that military and security forces should be controlled by the civilian institutions. Thus, the UN Human Rights Commission called upon states to strengthen the rule of law by 'ensuring that the military remains accountable to democratically elected civilian government.'[69] The Human Rights Committee has recommended the primacy and control of civil over military authorities.[70] The Committee against Torture made similar recommendations.[71] The Inter-American Commission on Human Rights has also recommended an independent, impartial and effective supervision of military police.[72]

***

[68] See above Chapter V, at IV.

[69] Resolution E/CN.4/RES/2000/47, 25 April 2000, para 1 (c) (ix).

[70] *Concluding Observations: Romania*, 28 July 1999. CCPR/C/79/Add.111. para 9; *Concluding Observations: Lesotho*, CCPR/C/79/Add. 106, 8 April 1999, para 14; *Concluding Observations: El Salvador*, CCPR/C/79/Add.34, 18 April 1994, para 8.

[71] *Conclusions and Recommendations: Chile*, 26 June 1995, A/50/44, paras 52-61, at 60 c).

[72] Report No. 55/01, Case 11.286 *et al*, *Aluísio Cavalcanti et al*, 16 April 2001 (Brazil), para 168 (6).

Summary

Human rights violations constitute violations of the state's obligations under international law. It therefore follows that, where the violation is ongoing, states have a duty to cease it.

The concept of guarantees of non-repetition as it is known from general international law, has now been clarified in the ambit of human rights law. The most important aspect of guarantees of non-repetition is their structural and wide-reaching nature. Thus, even in individual cases, a finding of violation by an international body means that the state not only has to cease violation in the particular case, but that it has to adopt further reaching measures in order to guarantee that the violation will not be repeated.

This may entail the adoption of legislative measures when violations result directly from domestic law. It may also imply the adoption of certain practices and policies, such as those to protect certain categories of persons at risk. Quite importantly, the need for education and training of all involved actors is a constant requirement voiced by all international bodies.

CHAPTER VII
RESTITUTION, COMPENSATION, REHABILITATION AND SATISFACTION

'It is a principle of international law that the breach of an engagement involves an obligation to make reparation in an adequate form. Reparation is therefore the indispensable complement of a failure to apply a convention and there is no necessity for this to be stated in the convention itself.'[1]

In 1927, the Permanent Court of International Justice, the world court established by the League of Nations, affirmed a fundamental principle of international law. It held, in the above-quoted passage, that a breach of an international obligation entails the obligation to repair the breach. It held that 'reparation is the indispensable complement of a failure to apply a convention and there is no necessity for this to be stated in the convention itself.' It is maybe the most important aspect of the Permanent Court's judgment that it saw the duty to repair as a necessary corollary to an international obligation. It essentially applied a principle of logic: what is being done in breach of international law must be undone.

It is important to recall this landmark judgment because it made clear that *all* violations of international law entail a duty to repair the violation, whether it is expressly mentioned or not, because the right to reparation is a right recognized by customary international law. While the Permanent Court of International Justice and subsequently the International Court of Justice did not address the question of individual reparation for human rights violations, the self-evident approach that reparation must be awarded

1 *Case Concerning the Factory at Chorzów (Jurisdiction)*, P.C.I.J. Series A, No 9 [8 i.e.], 26 July 1927, p 21.

to those affected by a breach of international law appears to be confirmed by the advisory opinion of the International Court of Justice *Legal consequences of the construction of a wall in the Occupied Palestinian Territory*. In this opinion, the Court held that reparation had to be made to all natural and legal persons concerned by breaches of human rights and international humanitarian law.[2] While it is clear that States have a duty to repair violations of human rights and humanitarian law, the modalities of the reparation may vary according to the right violated, the gravity of the violation, the harm done or the persons affected. Some of these aspects are clarified in the following.

***

This chapter describes different forms of reparation. The terminology regarding forms of reparation is taken from general public international law,[3] rather than from domestic systems. All the mentioned forms of reparation have been awarded by tribunals in disputes between states. As international human rights bodies have equally used this terminology, and referred to the reparation cases concerning inter-state disputes,[4] it is difficult to separate the case law on reparations between states and reparations to individuals.

While not in terms of human rights, but under their right to diplomatic protection, states have frequently sought reparations for injuries or other violations suffered by their nationals.[5] These claims are not made on behalf of the individual, but in the state's own right. However, the extent and content of the reparation and the amount of compensation was assessed with regard to the injury caused to the individual, and not to the state.[6] As

---

2 *Legal Consequences of the Construction of a Wall in the Occupied Palestinian Territory*, Advisory Opinion of 9 July 2004, paras 152-153.

3 See the discussion of terminology in *I. Brownlie*, Principles of Public International Law, 6th Edition, OUP 2003, pp. 441-449.

4 See, for instance, the Judgment of the Inter-American Court in *Velásquez Rodríguez v Honduras (Compensatory damages)*, 21 July 1989, Series C No7, para 25 and of the European Court of Human Rights in *Papamichalopoulos and others v Greece*, 31 October 1995, Series A No 330-B, para 36, both citing the *Chorzów Factory Case*.

5 See *P. Daillier/A. Pellet*, Droit International Public, 7th Edition, L.G.D.J., p. 793, No. 487.

6 Article 39 of the UN Draft Articles on Responsibility of States for Internationally Wrongful Acts implies this by stating that '[i]n the determination of reparation, account shall be taken to the contribution to the injury by [...] any person or entity in relation to whom reparation is sought.'

far as the content and forms of reparations are concerned, therefore, it is possible to seek guidance in the jurisprudence of the International Court of Justice, the Permanent Court of International Justice as well as arbitration tribunals and claims commissions. Moreover, the International Law Commission referred to the jurisprudence of human rights bodies, in particular the Inter-American and European Courts of Human Rights, to formulate its commentaries of the Draft Articles on Responsibility of States for Internationally Wrongful Acts.[7] Thus, these articles themselves were partly based on human rights jurisprudence, and the two fields of reparations, those to injured states and those to private parties, are closely intertwined. Likewise, the Inter-American Court of Human Rights has held since the *Aloeboetoe Case* that Article 63 (1) ACHR, which regulates the right to reparation, 'codifies a rule of customary law which, moreover, is one of the fundamental principles of current international law [...].'[8] It held:

> 'Reparations is a generic term that covers the various ways a State may make amends for the international responsibility it has incurred (*restitutio in integrum*, payment of compensation, satisfaction, guarantees of non-repetitions among others).'[9]

***

Reparation is an umbrella designation for many different forms of redress. It is important to stress that they are usually cumulative. This is not true, however, for restitution and compensation: compensation is due when restitution cannot be obtained – even though, of course, a violation may frequently entail restitution (for example of property) and also compensation for moral damage. But in general, while not all available forms of reparation are necessary in all cases, states cannot always choose to only award one form of reparation. This is also a general principle of law. Article 34 of the Draft Articles on Responsibility of States for Internationally Wrongful Acts says that full reparation shall take the form of restitution, compensation and satisfaction 'either singly or in combination'. The International Law Commission has noted that this formulation does not leave the form of repara-

7 See for instance Commentary to Article 36, para 19 and Commentary to Article 38, para 5.

8 Case *Aloeboetoe et al v Suriname (Reparations)*, Judgment of 10 September 1993, Series A No 15, para 43.

9 Case *Loayza Tamayo v Peru (Reparations)*, Judgment of 27 November 1998, Series C No 42, para 85.

tion to the discretion of the state, but rather clarifies that reparation may only be achieved in particular cases by the combination of different forms of reparation.[10] The Independent Expert on Impunity of the UN Commission on Human Rights, Diane Orentlicher, has likewise stressed that an important feature of an effective programme of reparations is its comprehensiveness.[11] The Human Rights Committee similarly understands reparation as encompassing 'restitution, rehabilitation and measures of satisfaction, such as public apologies, public memorials, guarantees of non-repetition and changes in relevant laws and practices, as well as bringing to justice the perpetrators of human rights violations.'[12]

***

Note on Terminology

Measures of reparations are recognized in many forms under international law: firstly in the Draft Articles on Responsibility of States for Internationally Wrongful Acts, in many human rights instruments[13] and by the interpretation of relevant provisions by all human rights bodies. It is impossible to find a coherent terminology for all systems or countries. One finds the general term 'reparation' (Article 34 of the Draft Articles on Responsibility of States for Internationally Wrongful Acts), 'compensation' (Article 9(5) ICCPR) 'remedy and compensation' (Article 63 ACHR), 'reparation' or 'just satisfaction' (Article 41 ECHR), 'redress and adequate compensation' (14 CAT), 'just and adequate reparation or satisfaction' (Article 6 CERD), 'compensation' (article 91 1st Add. Prot), 'reparation, including restitution, compensation and reha-

[10] Commentary to Article 34, para 2.

[11] *Independent Study on Impunity*, E/CN.4/2004/88, 27 February 2004, para 60.

[12] *General Comment No. 31 on the Nature of the General Legal Obligation Imposed on States Parties to the Covenant*, 26 May 2004, CCPR/C/21/Rev.1/Add.13, para 16.

[13] Article 9 (5) ICCPR; Article 14 CAT; Article 16 (4), (5) Indigenous and Tribal Peoples Convention 1989 (No. 169); Article 75 (1) and 85 Rome Statute of the International Criminal Court; Art. 106 Rules of Procedure and Evidence of ICTR and ICTY; Article 10, 63 (1) ACHR; Article 9 Inter-American Convention to Prevent and Punish Torture; Articles 5 (5), 41 ECHR; Articles 235, 288 (2), 285 ECT; Article 41 (3) EU Charter of Fundamental Rights; Article 21 (2) AfrCHPR; Article 27 (1) Protocol to the African Charter on Human and Peoples' Rights on the Establishment of an African Court on Human and Peoples' Rights; Article 19 Declaration on the Protection of all Persons from Enforced Disappearance; Principle 12 of the Declaration of Basic Principles of Justice for Victims of Crime and Abuse of Power; Article 9 (2) Declaration on Human Rights Defenders; Article 68 Third Geneva Convention; Article 91 First Additional Protocol to the Geneva Conventions.

bilitation' (Article 75 of the Rome Statute of the International Criminal Court), to name only some examples.

Note that the International Covenant on Civil and Political Rights does not contain a general reparations clause. The Human Rights Committee, however, relying on the right to a remedy in Article 2 (3) ICCPR has recognized that this right entails a duty of the state to grant reparation. This is an evolutive interpretation of this Article which, as the French and Spanish versions show, originally meant a right to a procedural remedy.[14]

However, it emerges from the practice and jurisprudence that under these different headings, many different measures have been ordered that can broadly be classified into the categories that have been chosen by the Special Rapporteur on the right to reparation in 1993: restitution, compensation, rehabilitation and satisfaction. Many of the measures fall under several categories, but are only described in this Guide under one category for brevity.

***

I. Restitution

Restitution is meant to reverse or annul the act that caused the violation and is recognized in a number of human rights instruments.[15] In accordance with the famous dictum in the *Chorzów Factory Case*, restitution or *restitutio in integrum* constitutes the primary objective of reparation.

> 'The essential principle contained in the actual notion of an illegal act – a principle which seems to be established by international practice and in particular in the decisions of arbitral tribunals – is that reparation must, as far as possible, wipe all of the consequences of the illegal act and re-establish the situation which would, in all probability, have existed if that act had not been committed.'[16]

It means the reconstitution of the *status quo ante*, the situation that would have existed if the violation had not occurred. There is a recognized excep-

[14] See in Spanish: 'recurso efectivo'; in French: 'recours utile'.

[15] Article 63 (1) ACHR; Article 41 ECHR ; Article 75 Rome Statute on the International Criminal Court; Principles 8-10 of the Declaration of Basic Principles of Justice for Victims of Crime and Abuse of Power.

[16] *Case Concerning the Factory At Chorzów (Claim for Indemnity) (The Merits)*, P.C.I.J., Series A No 17, 13 September 1928, p 47.

tion to this rule, stated in Article 35 of the Draft Articles on Responsibility of States for Internationally Wrongful Acts, when restitution is not materially possible or when it involves a 'burden out of all proportion to the benefit deriving from restitution instead of compensation'. This means that if restitution entails efforts or costs out of proportion, then instead of restitution, the state can pay compensation.

In a similar way, the European Court of Human Rights has considered reparation to be a consequence of the legally binding nature of its judgments and *restitutio in integrum* to be the primary means of reparation:

> 'The Court points out that by Article 53 of the Convention the High Contracting Parties undertook to abide by the decision of the Court in any case to which they were parties; furthermore, Article 54 provides that the judgment of the Court shall be transmitted to the Committee of Ministers which shall supervise its execution. It follows that a judgment in which the Court finds a breach imposes on the respondent State a legal obligation to put an end to the breach and make reparation for its consequences in such a way as to restore as far as possible the situation existing before the breach.'[17]

It has also recalled 'if *restitutio in integrum* is in practice impossible, the respondent states are free to choose the means whereby they comply with a judgment in which the Court has found a breach, and the Court will not make consequential orders or declaratory statements in this regard. It falls to the Committee of Ministers of the Council of Europe, acting under Article 54 of the Convention, to supervise compliance in this respect.'[18]

The UN Principles on Reparation define restitution as follows:

> 'Restitution should, whenever possible, restore the victim to the original situation before the violations of international human rights or humanitarian law occurred. Restitution includes, as appropriate: restoration of liberty, enjoyment of human rights, identity, family life and citizenship, return to one's place of residence, restoration of employment and return of property.'[19]

[17] Case *Papamichalopoulos and Others v Greece (Article 50)*, Judgment of 31 October 1995, Series A No. 330-B, para 34.

[18] Case *Selçuk and Asker v Turkey*, Judgment of 24 April 1998, Reports 1998-II, para 125; Case *Yöyler v Turkey*, Judgment of 24 July 2003, para 124; It is indeed the Committee of Ministers which supervises the compliance with judgments and measures of reparation.

[19] Principle 19.

Some of the measures of restitution are discussed below.

1. Right to Reopening of Criminal Proceedings

When the violation was caused by an act of the judiciary, it has to be reversed and the consequences arising out of it annulled, even if it was a binding judgment.[20] International jurisprudence has recognized that persons convicted pursuant to a miscarriage of justice have a right to re-trial or a right to commutation of sentence.

The Human Rights Committee has also demanded retrials of persons tried in contravention of the Covenant.[21] In the case of *Polay Campos v Peru*, in which the applicant had been convicted pursuant to an unfair trial, the Human Rights Committee considered that 'Mr. Polay Campos should be released unless Peruvian law provides for the possibility of a fresh trial that does offer all the guarantees required by article 14 of the Covenant.'[22] Similarly, it held in the case of *Semey v Spain* that the author should have an effective remedy according to Article 2 (3) ICCPR and should be entitled to have his conviction reviewed in conformity with the requirements of Article 14 (5) ICCPR.[23] The Committee has, moreover, considered that the simple pardon of convicted persons does not provide full redress. In the case of Peru it has recommended that the state 'revise all the convictions handed down by the military tribunals in treason and terrorism cases.'[24]

The Inter-American Court has ordered the re-trial of persons convicted in violation of the principles of fair trial.[25] The Inter-American Commission, in cases concerning capital punishment in which it found a violation of the American Convention on Human Rights, recommended that the state grant the victim an

---

20 *Affaire Martini (Italie c. Venezuela)*, sentence du 3 mai 1930, Recueil de sentences arbitrales, Volume II, p 975, at 1001.

21 Case *Raul Sendic Antonaccio v Uruguay*, Views of 28 October 1981, CCPR/C/14/D/63/1979, para 21.

22 Case *Polay Campos v Peru*, Views of 9 January 1998, CCPR/C/61/D/577/1994, para 10.

23 Case *Semey v Spain*, Views of 21 August 2003, CCPR/C/78/986/2001, para 9.2.

24 *Concluding Observations on Peru*, 18 November 1996, CCPR/C/79/Add.72, para 10; see also *Concluding Observations on Peru*, 15 November 2000, CCPR/CO/70/PER, para 11.

25 *Castillo Petruzzi et al Case*, Judgment of 30 May 1999, Series C No. 52, para 217-221.

effective remedy, including 're-trial in accordance with the due process protections prescribed under Article 8 of the Convention or, where a re-trial in compliance with these protections is not possible, his release, and compensation.'[26] In several cases concerning capital punishment, the Inter-American Commission found mandatory death penalty in violation of human rights. It recommended, as a consequence, that the state commute the sentence.[27]

The European Court has held under Article 41 ECHR that, '[w]here the Court finds that an applicant was convicted by a tribunal which was not independent and impartial within the meaning of Article 6 § 1, it considers that, in principle, the most appropriate form of relief would be to ensure that the applicant is granted in due course a retrial by an independent and impartial tribunal.'[28] However, it frequently refuses to give concrete indications as to the measures to be taken, since, according to Article 46 (2) ECHR, the supervision of the execution of judgments falls into the competence of the Committee of Ministers. The latter invited states parties to the Convention to 'ensure that there exist at national level adequate possibilities to achieve, as far as possible, *restitutio in integrum* and particularly 'to examine their national legal systems with a view to ensuring that there exist adequate possibilities of re-examination of the case, including reopening of proceedings, in instances where the Court has found a violation of the Convention [...].'[29]

---

[26] Report No. 127/01, Case 12.183, *Joseph Thomas* (Jamaica), 3 December 2001, para 153 (1) [right to a remedy, including re-trial or release]; Report No. 52/02, Merits, Case 11.753, *Ramón Martínez Villareal* (United States), 10 October 2002, para 101 (1) [*idem*].

[27] Report No. 55/02/, Merits, Case 11.765, *Paul Lallion* (Grenada), 21 October 2002, para 119 (1); Report No. 58/02, Merits, Case 12.275, *Denton Aitken*, 21 October 2002, para 161 (1).

[28] Case *Ükünç and Günes v Turkey*, Judgment of 18 December 2003, para 32; Case *Gençel v Turkey*, Judgment of 23 October 2003, para 27; Case *Somogyi v Italy*, Judgment of 18 May 2004, para 86; Case *Stoichkov v Bulgaria*, 24 March 2005, para 81.

[29] Recommendation No R (2000) 2, 19 January 2000, *on the re-examination o reopening of certain cases at domestic level following judgments of the European Court of Human Rights*. The recommendation encourages *restitutio in integrum* '[...]especially where:

(i) the injured party continues to suffer very serious negative consequences because of the outcome of the domestic decision at issue, which are not adequately remedied by the just satisfaction and cannot be rectified except by re-examination or reopening, and

(ii) the judgment of the Court leads to the conclusion that

(a) the impugned domestic decision is on the merits contrary to the Convention, or

(b) the violation found is based on procedural errors or shortcomings of such gravity that a serious doubt is cast on the outcome of the domestic proceedings complained of.'

The African Commission on Human and Peoples' Rights has also asked states to take appropriate measures to ensure the reopening of cases and re-trial.[30] In cases where it found that the military trials of civilians had contravened the African Charter on Human and Peoples' Rights, it urged states to permit civil re-trials.[31]

Recently in the *LaGrand Case*, the International Court of Justice held that:

> 'The Court considers in this respect that if the United States, notwithstanding its commitment [...], should fail in its obligation of consular notification to the detriment of German nationals, an apology would not suffice in cases where the individuals concerned have been subjected to prolonged detention or convicted and sentenced to severe penalties. In the case of such a conviction and sentence, it would be incumbent upon the United States to allow the review and reconsideration of the conviction and sentence by taking account of the violation of the rights set forth in the Convention. This obligation can be carried out in various ways. The choice of means must be left to the United States.'[32]

In the *Avena and other Mexican Nationals Case*, the International Court of Justice emphasised that the review and reconsideration had to take into account the violations, which included 'the question of the legal consequences of the violation upon the criminal proceedings that have followed the violation',[33] and that 'it is the judicial process that is suited to this task.'[34] It held that clemency proceedings did not meet these requirements as they did not fully examine and take into account the violation.[35] Thus, although the ICJ did not examine a case of human rights violations, it can

---

[30] Case *Civil Liberties Organisation v Nigeria*, Communication 151/96 (26th Ordinary Session, Nov 1999); Case *Avocats sans Frontières (on behalf of Gaëtan Bwampamye) v Burundi*, Communication 231/99 (28th Session, Nov 2000).

[31] Case *Civil Liberties Organisation v Nigeria*, Communication 151/96 (26th Ordinary Session, Nov 1999); Case *Media Rights Agenda v Nigeria*, Communication 224/98 (28th ordinary Session, Nov 2000), para 62.

[32] *LaGrand Case (Germany v the United States)*, Judgment of 27 June 2001, I.C.J. Reports 2001, p 514, para 125.

[33] Case of *Avena and other Mexican Nationals (Mexico v United States of America)*, Judgment of 31 March 2004, para 131.

[34] *Ibid*, para 140.

[35] *Ibid*, paras 138, 143.

be deduced from its judgment that in cases of human rights violations - such as violations of fair trial rights - leading to flawed criminal proceedings, both the sentence and the conviction must be subject to judicial review and reconsideration, because they are in breach of international law.

2. Restoration of Legal Rights

Beyond the re-opening of criminal proceedings, other legal rights may have to be restored. 'Restoration of legal rights' means the re-recognition of rights that were denied to the person as a result of a human rights violation. The most important example in this area is the rectification of a person's criminal record after a trial and conviction in violation of human rights. Human rights treaties provide that if a person has been convicted wrongfully and as a result of a miscarriage of justice, the state should provide him or her compensation.[36] However, the consequences of a conviction must be reversed if a person has been convicted wrongfully; mere compensation will not repair the harm done. This has been confirmed by international jurisprudence.

In the case of *Loayza Tamayo*, the petitioner had been detained and convicted in violation of the rights of the ACHR. The Inter-American Court held that all the consequences of the violations had to be annulled. This meant that all records of the trial and conviction and of the detention had to be annulled.[37] It decided similarly in the cases *Suárez Rosero* and *Cantoral Benavides*.[38]

In cases of convictions contrary to the Convention, the Committee of Ministers of the Council of Europe considered that the state had 'to take ad hoc measures allowing the consequences of the applicants' convictions contrary to the Convention in the above-mentioned cases to be rapidly and fully erased [...].'[39] Convictions based on unfair trials had to be erased.[40]

---

[36] Article 14(6) ICCPR, Article 3, Protocol 7 to the ECHR, Article 10 ACHR.

[37] Case *Loayza Tamayo v Peru (Reparations)*, Judgment of 27 November 1998, Series C No 42, para 122.

[38] Case *Suárez Rosero v Ecuador (Reparations)*, Judgment of 20 January 1999, Series C No 44, para 76; Case *Cantoral Benavides v Peru (Reparations)*, Judgment of 3 December 2001, Series C No 88, para 77, 78.

[39] Interim resolution DH (2001) 106, 23 July 2001, on *Violations of Freedom of expression in Turkey: Individual measures.*

[40] Interim Resolution ResDH(2004)13 concerning *Dorigo Paolo v Italy*, Interim Resolutions DH(99)258

3. Restoration of Liberty

In cases of detention in violation of international human rights law or of prison sentences resulting from unfair trials, international jurisprudence has found that persons must be released.[41] The Human Rights Committee has also found that if conditions of detention violate international human rights law, the detainee must be released if the conditions of detention do not improve.[42]

4. Restoration or Recognition of Citizenship

The UN Principles on Reparation list as one of the modalities of reparation the restoration of citizenship. Indeed, where someone is deprived of his or her nationality in violation of international law,[43] *restitutio in integrum* can be easily achieved through restoration or recognition of citizenship. This has been recognized, for example, by the Working Group on Enforced or Involuntary Disappearances[44] and the African Commission on Human and Peoples' Rights.[45]

of 15 January 1999 (finding of a violation) and DH(2002)30 of 19 February 2002 (reopening of judicial proceedings in violation of European Convention of Human Rights).

[41] Human Rights Committee: *Concluding Observations on Peru*, 15 November 2000, CCPR/CO/70/PER, para 11 (b); Case *Sarma v Sri Lanka*, Views of 31 July 2003, CCPR/C/78/D/950/2000, para 11; Case *Casafranca de Gómez v Peru*, Views of 20 August 2000, CCPR/C/78/D/981/2001, para 9; Case *Polay Campos v Peru*, Views of 9 January 1998, CCPR/C/61/D/577/1994, para 10; Case *Teillier Arredondo v Peru*, Views of 14 August 2000, CCPR/C/69/D/688/1996, para 12; ECtHR: Case *Assanidze v Georgia*, Judgment of 8 April 2004, paras 202-203; Case *Ilascu and others v Moldova and Russia*, Judgment of 8 July 2004, para 490; I/ACtHR: *Loayza Tamayo Case*, Judgment of 17 September 1997, Series C No 33, operative paragraph 5); AfrCmHPR: Case *Constitutional Rights Project and Civil Liberties Organisation v Nigeria*, Communication 102/93 (24th Ordinary Session, Oct 1998); Case *Centre for Free Speech v Nigeria*, Communication 206/97 (26th Ordinary Session, Nov 1999); Case *Constitutional Rights Project and Civil Liberties Organisation v Nigeria*, Communications 143/95, 150/96 (26th Ordinary Session, November 1999); Case *Constitutional Rights Project v Nigeria*, Communication 148/96 (26th Ordinary Session, November 1999).

[42] Case *Reece v Jamaica*, Views of 21 July 2003, CCPR/C/78/D/796/1998, para 9.

[43] The right to a nationality is enshrined in Article 15 (1) UDHR, Article 24 (3) ICCPR, Article 5 (d) (iii) of CERD Article 9 CEDAW, Article 8 CRC, Article 29 MWC.

[44] *General Comments on Article 19 of the Declaration on the Protection of All Persons from Enforced Disappearance*, 12 January 1998, E/CN.1/1998/43, para 75.

[45] Case *Malawi African Association et al. v Mauritania*, Communications 54/91, 61/91, 98/93, 164/97, 196/97, 210/98 (27th Ordinary Session, May 2000), Case *John K. Modise v Botswana*, Communication 97/93 (28th Ordinary Session, November 2000).

5. Return to One's Place of Residence

In a case where the state had omitted to protect the applicant against threats to his life and to investigate those threats so that the applicant had to live abroad, the Human Rights Committee held that the state had an obligation to 'take appropriate measures to protect his security of person and his life so as to allow him to return to the country.'[46] Similarly, the African Commission on Human and Peoples' Rights held that the state should ensure the return of an applicant who had been subject to political persecution and obliged to leave the country.[47] It also held that where persons have been expelled from the country in contravention of the AfrCHPR, the state should ensure their swift return.[48] This jurisprudence to a certain extent echoes the right to return to one's country enshrined in international law,[49] particularly the right to return of refugees.[50]

6. Restoration of Employment

In many cases, persons are dismissed from their employment in violation of their human rights. In these cases, *restitutio in integrum* can be achieved through restoration of employment. This has been increasingly reflected in international jurisprudence. The Human Rights Committee has held that the authorities should ensure restoration of employment or a similar employment so as to provide an effective remedy in the sense of Article 2 (3) ICCPR.[51] In the case of *Chira Vargas-Machuca v Peru* it held that the state

[46] Case *Jiménez Vaca v Colombia*, Views of 15 April 2002, CCPR/C/74/D/859/1999, para 9; see also Working Group on Enforced or Involuntary Disappearances, *General Comments on Article 19 of the Declaration on the Protection of All Persons from Enforced Disappearance*, 12 January 1998, E/CN.1/1998/43, para 75.

[47] Case *John D. Ouko v Kenya*, Communication 232/99 (28th Ordinary Session, November 2000).

[48] Case *Malawi African Association et al v Mauritania*, Communications 54/91, 61/91, 98/93, 164/97, 196/97, 210/98 (27th Ordinary Session, May 2000).

[49] See Article 13 (2) UDHR, Article 12 (4) ICCPR, Article 5 (d) (ii) CERD.

[50] This right has been reaffirmed in numerous Resolutions of the UN General Assembly: Resolutions 49/169 of 23 December 1994, operative paragraph 9; 50/152 of 21 December 1995, operative paragraph 17; 51/75 of 12 December 1996, operative paragraph 16; 52/103, 12 December 1997, operative paragraph 12; 53/125 of 9 December 1998, operative paragraph 11; 54/146, 17 December 1999, operative paragraph 12; 54/147, 17 December 1999, operative paragraph 16; 56/135, 19 December 2001, operative paragraph 19; 55/74, 4 December 2000, operative paragraph 15; 57/183, 18 December 2002, operative paragraph 22.

[51] Case *Busyo v Democratic Republic of Congo*, Views of 9 August 2003, CCPR/C/78/D/933/2000,

should ensure the applicant's 'effective reinstatement to his duties and to his post, with all the consequences that that implies, at the rank that he would have held had he not been dismissed in 1991, or to a similar post', and also 'compensation comprising a sum equivalent to the payment of the arrears of salary and remuneration that he would have received from the time at which he was not reinstated to his post.'[52] Similar findings have been reached by the Committee on the Elimination of Racial Discrimination,[53] the Working Group on Enforced or Involuntary Disappearances,[54] the African Commission on Human and Peoples' Rights[55] and the Inter-American Court of Human Rights.[56] They also held that if the restoration of employment is not possible, the state should provide compensation. In the case of *Loayza Tamayo*, the Inter-American Court found that the state had to ensure restoration of employment; if this was not possible because of the moral damage caused to the victim, then the authorities had to guarantee salary, social security and employment benefits.[57]

In sum, it may be retained that in case of loss of employment as a consequence of a human rights violation, it emerges from international human rights jurisprudence that the state has to grant *restitutio in integrum* in the form of restoration of this employment; if this is not possible, the victim must be ensured similar employment; and only as a last resort, if neither may be guaranteed, the authorities must grant compensation for the loss of employment.

7. Return of Property

As for deprivation of property in violation of human rights, *restitutio in integrum* in principle requires the return of property. In the case of unlawful

para 6.2; Case *Nyekuma Kopita Toro Gedumbe v Democratic Republic of the Congo*, Views of 1 August 1997, CCPR/C/75/D/641/1995, para 6.2.

52 Case *Félix Enrique Chira Vargas-Machuca v Peru*, Views of 26 July 2002, CCPR/C/75/D/906/2000, para 9.

53 Case *Yilmaz Dogan v the Netherlands*, Views of 29 September 1988, CERD/C/36/D/1/1984, para 10.

54 *General Comments on Article 19 of the Declaration on the Protection of All Persons from Enforced Disappearance*, 12 January 1998, E/CN.4/1998/43, para 75.

55 Case *Malawi African Association et al. v Mauritania*, Communications 54/91, 61/91, 98/93, 164/97, 196/97, 210/98 (27th Ordinary Session, May 2000).

56 Case *Baena Ricardo et al v Panama*, Judgment of 2 February 2001, Series C No 72, para 203.

57 Case *Loayza Tamayo v Peru (Reparations)*, Judgment of 27 November 1998, Series C No 42, paras 113-116.

expropriation, the European Court of Human Rights held that 'the best form of redress would in principle be for the state to return the land.'[58] The Human Rights Committee has also recommended restitution of property or equivalent compensation.[59] Likewise, the African Commission on Human and Peoples' Rights recommended the restitution of the looted belonging to the applicants.[60]

***

In sum, it is clear from international law and jurisprudence that the principle of *restitutio in integrum* is firmly rooted in international human rights law. Where the *status quo ante* can be returned to, the authorities have an obligation to ensure measures for its restoration. However, while restitution is, in principle, the primary form of reparation, in practice it is the least frequent, because it is mostly impossible to completely return to the situation before the violation, especially because of the moral damage caused to victims and their relatives. Where complete restitution is not possible, they have to take measures to achieve a status as approximate as possible, such as, for instance, re-employment in a similar position. Where this is not feasible either, the state has to provide compensation covering the damage arisen from the loss of the *status quo ante*.

II. Compensation

The UN Principles on Reparation have summarized the practice and jurisprudence into the following formulation.

> 'Compensation should be provided for any economically assessable damage, as appropriate and proportional to the gravity of the violation and the circumstances of each case, resulting from gross violations of international human rights law and serious violations of humanitarian law, such as:

[58] Case *Hentrich v France*, Judgment of 22 September 1994, Series A No 296-A, para 71; see also Case *Papamichalopoulos and Others v Greece (Article 50)*, Judgment of 31 October 1995, Series A No. 330-B, para 38; Case *Brumarescu v Romania* [GC], Judgment of 23 January 2001, Reports 2001-I, para 22.

[59] Case *Brok v Czeck Republic*, Views of 15 January 2002, CCPR/C/73/D/774/1997, paras 7.4, 9; Case *Des Fours Walderode*, Views of 2 November 2001, CCPR/C/73/D/747/1997, paras 8.4, 9.2.

[60] Case *Malawi African Association et al v Mauritania*, Communications 54/91 *et al* (27th Ordinary Session, May 2000).

a) Physical or mental harm;

b) Lost opportunities, including employment, education and social benefits;

c) Material damages and loss of earnings, including loss of earning potential;

d) Moral damage;

e) Costs required for legal or expert assistance, medicine and medical services, and psychological and social services.'[61]

The term compensation is used in varying forms in national legislations and practice; sometimes, the term indemnity is used, which can have a different meaning from compensation, particularly in French or Spanish.[62] On the international level, however, these terms are used synonymously. The term compensation will be understood here as the specific form of reparation seeking to provide economic or monetary awards for certain losses, be they of material or immaterial, of pecuniary or non-pecuniary nature.

1. Compensation in General

a) Treaties and other International Instruments

Initially, many human rights treaties contain an explicit individual right to 'compensation' for violations of human rights; in others, the right to compensation is read into other formulations such as 'reparation' or 'just satisfaction'. Some provisions include an explicit reference to 'compensation'.[63]

Beyond the general right to compensation for human rights violations, many treaties also enshrine the customary right to compensation for unlawful arrest, detention or conviction: Article 9 (5) ICCPR, Article 5 (5) ECHR,

---

[61] Principle 20.

[62] In French: "indemnisation", "compensation" or "indemnité"; in Spanish: "compensación", "indemnización" or "resarcimiento".

[63] Article 14 CAT, Articles 16 (4) and (5) of the Indigenous and Tribal Peoples Convention 1989 (No. 169), Article 75 (1) of the Rome Statute of the International Criminal Court, Article 19 of Declaration on the Protection of all Persons from Enforced Disappearance, Principle 12 of the Declaration of Basic Principles of Justice for Victims of Crime and Abuse of Power, Article 9 (2) of the Declaration on Human Rights Defenders. In the regional instruments, Article 63 (1) ACHR, Article 9 Inter-American Convention to Prevent and Punish Torture, Articles 288 (2) Treaty of the European Community, Article 41 (3) of the Charter of Fundamental Rights of the European Union, Article 21 (2) AfrCHPR, Article 27 (1) Protocol to the African Charter on Human and Peoples' Rights on the Establishment of an African Court on Human and Peoples' Rights.

Article 10 ACHR, Article 16 of the Arab Charter on Human Rights, and Article 85 of the Rome Statute of the International Criminal Court.

In humanitarian law, the right to compensation is enshrined in Article 91 of the 1st Additional Protocol to the Geneva Conventions, which stipulates that '[a] Party to the conflict which violates the provisions of the Conventions or of this Protocol shall, if the case demands, be liable to pay compensation.' Article 68 of the Third Geneva Convention relative to the Treatment of Prisoners of War prescribes the procedure to be followed for claim of compensation by prisoners of war for injury or other disability arising out of work or for personal effects, monies or valuables impounded by the Detaining Power.

b) Jurisprudence

For the Permanent Court of International Justice in the *Chorzów Factory Case*, compensation is a substitute for restitution in kind if it is impossible to fulfil. The amount must be based on the value equivalent to what restitution in kind would have offered, i.e. on the value lost as compared to the situation if the illegal act had not occurred:

> 'Restitution in kind, or, if this is not possible, payment of a sum corresponding to the value which a restitution in kind would bear; the award, if need be, of damages for loss sustained which would not be covered by restitution in kind or payment in place of it – such are the principles which should serve to determine the amount of compensation due for an act contrary to international law.'[64]

Also, it considered that the damage done to the private persons should be the measure for compensation.[65]

It should be noted that compensation for material and immaterial damage,[66] especially for wrongful death or deprivation of liberty has also been awarded by claims commissions.[67] A famous award in the *Lusitania Case* estimated amount of compensation as follows:

---

[64] *Case Concerning the Factory at Chorzów (Claim for Indemnity) (The Merits)*, P.C.I.J., Series A No 17, 13 September 1928, p. 47.

[65] *Ibid*, p 48 and following.

[66] This is also referred to as material and moral damage; pecuniary and non-pecuniary damage; patrimonial and non-patrimonial damage.

[67] See the references in Commentary to Article 36, para 18.

> 'It is a general rule of both the civil and the common law that every invasion of a private right imports an injury and that for every injury the law gives a remedy. Speaking generally, that remedy must be commensurate with the injury received. It is variously expressed as "compensation", "reparation", "indemnity", "recompense", and is measured by pecuniary standards, because, says Grotius, "money is the common measure of valuable things". [...]
>
> The amounts (a) which the decedent, had he not been killed, would probably have contributed to the claimant, add thereto (b) the pecuniary value to such claimant of the deceased's personal services in claimant's care, education, or supervision, and also add (c) reasonable compensation for such mental suffering or shock, if any, caused by the violent severing of family ties, as [the] claimant may actually have sustained by reason of such death. The sum of these estimates reduced to its present cash value, will generally represent the loss sustained by the claimant.'[68]

There is also guidance as to the appropriate compensation in the field of diplomatic protection, especially in cases of injury to the person or damage to or expropriation of property. As the International Law Commission notes, in the jurisprudence on diplomatic protection, '[c]ompensable personal injury encompasses not only associated material losses, such as loss of earnings and earning capacity, medical expenses and the like, but also non-material damage suffered by the individual (sometimes, though not universally, referred to as "moral damage" in national systems).'[69]

The treaty bodies of the United Nations have recognized a right to compensation even where it is not explicitly mentioned in the particular treaty. Indeed, the Human Rights Committee recommends, as a matter of practice, that states should award compensation.[70] The basis for this recommendation is Article 2 (3)(a) ICCPR, which guarantees the right to a remedy; the Committee interprets remedy as comprising compensation. It has ordered

[68] *Opinion in the Lusitania Cases*, 1 November 1923, Recueil de sentences arbitrales, Volume VII, p 32, at 35.

[69] Commentary to Article 36, para 16.

[70] *Concluding Observations on the Libyan Arab Jamahiriya*, 6 November 98, CCPR/C/79/Add.101, para 7; *Concluding Observations on Mexico*, 27 July 1999, CCPR/C/79/Add.109, para 6.; *Concluding Observations on Guatemala*, 27 August 2001, CCPR/CO/72/GTM, para 12; Case *Bleier v Uruguay*, Views of 23 May 1978, CCPR/C/15/D/30/1978, para 5; Case *Almeida de Quinteros et al v Uruguay*, Views of 21 July 1983, CCPR/C/19/D/107/1981, para 138; Case *Sterling v Jamaica*, Views of 18 October 1994, CCPR/C/57/D/598/1994, para 10; Case *Blanco v Nicaragua*, Views of 18 August 1994, CCPR/C/51/D/328/1988, para 11; Case *Sarma v Sri Lanka*, Views of 31 July 2003, CCPR/C/78/D/950/2000, para 11.

implementation of compensation measures in its conclusions on state reports.[71] The Human Rights Committee, however, unlike the European and Inter-American Courts of Human Rights, does not prescribe a defined amount of compensation to be awarded to the victim; it merely states that the compensation has to be 'adequate'.[72] The Committee against Torture similarly urges states to provide 'fair and adequate compensation'.[73] The Committee on the Elimination of Discrimination against Women, in its General Recommendation 19 stated that to combat violence against women, 'remedies, including compensation' should be provided.[74] The Committee on the Elimination of Racial Discrimination relies on Article 6 CERD and understands it to enshrine a right to 'just and adequate reparation or satisfaction [...] including economic compensation'.[75]

The right to compensation has also been recognized in numerous resolutions of the UN Commission on Human Rights[76] and its special procedures.[77] The Working Group on Enforced or Involuntary Disappearances has stressed that the compensation must be adequate, i.e. proportionate to the gravity of the violation.[78]

---

[71] *Concluding Observations on Colombia*, 25 March 2004, CCPR/CO/80/COL, para 10; *Concluding Observations on Germany*, CCPR/CO/80/DEU, 30 March 2004, para 15; *Concluding Observations on Suriname*, 30 March 2004, para 11; *Concluding Observations on Uganda*, CCPR/CO/80/UGA, 31 March 2004, paras 7, 16.

[72] Case *Sterling v Jamaica*, Views of 18 October 1994, CCPR/C/57/D/598/1994, para 10; Case *Blanco v Nicaragua*, Views of 18 August 1994, CCPR/C/51/D/328/1988, para 11; Case *Sarma v Sri Lanka*, Views of 31 July 2003, CCPR/C/78/D/950/2000, para 11.

[73] Case *Hajrizi Dzemajl et al v Yugoslavia*, Views of 2 December 2002, CAT/C/29/D/161/2000, para. 11; Pursuant to the Committee's findings in *Dzemajl*, the Government of Montenegro agreed to pay over 985,000 euros to 65 Romani victims of a 1995 violent pogrom, in which an entire Romani neighbourhood was destroyed. (Independent Study on Impunity, E/CN.4/2004/88, 27 February 2004, para 64). See also *Conclusions and recommendations on Saudi Arabia*, CAT/C/CR/28/5, 28 May 2002, para 8 f); and *Conclusions and recommendations on Brazil*, A/56/44, paras 115-120, 16 May 2001, para 120 f).

[74] *General Recommendation 19 on Violence against Women*, 29 January 1992, A/47/38, para 24 (i).

[75] Case *B.J. v Denmark*, Views of 10 May 2000, CERD/C/56/D/17/1999, para 6.2; see also Case *L.K. v the Netherlands*, Views of 16 March 1993, CERD/C/42/D/4/1991, para 6.9; Case *Habassi v Denmark*, Views of 6 April 1999, CERD/C/54/D/10/1997, para 11.2.

[76] Resolution E/CN.4/RES/2003/63 (extrajudicial, summary and arbitrary executions), 24 April 2003, para 4; E/CN.4/2003/32 (torture), 23 April 2003, para 10.

[77] *Report of the Special Rapporteur on violence against women on cultural practices in the family that are violent towards women*, E/CN.4/2002/83, 31 January 2002, paras 116, 119; *Report of the Special Rapporteur on torture*, E/CN.4/2003/68, 17 December 2002, para 26 (l).

[78] *General Comments on Article 19 of the Declaration on the Protection of All Persons from Enforced*

Like the UN treaty bodies, the Inter-American Commission on Human Rights[79] and the African Commission on Human and Peoples' Rights[80] recommend compensation, but do not define a specific amount. The Inter-American and European Courts on Human Rights, on the other hand, have developed a rather detailed, if somewhat incoherent, jurisprudence on compensation, awarding specific amounts for damages that they divide into pecuniary and non-pecuniary.[81]

Compensation must also be paid for violations of humanitarian law. In its Resolution on the *Protection of the civilian population in period of armed conflict*, the 26th International Conference of the Red Cross and Red Crescent reaffirmed 'that any party to an armed conflict which violates international humanitarian law shall, if the case demands, be liable to pay compensation.'[82] The members of the 27th International Conference of the Red Cross and Red Crescent adopted the Plan of Action for the years 2000-2003, in which they propose that, in order to achieve the goal to set 'an effective barrier against impunity through the combination of relevant international treaties and national laws concerning the repression of violations of international humanitarian law, and the examination of an equitable system of reparations [...], States examine mechanisms for making reparations for damage inflicted on the victims of violations of international humanitarian law.'[83]

Disappearance, 12 January 1998, E/CN.1/1998/43, para 73.

79 See, for example, Report No. 61/01, Case 11.771, *Samuel Alfonso Catalán Lincoleo* (Chile), 16 April 2001, para 96 (3) [compensation for physical and non-physical damages, including moral damages, for members of family]; Report No. 54/01, Case 12.051, *Maria Da Penha Maia Fernandes* (Brazil), 16 April 2001, para 61 (3) [symbolic and actual compensation for state failure to prevent domestic violence]; Report No 101/01, Case 10.247 *et al*, *Extrajudicial Executions and Forced Disappearances of Persons* (Peru), 11 October 2001, para 253 (3); Case *Lucio Parada Cea et al* (El Salvador), Report No 1/99, 27 January 1999, para 160 (3).

80 Case *Malawi African Association et al v Mauritania*, Communications 54/91, 61/91, 98/93, 164/97, 196/97, 210/98 (27th Ordinary Session, May 2000); Case *Mouvement Burkinabé des Droits de l'Homme et des Peuples v Burkina Faso*, Communication 204/97 (29th Ordinary Session, May 2001); Case *The Social and Economic Rights Action Center and the Center for Economic and Social Rights v Nigeria*, Communication 155/96 (30th Ordinary Session, October 2001), paras 57, 61; Case *John K. Modise v Botswana*, Communication 97/93 (28th Ordinary Session, November 2000), para 96.

81 See the jurisprudence referred to below at 2 and 3.

82 Resolution 2 on the *Protection of the civilian population in period of armed conflict* adopted at the 26th International Conference of the Red Cross and Red Crescent, Geneva 1995.

83 Plan of Action for the years 2000-2003 adopted by the 27th International Conference of the Red Cross and Red Crescent, Geneva, 31 October to 6 November 1999, para 11, reprinted in: IRRC No. 836 (1999), pp. 880-895.

In the following, it will be shown that international jurisprudence has divided compensation into material damages, including loss of earnings and other material damage, and moral damages, quite in the same way as the *Lusitania* award did.

2. Material Damages

Firstly, compensation is granted for so called material damages, i.e. for economic losses resulting from the violation of human rights. Violations may indeed result in loss of actual or future earnings, loss of movable and immovable property, and costs arising from legal assistance, the pursuit of investigations or lawsuits, medical and psychological assistance, all immediate or removed consequences of the violation.

a) Loss of Earnings

International jurisprudence is unanimous in granting victims compensation for lost earnings. In cases in which the human rights violation consisted of the loss of employment, the Human Rights Committee, while not calculating itself the amounts to be compensated, considers that the authorities should compensate lost earning based on the salaries that the victim would have received.[84]

The European Court of Human Rights considers that 'there must be a clear causal connection between the damage claimed by the applicant and the violation of the Convention and that this may, in the appropriate case, include compensation in respect of loss of earnings.'[85] With respect to pecuniary losses, it has considered that, while the damage flowing from the violation was of an inherently uncertain character, the Court was not prevented from making an award of past and future pecuniary losses on the basis of equity.[86] In the case of *Isayeva v Russia*, it followed the applicant's

[84] Case *Busyo v Democratic Republic of Congo*, Views of 9 August 2003, CCPR/C/78/D/933/2000, para 6.2; Case *Nyekuma Kopita Toro Gedumbe v Democratic Republic of the Congo*, Views of 1 August 1997, CCPR/C/75/D/641/1995, para 6.2; Case *Adimayo M. Aduayom et al v Togo*, Views of 12 July 1996, CCPR/C/57/D/422/1990, 423/1990 and 424/1990, para 9; and Case *Félix Enrique Chira Vargas-Machuca v Peru*, Views of 26 July 2002, CCPR/C/75/D/906/2000, para 9.

[85] Case *Çakici v Turkey*, Judgment of 8 July 1999, reports 1999-IV, para 127; Case *Selçuk and Asker v. Turkey*, Judgment of 24 April 1998 , Reports 1998-II, para 112; and Case *Orhan v Turkey*, Judgment of 18 June 2002, para 430. See also Case *Aktas v Turkey*, Judgment of 24 April 2003 and Case *Ipek v Turkey*, Judgment of 17 February 2004.

[86] Case *Lustig-Prean and Beckett v the United Kingdom (Article 41)*, Judgment of 25 July 2000, paras 22-

reasoning that there was a causal link between her son's death in violation of Article 2 and the loss by the applicant of the financial support which he could have provided her. She had claimed that she could have counted on receiving a third of her son's income for the rest of her life if he had not been killed and calculated the sum of lost earnings on the basis of the average life expectancy in Russia.[87]

The Inter-American Court has developed the most elaborate calculations of lost earnings. Lost earnings are based on the victim's earnings before the violation.[88] When the victim has died, compensation for lost earnings is awarded to relatives and other third parties. As mentioned above,[89] to award compensation to relatives of the victim or other persons, the Inter-American Court has established certain criteria: first, the payment sought must be based on effective and regular contributions made by the victim to the claimant, regardless of whether or not they constituted a legal obligation to pay support; second, the nature of the relationship between the victim and the claimant should be such that it provides some basis for the assumption that the payments would have continued, had the victim not been killed; third, the contributions must been based on a financial need of the recipient.[90] The reference is the average life expectancy in the state in question.[91] Where there is no detailed or reliable information, the reference for the Court is the minimum wage in national law[92] and the Court determines loss of earnings 'in fairness'.[93] The Court then calculates the lost earnings on the basis of twelve monthly sala-

---

23; and Case *Orhan v Turkey*, Judgment of 18 June 2002, paras 431-434. See also Case *Aktas v Turkey*, Judgment of 24 April 2003 and Case *Ipek v Turkey*, Judgment of 17 February 2004.

[87] Case *Isayeva v Russia*, Judgment of 24 February 2005, para 234 ; Case *Karakoc v Turkey*, 15 October 2002, para 285.

[88] Case *Loayza Tamayo v Peru (Reparations)*, Judgment of November 27, 1998, Series C No. 42, para 129.

[89] See Chapter II at I.2.

[90] Case *Aloeboetoe et al v Suriname (Reparations)*, Judgment of 10 September, 1993, Series C No 15, paras 67, 68.

[91] Case *Bámaca Velásquez v Guatemala (Reparations)*, Judgment of 22 February, 2002, Series C No. 91, para 51.b).

[92] *Villagrán Morales et al v Guatemala, Street Children Case (Reparations)*, Judgment of 26 May 2001, Series C No 77, para 79; *Case of Caracazo v Venezuela, (Reparation)*, Judgment of 29 August 2002, Series C No 95, para 88; *Case of Panel Blanca v Guatemala (Reparations)*, Judgment of 25 May 2001, Series C No 76, paras 116-117; Case *Castillo Páez v Peru (Reparations)*, Judgment of 27 November 1998, Series C No 43, para 75.

[93] Case *Neira Alegría et al v Peru (Reparations)*, Judgment of 19 September 1996, Series C No 29, paras 49-52; Case *Maritza Urrutia v Guatemala*, Judgment of 27 November, 2003, Series C No 103, para 158.

ries and the benefits granted under national legislation, less 25% for personal expenses, to which it adds current interests.[94] In the case of *Cantoral Benavides*, the Court awarded lost earnings to the victim, who at the time of his detention was a biology student, with reference to the income he would have had in his profession had he not been detained and prevented from pursuing his studies.[95] In the case of *Bámaca Velásquez*, who was a *guerilla* fighter at the time in which he was disappeared, the Court did not award compensation for lost income of his activity as a *guerilla* fighter. It considered, however, that after the peace accords in Guatemala in 1996, he would have joined the labour force and had an income. For the fictitious life span after the peace accords (based on the average life expectancy), the Court awarded an amount for lost earnings in equity.[96]

Lastly, it should be mentioned that in the case of *Bámaca Velásquez*, the Inter-American Court also awarded direct compensation to the wife of the disappeared victim for lost earnings, since she had 'spent much of her time taking steps to determine the whereabouts of her husband as well as struggling against the obstructions and acts of denial of justice, which did not allow her to practice her profession.' The amount was determined in equity.[97]

Like the Court, the Inter-American Commission on Human Rights has recognized that material damage includes 'consequential damages' and 'lost profit'.[98]

*

In sum, lost earnings must be compensated in cases of violations of human rights resulting in loss of employment or salary. It is important to note that international jurisprudence has not hesitated to award compensation for lost

94 *Villagrán Morales et al v Guatemala, Street Children Case (Reparations)*, Judgment of 26 May 2001, Series C No 77, para 79; *Case of Caracazo v Venezuela, (Reparation)*, Judgment of 29 August 2002, Series C No 95, para 81; *Case of Panel Blanca v Guatemala (Reparations)*, Judgment of 25 May 2001, Series C No 76, paras 95, 117, 132, 151, 166.

95 Case *Cantoral Benavides v Peru (Reparations)*, Judgment of 3 December 2001, Series C No 88, paras 47-49; see the similar decision in Case *Trujillo Oroza v Bolivia (Reparations)*, Judgment of 27 February 2002, Series C No 92, paras 71-73.

96 Case *Bámaca Velásquez v Guatemala (Reparations)*, Judgment of 22 February, 2002, Series C No 91, para 51 (b).

97 Case *Bámaca Velásquez v Guatemala (Reparations)*, Judgment of 22 February, 2002, Series C No 91, para 54 (a).

98 *Report on the Situation of Human Rights in Amayampa, Llallagua and Capasirca, Northern Potosi, Bolivia, December 1996*, 29 July 1997, OEA/Ser.L/V/II, Doc 8 rev 1, para 204.

earnings only because of lack of evidence about the actual earnings. Where evidence has been insufficient, it has awarded compensation on the basis of an assessment in equity. It is also noticeable that loss of earnings is not only awarded to the victims, but also to their relatives or other dependants when these suffer economic harm from the loss of income of the direct victim.

b) Other Material Damage, including Legal Costs

Beyond lost earnings, victims, their relatives or other persons may suffer other forms of direct material damage resulting from the violation. Some of these have been addressed in jurisprudence.

The European Court of Human Rights awards compensation for such material damages as loss of house and other property,[99] loss of livestock,[100] additional expenditures,[101] costs of alternative housing,[102] costs of removals, or higher living costs in a new residence resulting from the violations.[103] Where it does not have sufficiently detailed evidence on the material damages, it nevertheless awards these on an equitable basis.[104] It also orders the reimbursement of legal costs and expenses for the proceedings as a matter of practice, in so far as they are necessary, reasonable and actually incurred.[105]

The Inter-American Court considers that compensation covers both past and future costs for medical care and psychological assistance.[106] In the case

[99] Case *Selçuk and Asker v Turkey*, Judgment of 24 April 1998, Reports 1998-II, para 106; Case *Bilgin v Turkey*, Judgment of 16 November 2000, paras 138-152.

[100] Case *Ipek v Turkey*, Judgment of 17 February 2004, paras 228, 229.

[101] Case *Ipek v Turkey*, Judgment of 17 February 2004, paras 232, 233.

[102] Case *Selçuk and Asker Turkey*, Judgment of 24 April 1998, paras 104-115.

[103] Case *Orhan v Turkey*, Judgment of 18 June 2002, para 438.

[104] Case *Selçuk and Asker v Turkey*, Judgment of 24 April 1998, Reports 1998-II, para 106.

[105] Case *Selçuk and Asker Turkey*, Judgment of 24 April 1998, paras 120-122.

[106] Case *Durand and Ugarte v Peru (Reparations)*, Judgment of 3 December 2001, Series C No 89, paras 36, 37 and operative paragraph 3; Case *Loayza Tamayo v Peru (Reparations)*, Judgment of 27 November 1998, Series C No 42, para 129 d); Case *Barrios Altos v Peru (Reparations)*, Judgment of 30 November 2001, Series C No 87, para 42 and operative paragraph 3; Case *Bámaca Velásquez v Guatemala (Reparations)*, Judgment of 22 February 2002, Series C No 91, para 52; Case *Blake v Guatemala (Reparations)*, Judgment of 22 January 1999, Series C No 48, para 50; Case *Cantoral Benavides v Peru (Reparations)*, Judgment of 3 December 2001, Series C No 88, para 51; Case *Trujillo Oroza v Bolivia (Reparations)*, Judgment of 27 February 2002, Series C No 92, para 74 b).

of *Suárez Rosero* it ordered compensation for domestic aid for the physically disabled victim, and for physical and psychological treatment.[107] It has also ordered compensation for numerous other pecuniary damages, including, for instance, the expenses incurred to locate disappeared victims,[108] expenses for family visits and relatives' expenditure for medical care in prison,[109] or expenses for moving to another village.[110] In the *Caracazo Case*, the Court summarized so-called consequential damages, i.e. material damages other than lost earnings, as including patrimonial damage to the household; expenses in relation to search of mortal remains; medical treatment; exhumation costs; lost earnings; patrimonial losses, such as reduced family income or bankruptcy; burial and funerary services, *etc.*[111] The Court orders reimbursement of costs and expenses of the legal proceedings; in one case it also ordered reimbursement of costs to NGOs who had assisted the victims.[112] In the case of a massacre where most victims had lost their houses, the Court ordered the state to put in place a programme for adequate housing over a period of five years.[113]

The African Commission on Human and Peoples' Rights also awards compensation for material damage. In the case concerning the destruction of Ogoniland through ransacking and destruction of villages and food sources and pollution of water and soil, the African Commission appealed to the government to ensure 'adequate compensation to victims of human rights violations, including relief and resettlement assistance to victims of government sponsored raids.'[114]

---

[107] Case *Suárez Rosero v Ecuador (Reparations)*, Judgment of 20 January 1999, Series C No. 44, para 60.

[108] Case *Bámaca Velásquez v Guatemala (Reparations)*, Judgment of 22 February 2002, Series C No 91, para 52; Case *Blake v Guatemala (Reparations)*, Judgment of 22 January 1999, paras 47-50; Case *Trujillo Oroza v Bolivia (Reparations)*, Judgment of 27 February, 2002, Series C No 92, paras 72-76; *Juan Humberto Sánchez Case*, Judgment of 7 June, 2003, Series C No 99, para 166.

[109] Case *Loayza Tamayo v Peru (Reparations)*, Judgment of 27 November 1998, Series C No 42, para 129; *Cantoral Benavides v Peru (Reparations)*, Judgment of 3 December 2001, Series C No 88, paras 47-52.

[110] *Juan Humberto Sánchez v Honduras*, Judgment of 7 June, 2003, Series C No 99, para 166.

[111] *Case of Caracazo v Venezuela (Reparation)*, Judgment of 29 August 2002, Series C No 95, para 80.

[112] *Villagrán Morales et al v Guatemala, Street Children Case (Reparations)*, Judgment of 26 May 2001, Series C No 77, operative para 9 [of the costs and expenses, some have to be paid to the NGOs Casa Alianza and CEJIL].

[113] Case of *Plan de Sánchez Massacre* (Reparations), Judgment of 19 November 2004, Series C No 116, para 105.

[114] Case *The Social and Economic Rights Action Center and the Center for Economic and Social Rights v*

c) Lost Opportunities, including Employment and Education (and the Concept of 'Proyecto de Vida'*)*

The UN Principles on Reparation consider that compensation must cover 'lost opportunities, including employment, education and social benefits' (Principle 20). Of these, the loss of educational opportunities has been addressed by the Inter-American Court in particular. Indeed, in one of its first judgments on reparations, the *Aloeboetoe et al Case*, the Court ordered that the heirs of the victims must receive compensation to be able to study. But it also considered that it was not sufficient to just grant compensation; rather, there also had to be a school available for the children; consequently, it ordered that the state should reopen the local school and staff it with teachers and administrative personnel.[115]

In the case of *Loayza Tamayo*, who was victim of an unfair trial, unlawful detention and torture by the state of Peru and lived in exile in Chile, the Inter-American Court developed the concept of '*proyecto de vida*' ('life plan'). It considered that, beyond the material loss resulting from the loss of income due to her detention, the applicant had suffered harm to her life plan. This concept, in the understanding of the court, resembles that of personal fulfilment; it deals with the 'full self-actualisation of the person concerned and takes account of her calling in life, her particular circumstances, her potentialities, and her ambitions, thus permitting her to set for herself, in a reasonable manner, specific goals, and to attain those goals.'[116] While in the *Loayza Tamayo* case the Court refused to make an economic assessment of the harm suffered to the life plan and considered that access to international jurisdiction and judgment of international tribunal contributed to satisfaction for the applicant, it subsequently changed its jurisprudence with the case of *Cantoral Benavides*. In this case, it decided to order compensation for the damage to the life plan of the victim, who had been prevented from pursing his studies by being unlawfully detained. The Court thus ordered the state to secure him a scholarship to pursue his studies of biology.[117] Similarly, in the case of *Barrios Altos*, the Court ordered

Nigeria, Communication 155/96 (30th Ordinary Session, October 2001), recommendations.

[115] Case *Aloeboetoe et al v Suriname (Reparations)*, Judgment of 10 September, 1993, Series C No 15, para 96.

[116] Case *Loayza Tamayo v Peru (Reparations)*, Judgment of 27 November 1998, Series C No 42, para 147.

[117] Case *Cantoral Benavides v Peru (Reparations)*, Judgment of 3 December 2001, Series C No 88, paras 60, 80.

that, pursuant to an agreement reached by the victims and the state, the state had to grant the victims scholarships for education, support to those who wanted to continue their studies, and educational material.[118]

***

The economic consequences of human rights violations are so numerous and varied in nature that it is difficult to classify them for the purposes of compensation. International jurisprudence seeks to make findings in which they address the real losses incurred by victims. These may vary and the jurisprudence is in constant evolution. It emerges from the jurisprudence that no economically assessable loss is excluded *per se* from compensation, as long as the conditions for reparation are fulfilled, in other words, as long as there is a causal link between the violation and the damage.

As far as the existence of material damage can be demonstrated, the award does not depend on whether the victim can give detailed evidence of the precise amounts, as it is frequently impossible to prove such exact figures. In the absence of detailed information, compensation is granted on the basis of equity.

***

3. Immaterial/Moral Damage: Physical and Mental Harm

While compensation consists in financial reparation, and is awarded for 'economically assessable' damage, this does not mean that it only concerns damage to material goods or other economic assets. Quite to the contrary, one of the main functions of compensation is to provide redress for harm to the physical and mental well-being of a person, given that there is no possibility of *restitutio in integrum* for such damage. This is particularly true in case of gross human rights violations, as they often cause considerable physical harm, psychological damage and trauma. Such damage is sometimes easily 'economically assessable' when it leads to costs for medical or psychological treatment, medicine, etc. However, it can also be measured on the basis of 'equity', which is a recognized method of assessment for damages in

118 Case *Barrios Altos v Peru (Reparations)*, Judgment of 30 November 2001, Series C No 87, para 43 and operative para 4.

comparative law, when no such obvious figures can be shown. It will usually be the only method to assess harm resulting from pain, suffering, anguish and distress, and for harm done to the reputation and dignity of the person. In the *Janes Case*, the arbitration tribunal held that 'the individual grief of the claims should be taken into account'[119] and in the *Lusitania* award, the arbitration tribunal held:

> 'Mental suffering is a fact just as real as physical suffering, and susceptible of measurement by the same standards. [...] there can be no doubt of the reality of mental suffering, of sickness of mind as well as sickness of body, and of its detrimental and injurious effect on the individual and on his capacity to produce. Why, then, should he be remediless for this injury?.'[120]

The right to compensation for physical and mental damage has been recognized widely, even by those human rights bodies that do not determine the exact amount of compensation.

Thus, the Human Rights Committee, for instance, recommends compensation for the relatives of disappeared persons. In those cases, it recognizes that those persons have suffered harm in their own person that amounts to treatment contrary to Article 7 of the Covenant, because of the anguish and stress caused by the disappearance.[121] In the case of *Coronel v Colombia*, the Committee did not explicitly find a violation of Article 7 for the relatives, but nonetheless recommended that they be granted compensation, implicitly presuming their mental harm.[122]

In the case of *B.J. v Denmark*, the Committee for the Elimination of Racial Discrimination recommended 'that the State party take the measures necessary to ensure that the victims of racial discrimination seeking just and adequate reparation or satisfaction in accordance with article 6 of the Convention, including economic compensation, will have their claims consi-

[119] Case *Laura M.B. Janes et al (USA) v the United Mexican States*, award of 16 November 1925, Recueil de sentences arbitrales, Volume IV, p 82, at 89, para 25.

[120] *Opinion in the Lusitania Cases*, 1 November 1923, Recueil de sentences arbitrales, Volume VII, p 32, at 36.

[121] Case *Almeida de Quinteros et al v Uruguay*, Views of 15 October 1982, Communication No. 107/1981, 21 July 1983, CCPR/C/19/D/107/1981, paras 14, 16; Case *Sarma v Sri Lanka*, Views of 31 July 2003, CCPR/C/78/D/950/2000, paras 9.5, 11.

[122] Case *Coronel et al v Colombia*, Views of 29 November 2002, CCPR/C/76/D/778/1997, para 10.

dered with due respect for situations where the discrimination has not resulted in any physical damage but humiliation or similar suffering.'[123]

The Inter-American Court of Human Rights has awarded so called 'moral damage' to victims since its very first judgment on reparations and based this award on equity.[124] Since this judgment, the jurisprudence has undergone considerable refinement, if not always in a consistent manner. It appears that one can extract the following principles from the awards in equity made by the Court: Moral damage is awarded to the victims and his or her family members (not only in cases of disappearances, but also, for instance, in cases in which the victim is imprisoned and tortured). The closer the family link, the higher the award, so that spouses, parents and children are normally granted higher awards than siblings or other family members.[125] Another important feature is the fact that close family members of victims of gross violations are awarded moral damage without having to prove the actual damage, because they are presumed to have a very close relationship to the victim; this is clear for parents, children, spouses and permanent partners of the victim; for siblings or their dependents or claimants, the jurisprudence is not uniform: the Court has sometimes presumed their moral damage, sometimes not,[126] but it appears that in recent jurispru-

---

[123] Case *B.J. v Denmark*, Views of 10 May 2000, CERD/C/56/D/17/1999, para 7.

[124] Case *Velásquez Rodríguez v Honduras (Compensatory damages)*, Judgment of 21 July 1989, Series C No7, paras 50-52 [moral damage] and para 27 [based on the principle of equity].

[125] Case *Loayza Tamayo v Peru (Reparations)*, Judgment of 27 November 1998, Series C No 42, paras 138-145 [different awards for victim, children, siblings]; *Villagrán Morales et al. v Guatemala, Street Children Case (Reparations)*, Judgment of 26 May 2001, Series C No 77, para 93 [amount awarded to mothers and grandmothers is higher than amount awarded to siblings]; Case *Cesti Hurtado v Peru (Reparations)*, Judgment of 31 May 2001, Series C No 78, paras 54-56 [for wife and children pecuniary compensation for moral damage; for father and godmother the judgement constitutes just satisfaction]; Case *Bámaca Velásquez v Guatemala (Reparations)*, Judgment of 22 February 2002, Series C No 91, paras 60-67 [different amounts to victim, widow, parents, sisters]; Case *Trujillo Oroza v Bolivia (Reparations)*, Judgment of 27 February 2002, Series C No 92, para 89 [different amounts to victim, mother, adoptive father, brothers]; *Case of Caracazo v Venezuela (Reparation)*, Judgment of 29 August 2002, Series C No 95, para 110 [in different amounts victims and next of kin; higher awards for those family members, to whom the bodies of their relatives have not been returned]; Case *Juan Humberto Sánchez v Honduras*, Judgment of 7 June 2003, Series C No 99 [different amounts victims and next of kin].

[126] Case *Aloeboetoe et al v Suriname (Reparations)*, Judgment of 10 September 1993, Series C No 15, paras 54, 71, 75 [presumption of moral damage for relatives of the victims; other claimants and dependents must prove moral damage]; Case *Garrido and Baigorria v Argentina (Reparations)*, Judgment of 27 August 1998, Series C No 39, paras 62, 63 [mother without further proof; brothers did not show that they had very close relation to disappeared, so that moral damage not very grave]; Case *Castillo Páez v Peru(Reparations)*, Judgment of 27 November 1998, Series C No 43, paras 88, 89 [parents need not prove

dence it explicitly stated that the suffering of siblings was presumed as well as that of parents and children.[127] It is important to note that the Court does not explicitly have to find a violation of the human rights concerning the relatives themselves in order to grant them compensation.

The Inter-American Commission on Human Rights has a similar jurisprudence to that of the Inter-American Court, even though it does not award specific amounts. In its reports, it recommends compensation not only for the victims, but also for the relatives, particularly, but not only, in the case of enforced disappearances,[128] for their anguish and stress.[129]

The European Court of Human Rights orders compensation to victims for non-pecuniary damage when it finds that they have suffered anguish, distress or other mental or physical harm. Where the victims are disappeared or dead, the Court has awarded non-pecuniary damages to the victims' heirs.[130] The mental harm must not necessarily be demonstrated by the victim, but may be presumed by the simple fact of a gross violation: In some cases, such as *Orhan v Turkey* or *Selçuk and Asker v Turkey*, the European Court of Human Rights awarded 'non-pecuniary damages' on account of the 'gravity of the breaches in question'[131] or, in cases of gross violations such as torture, on account of the simple finding of the violation.[132]

---

moral damage; in present case, moral damage of sister was based on proof]; Case *Blake v Guatemala (Reparations)*, Judgment of 22 January 1999, para 37 [parents and brothers and sisters of disappeared person, without differentiation in proof]; Case *Panel Blanca v Guatemala (Reparations)*, Judgment of 25 May 2001, Series C No 76, paras 106-110 [closest members of the family, i.e. parents and children, without further proof; for siblings and sisters in law because of close relationship with victim].

127 Case *Maritza Urrutia v Guatemala*, Judgment of 27 November 2003, Series C No. 103, para 169 a), b) and c).

128 Report No 51/99, Cases 10.471, *Anetro Castillo Pero et al* (Peru), 13 April 1999, para 151 (3).

129 Report No. 61/01, Case 11.771, *Samuel Alfonso Catalán Lincoleo* (Chile), 16 April 2001, para 96 (3) [compensation for physical and non-physical damages, including moral damages, for members of family]; Report No. 54/01, Case 12.051, *Maria Da Penha Maia Fernandes* (Brazil), 16 April 2001, para 61 (3) [symbolic and actual compensation for state failure to prevent domestic violence]; Report No 101/01, Case 10.247 *et al*, *Extrajudicial Executions and Forced Disappearances of Persons* (Peru), 11 October 2001, para 253 (3); *Report on the Situation of Human Rights in Amayampa, Llallagua and Capasirca, Northern Potosi, Bolivia, December 1996*, 29 July 1997, OEA/Ser.L/V/II, Doc 8 rev 1, para 204.

130 See Case *Ipek v Turkey*, Judgment of 17 February 2004, para 237; Case *Aktas v Turkey*, Judgment of 24 April 2003, para 361.

131 Case *Orhan v Turkey*, Judgment of 18 June 2002, para 443; Case *Selçuk and Asker v Turkey*, Judgment of 24 April 1998, Reports 1998-II, para 118.

132 Case *Orhan v Turkey*, Judgment of 18 June 2002, para 443.

Beyond the award ordered for relatives or other persons as claimants in the name of the victim, they may also claim compensation in their own right. In the words of the Court, they may be an 'injured party' in the sense of Article 41 ECHR without being victims.[133] While in the case of *Kurt v Turkey*, the Court found that the mother of the disappeared has suffered a violation of Article 3 ECHR and was therefore entitled to compensation for her suffering,[134] the Court also sometimes awards relatives of victims compensation without their being themselves victims of a violation. This was the case in the judgment of *Aksoy v Turkey*, where the Court, 'in view of the extremely serious violations of the Convention suffered by Mr *Zeki Aksoy* and the anxiety and distress that these undoubtedly caused to his father', awarded the full amount of compensation sought to the father of the victim.[135] In other cases, the Court considered that the relatives suffered 'feelings of frustration, distress and anxiety' from the non-existence or inefficiency of the investigation.[136] In some cases, the Court accepts that relatives have suffered 'non-pecuniary damage' without describing it further, possibly presuming moral suffering from the lack of investigation.[137]

As mentioned above, numerous awards have been made in claims commissions for deprivation of liberty. The ILC notes that in those cases, arbitrators sometimes awarded a set amount for each day spent in detention. Awards were often increased when abusive conditions of confinement accompanied the wrongful arrest and imprisonment, resulting in particularly serious physical or psychological injury.[138]

[133] Case *Çakici v Turkey*, 8 July 1999, Reports 1999-IV, para 130; Case *Aktas v Turkey*, Judgment of 24 April 2003, para 364, see above Chapter I at I 2.

[134] Case *Kurt v Turkey*, Judgment of 25 May 1998, Reports 1998-III, para 175; see also Case *Orhan v Turkey*, Judgment of 18 June 2002, para 443; Case *Cyprus v Turkey*, Judgment of 10 May 2001, Reports 2001-IV, paras 156-158; Case *Ipek v Turkey*, Judgment of 17 February 2004, para 238.

[135] Case *Aksoy v Turkey*, Judgment of 18 December 1996, Reports 1996-VI, para 113.

[136] Case *McKerr v the United Kingdom*, Judgment of 4 May 2001, Reports 2001-III, para 181; Case *Shanaghan v the United Kingdom*, 4 May 2001, Reports 2001-III, para 181; Case *Hugh Jordan v the United Kingdom*, Judgment of 4 May 2001, Reports 2001-III, para 170; Case *Kelly v the United Kingdom*, Judgment of 4 May 2001, Reports 2001-III, para 164.

[137] Case *Ogur v Turkey*, Judgment of 20 May 1999, reports 1999-III, para 98; Case *Mahmut Kaya v Turkey*, Judgment of 28 March 2000, para 139 [brother of the victim]; Case *Aktas v Turkey*, Judgment of 24 April 2003, para 364: although the brother of the victim was not a 'victim', the Court considered him an 'injured party' in the sense of Article 41 ECHR.

[138] See references in Commentary to Article 36, para 18.

4. Collective Compensation/Reparation

For some communities, it is important to receive collective compensation. This has been recognized in Article 16 (4) of the Indigenous and Tribal Peoples Convention 1989 (No. 169), which concerns removal of indigenous communities from their lands. It stipulates that when their return is not possible 'these peoples shall be provided in all possible cases with lands of quality and legal status at least equal to that of the lands previously occupied by them, suitable to provide for their present needs and future development. Where the peoples concerned express a preference for compensation in money or in kind, they shall be so compensated under appropriate guarantees.' This provision grants compensation to peoples, not to individuals.

The Inter-American Commission on Human Rights and the African Commission on Human and Peoples' Rights have also recognized the need for collective reparation. In the case of the *Caloto Massacre*, in which members of an indigenous community were massacred with the participation of the police, the Inter-American Commission recommended that the state 'adopt the measures necessary to carry out the commitments regarding social reparations on behalf of the Paez indigenous community of northern Cauca.'[139] It referred to the recommendations of a Committee set up for the settlement of the case, which recommended 'full implementation of [existing] agreements on adjudication of lands through more expeditious procedures and within a reasonable time, in conjunction with the indigenous communities';[140] it had concluded 'that the Caloto massacre affected the entirety of the Paez indigenous community of northern Cauca' and 'that the State should attend to its obligation to protect the fundamental rights of the indigenous peoples, whose first right, the right to life, should be understood in collective terms, as well as the right to ethnic and cultural reproduction, the right to territory, and the right to self-determination.'[141]

The Inter-American Court, without always calling them collective reparations, has recognised that where a whole community is affected, a reparation scheme benefiting the whole community will be appropriate. In the

[139] Report No. 36/00, Case 11.101, "*Caloto Massacre*" (Colombia), 13 April 2000, para 75 (3).

[140] *Ibid*, para 28.

[141] *Ibid*, para 23.

Aloeboetoe v Suriname case it ordered the reopening of a school and a medical dispensary in the village where the massacre occurred.[142] In the *Plan de Sánchez Massacre* case, it ordered the state to adopt a five year development plan for education, health, infrastructure (drinking water) and production.[143]

In the case of the *Mayagna (Sumo) Awas Tingni Community*, in which the Inter-American Court of Human Rights found a violation of the right of an indigenous community to respect of its land, the Court found that 'in equity, the State must invest, as reparation for immaterial damages, in the course of 12 months, the total sum of US$ 50,000 in works or services of collective interest for the benefit of the Mayagna (Sumo) Awas Tingni Community, by common agreement with the Community and under supervision by the Inter-American Commission of Human Rights' and that 'in equity, the State must pay the members of the Mayagna (Sumo) Awas Tingni Community, through the Inter-American Commission of Human Rights, the total sum of US$ 30,000 for expenses and costs incurred by the members of that Community and their representatives, both those caused in domestic proceedings and in the international proceedings before the inter-American system of protection.'[144]

In the case of *The Social and Economic Rights Action Center and the Center for Economic and Social Rights v Nigeria,* the African Commission on Human and Peoples' Rights found multiple violations of the rights of the Ogoni Communities in Nigeria by oil companies with the acquiescence of the government, particularly of Article 21 AfrCHPR which guarantees the right of *peoples* to freely dispose of their wealth and natural resources.[145] It appealed to the government 'to ensure protection of the environment, health and livelihood of the people of Ogoniland' by, amongst others, 'stopping all attacks on Ogoni *communities* and leaders [...]', 'ensuring adequate compen-

---

142 Case *Aloeboetoe et al v Suriname (Reparations)*, Judgment of 10 September 1993, Series C No 15, para 96.

143 Case of *Plan de Sánchez Massacre* (Reparations), Judgment of 19 November 2004, Series C No 116, paras 109-111.

144 Case *The Mayagna (Sumo) Awas Tingni Community v Nicaragua*, Judgment of 31 August 2001, Series C No 79, operative paras 6 and 7.

145 Case *The Social and Economic Rights Action Center and the Center for Economic and Social Rights v Nigeria*, Communication 155/96 (30th Ordinary Session, October 2001), paras 55-59.

sation to victims of the human rights violations [...] and undertaking a comprehensive cleanup of lands and rivers damaged by oil operations.'[146] Here again, the reparation is both individual and collective, and takes into account the damage done to the lands and lives of the whole community and not only its individual members.

5. Compensation Claims and Statutes of Limitations

In his final report to the Sub-Commission, the Special Rapporteur on the right to reparation recalled that 'for many victims of gross violations of human rights, the passage of time has no attenuating effect; on the contrary, there is an increase in post-traumatic stress, requiring all necessary material, medical, psychological and social assistance and support over a long period of time', so that statutory limitation constituted a real obstacle for reparation.[147] Similarly, the UN Principles on Impunity state that statutes of limitation shall not be effective against civil or administrative actions brought by victims seeking reparation for their injuries.[148] The Working Group on Enforced or Involuntary Disappearances insists that '[c]ivil claims for compensation shall not be [...] made subject to statutes of limitation.'[149]

The European Court of Human Rights has had to assess the legitimacy of statutes of limitations for civil claims under Article 6 ECHR. It has held that Article 6 embodied 'the "right to a court", of which the right of access, that is, the right to institute proceedings before a court in civil matters, constitutes one aspect.'. It held that while this right was not absolute, any restriction to it had to be proportionate and could 'not restrict or reduce the access left to the individual in such a way or to such an extent that the very essence of the right is impaired.'[150]

[146] *Ibid*, recommendations, emphasis added.

[147] *Final report submitted by the Special Rapporteur on the right to restitution, compensation and rehabilitation for victims of gross violations of human rights and fundamental freedoms*, E/CN.4/Sub.2/1993/8, 2 July 1993, para 135.

[148] Principle 23 of the UN Principles on Impunity.

[149] *General Comments on Article 19 of the Declaration on the Protection of All Persons from Enforced Disappearance*, E/CN.4/1998/43, para 73.

[150] Case *Stubbings and others v the United Kingdom*, Judgment of 22 October 1996, Report 1996-IV, para 50.

The case of *Forti v Suarez Mason* is reminiscent of Article 17 (2) of the Declaration on the Protection of All Persons from Enforced Disappearance – although this Article deals with criminal proceedings. Victims sued an Argentinian ex-general for torture, arbitrary detention and disappearances in violation of international human rights law under the Alien Tort Claims Act. The Court considered that the statute of limitation applicable could not run during the period of 1977 to 1984 because plaintiffs were denied access to Argentine courts, nor during the period of 1984 to 1987 because the defendant was in hiding. Based on this, the plaintiffs claims were not time-barred.[151] Prescription cannot run while there is no effective remedy for the victim.[152]

It should be noted that many national systems do not know statutes of limitations, either for civil claims or for criminal proceedings. This is one of the reasons why there is no clear rule in international law on statutes of limitation. But while international law does not clearly prohibit statutory limitations for compensation claims in cases of gross human rights violations, it is clear that they constitute a major and frequent obstacle to the claims of victims, who are, in effect, barred from their right to reparation.

***

In conclusion, it is difficult to find guidance in international law and jurisprudence on the amount of compensation, since the amounts awarded by different human rights bodies vary considerably.[153] However, it is beyond doubt that the right to compensation is an individual right under international law. The evaluation of the amount of compensation must always be done in reference to international, never to national, rules, and will often have to have recourse to notions of equity. Again, the award in the *Lusitania* case may be cited:

> 'In many tort cases, including those for personal injury or for death, it is manifestly impossible to compute mathematically or with any degree of accu-

[151] Case *Forti v Suarez Mason*, 672 F. Supp. 1531, 1987, District Court for the Northern District of California.

[152] See also the decision in the case of *Alvaro Saravia*, found guilty for the murder of Archbishop Oscar Romero, Independent on Sunday (London), 5 September 2004, US Court Orders Man Behind Death-Squad Killing of El Salvador's Archbishop to Pay $ 10M in Damages.

[153] See also Commentary to Article 36 para 20.

racy or be the use of any precise formula the damage sustained [...]. This, however, furnishes no reason why the wrongdoer should escape repairing his wrong or why he who has suffered should not receive reparation therefore measured by rules as nearly approximating accuracy as human ingenuity can devise. To deny such reparation would be to deny the fundamental principle that there exists a remedy for the direct invasion of every right.'[154]

It may be retained that compensation must not only cover directly economically assessable damage such as lost earning or other patrimonial damages.

- Compensation must also encompass financial reparation for physical or mental suffering. As this damage is not economically quantifiable, the assessment must be made in equity.
- Since it is difficult to provide evidence for certain moral or psychological effects of violations, mental harm should always be presumed as a consequence of gross violations of human rights such as torture, ill-treatment, unlawful killings or disappearances.
- For persons other than close relatives (who should include parents, children, and siblings), harm may have to be shown so as to limit the number of persons who may claim compensation. However, here again, moral damage will be difficult to demonstrate, so that the conditions for claiming compensation should not be impossible to meet.

***

III. REHABILITATION

Rehabilitation is guaranteed in many universal treaties and declarations. Particularly, Article 14 (1) CAT provides that 'each State Party shall ensure in its legal system that the victim of an act of torture obtains redress and has an enforceable right to fair and adequate compensation, including the means for as full rehabilitation as possible.' Article 39 CRC states that 'States Parties shall take all appropriate measures to promote physical and psychological recovery and social reintegration of a child victim [...].'[155]

[154] *Opinion in the Lusitania Cases*, 1 November 1923, Recueil de sentences arbitrales, Volume VII, p 32, at 36.

[155] Rehabilitation is also referred to in, amongst others, Article 75 of the Rome Statute on the International Criminal Court, Article 6 (3) of the Protocol to Prevent, Suppress and Punish Trafficking in

Rehabilitation measures are often considered within compensation awards, and there is an overlap between findings directly requiring that the authorities adopt measures of rehabilitation and findings that states afford compensation for rehabilitation measures. Often, it is simply ordered that the state compensate the costs of rehabilitation. This is reflected in Article 14 CAT, which refers to 'compensation, including the means for as full rehabilitation as possible'. In this sense, the Special Rapporteur on torture recommends that states ensure 'fair and adequate compensation, including the means for the fullest rehabilitation possible'.[156] The Special Rapporteur also encourages states to 'support and assist rehabilitation centres that may exist in their territory to ensure that victims of torture are provided the means for as full a rehabilitation as possible.'[157] Similarly, the Human Rights Committee holds that states have to afford the necessary medical assistance to victims.[158] The Committee against Torture has recommended rehabilitation measures for victims of torture.[159] The Committee on the Elimination of Discrimination against Women has listed rehabilitation in its General Recommendation 19 on Violence against Women.[160] The Working Group on Enforced or Involuntary Disappearances understands rehabilitation as, amongst others, 'medical care and rehabilitation for any form of physical or mental damage.'[161]

Persons, especially Women and Children, supplementing the United Nations Convention against Transnational Organized Crime, Article 19 of the Declaration on the Protection of all Persons from Enforced Disappearance, Article 4 (g) of the Declaration on the Elimination of Violence against Women, and Principles 14-17 of the Declaration of Basic Principles of Justice for Victims of Crime and Abuse of Power.

[156] *Report of the Special Rapporteur on torture*, E/CN.4/2003/68, 17 December 2002, para 26 (l).

[157] *Report by the Special Rapporteur on torture*, A/54/426, 1 October 1999, para 50.

[158] Case *Raul Sendic Antonaccio v Uruguay*, Views of 28 October 1981, CCPR/C/14/D/63/1979, para 21; Case *Elena Beatriz Vasilskis v Uruguay*, Views of 31 March 1983, CCPR/C/18/D/80/1980, para 12; Case *Gustavo Raul Larrosa Bequio v Uruguay*, Views of 29 March 1983, CCPR/C/18/D/88/1981, para 13; and *Concluding Observations on Mexico*, 27 July 1999, CCPR/C/79/Add.109, para 15.

[159] *Conclusions and recommendations on Brazil*, A/56/44, paras 115-120, 16 May 2001, para 120 f); *Conclusions and recommendations on Zambia*, CAT/C/XXVII/Concl.4, 23 November 2001, para 8 g); *Conclusions and recommendations on Indonesia*, CAT/C/XXVII/Concl.3, 22 November 2001, para 10 n); *Conclusions and recommendations on Turkey*, 27 May 2003, CAT/C/CR/30/5, para 7 (h); *Conclusions and recommendations on Cambodia*, 27 May 2003, CAT/C/CR/30/2, para 7 (k).

[160] *General Recommendation 19 on Violence against Women*, 29 January 1992, A/47/38, para 24 (a), (b).

[161] *General Comments on Article 19 of the Declaration on the Protection of All Persons from Enforced Disappearance*, 12 January 1998, E/CN.4/1998/43, para 75.

The Inter-American Court of Human Rights refers to medical assistance within its compensation awards. Sometimes, however, it refers more directly to measures of rehabilitation. Thus, in the *Aloeboetoe Case*, the Court ordered the reopening of a medical dispensary in a village affected by gross human rights violations.[162] In the case of the *Plan de Sánchez Massacre*, it ordered the state to award free medical aid and medicine to the victims and to establish a programme of psychological and psychiatric treatment free of cost.[163]

It should be noted that rehabilitation is not only relevant for physical or psychological damages. Rehabilitation can also be of a social nature. Victims are entitled to rehabilitation of their dignity, their social situation and their legal situation.[164] Some of these measures, such as legal rehabilitation through rectification of criminal records, or invalidation of unlawful convictions are mentioned above under 'restitution'. As said above, these measures often fall into more than one category.

***

IV. SATISFACTION

While compensation for immaterial damage is a form of monetary reparation for physical or mental suffering, distress, harm to the reputation or dignity or other moral damage, satisfaction is a different, non-financial form of reparation for moral damage or damage to the dignity or reputation. Measures of satisfaction have been recognized by the International Court of Justice. In its judgment in the *Corfu Channel Case*, for instance, it held that its declaration constituted in itself just satisfaction.[165]

[162] Case *Aloeboetoe et al v Suriname (Reparations)*, Judgment of 10 September, 1993, Series C No 15, para 96.

[163] Case of *Plan de Sánchez Massacre* (Reparations), Judgment of 19 November 2004, Series C No 116, paras 106-108, 117.

[164] See *General Comments on Article 19 of the Declaration on the Protection of All Persons from Enforced Disappearance*, 12 January 1998, E/CN.4/1998/43, para 75, which speaks of 'legal and social rehabilitation'.

[165] *Corfu Channel Case (Merits)*, Judgment of 9 April 1949, I.C.J. Reports 1949, p 1, at 35.

1. Satisfaction through Judicial Decisions

In many cases, international tribunals have decided that a condemnatory judgment constitutes satisfaction in itself, since an independent and impartial tribunal states with legal authority that the victim has suffered a violation of his or her human rights.[166]

The Inter-American Court, however, considers that in cases of gross human rights violations, a judgment alone does not suffice to constitute adequate reparation; such violations call for compensation.[167] In cases of gross human rights violations, a mere declaration by a Court will usually fail to do justice to the victim.[168]

2. Apology, Public Acknowledgment, and Acceptance of Responsibility

One of the most important forms of reparations is the search for and the acknowledgement of truth, but also of responsibility and indeed fault. In this sense, it is intrinsically linked to the right to an investigation and the right to truth. The UN Principles on Reparation list as measures of reparation the '[v]erification of the facts and full and public disclosure of the truth to the extent that such disclosure does not cause further unnecessary harm or threaten the safety of the victim, witnesses, or others', the 'search for the whereabouts of the disappeared and for the bodies of those killed, and assistance in the recovery, identification and reburial of the bodies in accordance with the cultural practices of the families and communities', '[a]pology, including public

[166] See only ECtHR: Case *Golder v the United Kingdom*, Judgment of 21 February 1975, Series A No 18, para 46; Case *Oçalan v Turkey*, Judgment of 12 March 2003, para 250; I/ACtHR: *Cesti Hurtado Case (Reparations)*, Judgment of 31 May 2001, Series C No 78, para 59 [judgment constitutes satisfaction with regard to the reputation and honour of the victim].

[167] Case *El Amparo v Venezuela (Reparations)*, Judgment of 14 September 1996, Series C No 28, para 35; Case *Neira Alegría et al v Peru (Reparations)*, Judgment of 19 September 1996, Series C No 29, para 56; Case *Castillo Páez v Peru (Reparations)*, Judgment of 27 November 1998, Series C No 43, para 84; Case *Blake v Guatemala (Reparations)*, Judgment of 22 January 1999, para 55; Case of *Panel Blanca v Guatemala (Reparations)*, Judgment of 25 May 2001, Series C No 76, para 105.

[168] *Villagrán Morales et al v Guatemala, Street Children Case (Reparations)*, Judgment of 26 May 2001, Series C No 77, para 88; Case of *The Mayagna (Sumo) Awas Tingni Community v Nicaragua*, Judgment of 31 August 2001, Series C No 79, para 166; Case *Cantoral Benavides v Peru (Reparations)*, Judgment of 3 December 2001, Series C No 88, para 79; Case *Bámaca Velásquez v Guatemala (Reparations)*, Judgment of 22 February 2002, Series C No 91, para 84.

acknowledgement of the facts and acceptance of responsibility', and '[i]nclusion of an accurate account of the violations that occurred in international human rights and humanitarian law training and in educational material at all levels.'[169] The search for, the acknowledgment and the publication of the truth and the recognition of responsibility are indeed forms of moral, non-monetary reparation and thus of satisfaction. Similarly, the punishment of the authors of the violation is a form of satisfaction.[170]

Beyond the right to investigation and truth, public acknowledgement, apology and acceptance of responsibility are important forms of reparation. Along these lines, the UN Principles on Impunity recommend that the final report of truth commissions should be made public.[171] Similarly, the UN Human Rights Commission's resolutions on impunity recognize that 'for the victims of human rights violations, public knowledge of their suffering and the truth about the perpetrators, including their accomplices, of these violations are essential steps towards rehabilitation and reconciliation.'[172]

International courts and bodies, such as the Human Rights Committee,[173] the African Commission on Human and Peoples' Rights,[174] and the Inter-American Court of Human Rights[175] have asked states to make their judg-

[169] Principle 22 (b), (c), (e), (h) of the UN Principles on Reparation.

[170] Principle 22 (f) of the UN Principles on Reparation.

[171] Principle 13.

[172] Resolutions on Impunity E/CN.4/RES/2001/70, 25 April 2001, para 8; E/CN.4/RES/2002/79, para 9; E/CN.4/RES/2003/72 I, para 8.

[173] Case *Félix Enrique Chira Vargas-Machuca v Peru*, Views of 26 July 2002, CCPR/C/75/D/906 2000, para 10; Case *Sarma v Sri Lanka*, Views of 31 July 2003, CCPR/C/78/D/950/2000, para 12; Case *Busyo v Democratic Republic of Congo*, Views of 9 August 2003, CCPR/C/78/D/933/2000, para 6.3; Case *Nyekuma Kopita Toro Gedumbe v Democratic Republic of the Congo*, Views of 1 August 1997, CCPR/C/75/D/641/1995, para 6.3.

[174] Case *Krishna Achuthan on behalf of Aleka Banda, Amnesty International on behalf of Orton and Vera Chirwa v Malawi*, Communications 64/92, 68/92 and 78/92, para 18.

[175] Case *Trujillo Oroza v Bolivia (Reparations)*, Judgment of 27 February 2002, Series C No 92, para 119; Case of *Barrios Altos v Peru (Reparations)*, Judgment of 30 November 2001, Series C No 87, para 44 (d) and operative paragraph 5 d); Case *Cantoral Benavides v Peru (Reparations)*, Judgment of 3 December 2001, Series C No 88, para 79; Case *Durand and Ugarte v Peru (Reparations)*, Judgment of 3 December 2001, Series C No 89, para 39 a) and operative paragraph 3 a); Case *Bámaca Velásquez v Guatemala (Reparations)*, Judgment of 22 February 2002, Series C No 91, para 84; Case of *Caracazo v Venezuela (Reparations)*, Judgment of 29 August 2002, Series C No 95, para 128; Case *Juan Humberto Sánchez v Honduras*, Judgment of 7 June 2003, Series C No 102, para 188.

ments public. The Inter-American Court as a matter of practice orders its judgments to be published in the official newspaper of the country concerned[176] and, in relevant cases, have them translated into the language of the person most affected (for example in Maya for victims of a massacre committed against Maya communities in Guatemala).[177]

Beyond the mere finding and publication of facts, apology and recognition of responsibility - in other words the recognition that those facts are not ethically neutral - is an essential part of satisfaction. This has been recognized by the Inter-American Court of Human Rights, which has ordered such recognition of responsibility and public apology.[178] Apology may also consist in restoring the honour, reputation or dignity of a person.[179]

3. Public Commemoration

Another important aspect of reparation that can provide a measure of satisfaction to victims is public commemoration. This is particularly important in cases of violations of the rights of groups or a high number of persons, sometimes not individually identified, or in cases of violations that occurred a long time in the past. Public commemoration in these cases has a symbolic value and constitutes a measure of reparation for current but also future generations. The Inter-American Court, for instance, has ordered public commemoration in individual cases, such as the naming of a street

---

[176] *Ibidem.*

[177] Case of *Plan de Sánchez Massacre (Reparations)*, Judgment of 19 November 2004, Series C No 116, para 102.

[178] Case of *Barrios Altos v Peru (Reparations)*, Judgment of 30 November 2001, Series C No 87, para 44 e) and operative paragraph 5 e); Case *Cantoral Benavides v Peru (Reparations)*, Judgment of 3 December 2001, Series C No 88, para 81; Case *Durand and Ugarte v Peru (Reparations)*, Judgment of 3 December 2001, Series C No 89, para 39 b) and operative paragraph 4 b); Case *Bámaca Velásquez v Guatemala (Reparations)*, Judgment of 22 February 2002, Series C No 91, para 84; Case *Juan Humberto Sánchez v Honduras*, Judgment of 7 June 2003, Series C No 99, para 188; Case of *Plan de Sánchez Massacre (Reparations)*, Judgment of 19 November 2004, Series C No 116, para 100. Guatemala apologized publicly for the massacre: AP Guatemala Apologizes for 1982 Massacre [available at http://news.yahoo.com/s/ap/20050719/aponrelaamca/guatemala_human_rights].

[179] I/ACtHR: Case *Cesti Hurtado v Peru (Reparations)*, Judgment of 31 May 2001, Series C No 78, para 59 [judgment constitutes satisfaction with regard to the reputation and honour of the victim]; I/ACmHR: Report No 20/99, Case 11.317, *Rodolfo Robles Espinoza and sons* (Peru), 23 February 1999, para 176 (1, 2) [restore honour and reputation of Major General after defamation campaign]; Case of *Plan de Sánchez Massacre* (Reparations), Judgment of 19 November 2004, Series C No 116, para 101.

and educational centre[180] or the dedication of a public monument[181] to the victims. The Special Rapporteur of the Sub-Commission on the question of impunity has equally recommended such public commemoration.[182]

***

Summary

While the different forms of reparation have been recognized in public international law for some time, human rights law is somewhat erratic in its terminology on reparations. Interpretation of the treaties and other norms concerning reparation have, however, clarified many of the concepts. It is now beyond doubt that victims of human rights violations have a right to restitution, compensation, rehabilitation and satisfaction. International jurisprudence converges in substance, if not always in terminology, in the rights it recognizes to victims.

The different forms of reparation must be complementary to achieve to the fullest extent possible reparation for material and moral damage suffered:

- Restitution is the ideal form of reparation as it wipes out the consequences of the violation. However, it is often not possible and other forms of reparation have to be resorted to.
- Compensation must be based on the material loss actually incurred; it must also provide redress for moral damages, which should be assessed in equity.
- Rehabilitation should seek to physically and mentally help the victim to overcome the damage suffered by the violation.
- Satisfaction should help to restore a person's dignity, mental well-being, and reputation.

180 *Villagrán Morales et al. v Guatemala, Street Children Case (Reparations)*, Judgment of 26 May 2001, Series C No 77, para 103; Case *Trujillo Oroza v Bolivia (Reparations)*, Judgment of 27 February 2002, Series C No 92, para 122.

181 Case of *Barrios Altos v Peru (Reparations)*, Judgment of 30 November 2001, Series C No 87, para 44 f) and operative paragraph 5 f).

182 *Report of the Special Rapporteur on the question of impunity of perpetrators of human rights violations (civil and political)*, 2 October 1997, E/CN.4/Sub.2/1997/20/Rev1, para 17.

While the assessment of damage is not always easy because evidence is lacking, international case law has made clear that this is not an obstacle for granting reparation. Damages may have to be presumed from the violation as such, because it is hardly conceivable that a gross human rights violation will leave a person unaffected either materially or morally. As far as financial compensation is concerned, it may often have to be assessed in equity.

Relatives of the victims, or other persons or groups may likewise have a right to be granted these different forms of reparation, either in the name of the victim or in their own name when they have themselves suffered material or moral damage.

CHAPTER VIII
THE OBLIGATION TO PROSECUTE AND PUNISH

'[...] it cannot be ignored that a clear nexus exists between the impunity of perpetrators of gross violations of human rights and the failure to provide just and adequate reparation to the victims and their families or dependants. In many situations where impunity has been sanctioned by the law or where de facto impunity prevails with regard to persons responsible for gross violations of human rights, the victims are effectively barred from seeking and receiving redress and reparation. In fact, once the State authorities fail to investigate the facts and to establish criminal responsibility, it becomes very difficult for victims or their relatives to carry on effective legal proceedings aimed at obtaining just and adequate reparation.'[1]

The international obligation to prosecute and punish violations of human rights has existed at least since the international law on diplomatic protection which preceded the international human rights regime. This is illustrated in the famous dictum by Max Huber in the *Spanish Morroco case*, in which he states that the responsibility of the state can be engaged for denial of justice when they lack due diligence in the pursuit of criminals.[2] Likewise, in the *Janes case*,[3] the United States presented a claim *on behalf* of the relatives of Mr *Janes*, an American citizen, based on the failure of Mexico to

[1] Theo Van Boven, *Study concerning the right to restitution, compensation and rehabilitation for victims of gross violations of human rights and fundamental freedoms*, E/CN.4/Sub.2/1993/8, 2 July 1993, paras 126-127.

[2] *Affaires des biens britanniques au Maroc Espagnol (Espagne c. Royaume-Uni)*, Sentence du 1er mai 1925, Recueil de sentences arbitrales, Volume II, p 615, at 645.

[3] Case *Laura M.B. Janes et al (USA) v the United Mexican States*, award of 16 November 1925, Recueil de sentences arbitrales, Volume IV, p 82.

apprehend his murderer. The Claims Commission based its award of compensation on the damage caused to the relatives for the 'indignity' caused by the non-punishment of the murderer.[4]

The obligation to prosecute and punish is often described as a correlative to the 'right to justice'[5] of victims and as a fundamental duty of the state in the obligation to combat impunity. There are few definitions of the concept of impunity. One definition is used in the jurisprudence of the Inter-American Court, which understands impunity as 'the total lack of investigation, prosecution, capture, trial and conviction of those responsible for violations of the rights protected by the American Convention, in view of the fact that the state has the obligation to use all the legal means at its disposal to combat that situation, since impunity fosters chronic recidivism of human rights violations, and total defenselessness of victims and their relatives.'[6] Another is used by the Special Rapporteur on the question of impunity and reads as follows: 'Impunity means the impossibility, *de jure* or *de facto*, of bringing the perpetrators of human rights violations to account – whether in criminal, civil, administrative or disciplinary proceedings – since they are not subject to any inquiry that might lead to their being accused, arrested, tried and, if found guilty, convicted, and to reparations being made to their victims.'[7]

The obligation to prosecute and punish perpetrators of gross human rights violations is not necessarily a part of the victim's right to reparation. It exists independently of the rights of the victim as an obligation of the state. Nevertheless, the accountability of perpetrators is one of the most important measures of redress for victims, which is why it is sometimes described as their right to justice. This has been stressed by the Special Rapporteur on the right to reparation.[8] The General Assembly of the United Nations has similarly emphasized this link when it stated that 'the accountability of in-

---

4 *Ibid.*

5 *Revised final report of the Special Rapporteur on the question of impunity of perpetrators of human rights violations (civil and political)*, 2 October 1997, E/CN.4/Sub.2/1997/20/Rev1, Annex II, Section II.

6 Case of "*Panel Blanca*" *v Guatemala*, Judgment of 8 March 1998, Series C No 37, para 173; Case *Bámaca Velásquez v Guatemala*, Judgment of 25 November 2000, Series C No 79, para 211.

7 *Revised final report of the Special Rapporteur on the question of impunity of perpetrators of human rights violations (civil and political)*, 2 October 1997, E/CN.4/Sub.2/1997/20/Rev1, Annex II, pp 13-14.

8 See above, footnote 1.

dividual perpetrators of grave human rights violations is one of the central elements of any effective remedy for victims of human rights violations and a key factor in ensuring a fair and equitable justice system and, ultimately, reconciliation and stability within a State.'[9]

As shall be demonstrated, international human rights law requires that those responsible for gross human rights violations such as extrajudicial executions, torture and ill-treatment, enforced disappearances, genocide, crimes against humanity, war crimes, and other gross human rights violations, should be brought to justice. Further, international law has addressed some of the impediments to an effective prosecution of those responsible, such as amnesty laws, statutes of limitations and impunity perpetuated through the military justice system (these are dealt with in Chapters IX).

***

I. The Obligation to Prosecute and Punish Gross Human Rights Violations

1. State Obligation to Prosecute and Punish

All States have an obligation to prosecute and punish perpetrators of gross human rights violations and to combat impunity. This is accepted by the highest organs of the United Nations, the Security Council[10] and the General Assembly.[11] Before turning to the specific rights whose violation must be prosecuted and punished, the general approach of international human rights bodies with regard to impunity should be described.

a) UN Commission on Human Rights

The resolutions of the Human Rights Commission on impunity emphasize the importance of combating impunity and the importance to hold ac-

[9] Resolution A/RES/57/228 on *Khmer Rouge trials* of 18 December 2002.

[10] Resolution on the question concerning Haiti, S/RES/1529 (2004), 29 February 2004, para 7; Resolution on the situation in Côte d'Ivoire, S/RES/1479 of 13 May 2003, para 8.

[11] A/RES/57/228 of 27 February 2002, on *Khmer Rouge trials*, p 3; the General Assembly has asked to bring those responsible of child abduction to justice: A/RES/57/190, 19 February 2003, para 11.

countable perpetrators, including their accomplices, of violations of international human rights and humanitarian law. It recognizes that amnesties should not be granted to those who commit violations of international humanitarian and human rights law that constitute serious crimes and urges states to take action in accordance with their obligations under international law.[12] Special Rapporteurs of the Commission have also asked for the punishment of perpetrators of gross human rights violations.[13]

b) Human Rights Committee

The Human Rights Committee has developed jurisprudence on the duty to prosecute and punish violations of human rights since its first individual cases concerning Uruguay. For example, in the case of *Bleier v Uruguay* the Human Rights Committee urged the Government 'to bring to justice any persons found to be responsible for his death, disappearance or ill-treatment.'[14] Similar findings can be found in many cases of the Human Rights Committee[15] and in its concluding observations on state party reports.[16] It considers that a climate of impunity for human rights violations (for example through amnesties) consti-

[12] Resolutions E/CN.4/RES/2003/72, paras 2, 10; E/CN.4/RES/2002/79, paras 2, 11; E/CN.4/RES/2001/70, para 2; E/CN.4/RES/2000/68, para 4; E/CN.4/RES/1999/34, para 4; E/CN.4/RES/1998/53, para 4.

[13] *Report of the Special Rapporteur on the independence of judges and lawyers on his mission to Guatemala*, 21 December 2001, E/CN.4/2002/72/Add.2, recommendation a); *Report on the independence of judges and lawyers on the mission to Mexico*, 24 January 2000, E/CN.4/2002/72/Add.1, recommendations j), k), p).

[14] Case *Bleier v Uruguay*, Views of 29 March 1982, CCPR/C/15/D/30/1978, para 11.

[15] Case *Almeida de Quinteros et al v Uruguay*, Views of 21 July 1983, CCPR/C/OP/2, para 16 (b); Case *Dermit Barbato v Uruguay*, Views of 21 October 1982, CCPR/C/17/D/84/1981, para 11; Case *Celis Laureano v Peru*, Views of 16 April 1996, CCPR/C/56/D/540/1993, para 10; Case *Sarma v Sri Lanka*, Views of 31 July 2003, CCPR/C/78/D/950/2000, para 11; Case *Nydia Erika Bautista v Colombia*, Views of 13 November 1995, CCPR/C/55/D/563/1993, paras 8.6, 10; Case *José Vicente y Amado Villafañe Chaparro v Colombia*, Views of 29 July 1997, CCPR/C/60/D/612/1995, para 8.2; Case *Coronel et al v Colombia*, Views of 13 October 2000, CCPR/C/70/D/778/1997, para 10.

[16] *Concluding Observations on the Libyan Arab Jamahiriya*, 6 November 1998, CCPR/C/79/Add.101, paras 7, 10; *Concluding Observations on Mexico*, 27 July 1999, CCPR/C/79/Add.109, para 6; *Concluding Observations on Algeria*, 18 August 1998, CCPR/C/79/Add.95, paras 6, 7, 9; *Concluding Observations on Argentina*, 3 November 2000, CCPR/CO/70/ARG, paras 9, 13; *Concluding Observations on the Kyrgyz Republic*, 24 July 2000, CCPR/CO/69/KGZ, para 7; *Concluding Observations on Guatemala*, 27 August 2001, CCPR/CO/72/GTM, para 12; *Concluding Observations on Venezuela*, 26 April 2001, CCPR/CO/71/VEN, para 8; *Concluding Observations on Hungary*, 19 April, 2002, CCPR/CO/74/HUN, para 12; *Concluding Observations on Colombia*, 5 May 1997, CCPR/C/79/Add.76, para 32; *Concluding Observations on Argentina*, 3 November 2000, CCPR/CO/70/ARG, paras 9, 13.

tutes a breach of the obligations of states under the Covenant.[17] In its *General Comment No 31 on Article 2 of the Covenant*, it held that:

> 'Where the investigations referred to in paragraph 15 reveal violations of certain Covenant rights, States Parties must ensure that those responsible are brought to justice. As with failure to investigate, failure to bring to justice perpetrators of such violations could in and of itself give rise to a separate breach of the Covenant. These obligations arise notably in respect of those violations recognized as criminal under either domestic or international law, such as torture and similar cruel, inhuman and degrading treatment, summary and arbitrary executions and enforced disappearance. Indeed, the problem of impunity for these violations, a matter of sustained concern by the Committee, may well be an important contributing element in the recurrence of the violations. When committed as part of a widespread or systematic attack on a civilian population, these violations of the Covenant are crimes against humanity.'[18]

While the Human Rights Committee considers that criminal sanctions are the primary obligation of states with regard to gross human rights violations,[19] it considers that disciplinary measures are complementary to penal sanctions. It considers that persons found guilty of serious human rights violations should be 'dismissed from public service in addition to any other punishment.'[20]

17 *Concluding Observations on Uruguay*, 5 May 1993, CCPR/C/79/Add.19, para 7; *Concluding Observations on Chile*, 30 March 1999, CCPR/C/79/Add.104, para 7; *Concluding Observations on Lebanon*, 1 April 1997, CCPR/C/79/Add.78, para 12; *Concluding Observations on El Salvador*, 18 April 1994, CCPR/C/79/Add.34, para 7; *Concluding Observations on Haiti*, 3 October 1995, A/50/40, paras 224-241, at 230; *Concluding Observations on Peru*, 15 November 2000, CCPR/CO/70/PER, para 9; *Concluding Observations on France*, 4 August 1997, CCPR/C/79/Add.80, para 13; *Concluding Observations on Argentina*, 5 April 1995, CCPR/C/79/Add.46, para 146 and 3 November 2000, CCPR/CO/70/ARG, para 9; *Concluding Observations on Croatia*, 4 April 2001, CCPR/CO/71/HRV, para 11; *Concluding Observations on Guatemala*, 27 August 2001, CCPR/CO/72/GTM, para 12.

18 *General Comment No 31 on Article 2 of the Covenant: The Nature of the General Legal Obligation Imposed on States Parties to the Covenant*, 21 May 2004, CCPR/C/74/CRP.4/Rev.6, para 18 (references omitted).

19 Case *Nydia Erika Bautista v. Colombia*, Views of 13 November 1993, CCPR/C/55/D/563/1993, para 8.2; Case *José Vicente y Amado Villafañe Chaparro et al v Colombia*, Views of 29 July 1997, CCPR/C/60/D/612/1995, para 8.2.

20 *Concluding Observations on Serbia and Montenegro*, CCPR/CO/81/SEMO, 12 August 2004, para 9.

c) Inter-American Court and Commission of Human Rights

The Inter-American Court of Human Rights holds that the duty to punish, along with the obligations to prevent, investigate and compensate, forms part of the holistic duty of the state to 'ensure' the full enjoyment of human rights. It considers that the duty to prevent human rights violations includes 'all those means of a legal, political, administrative and cultural nature that promote the protection of human rights and ensure that any violations are considered and treated as illegal acts, which, as such, may lead to the punishment of those responsible and the obligation to indemnify the victims for damages.'[21] It has indicated that the state 'has the obligation to combat [impunity] through all legal means at its disposal because [it] fosters chronic recidivism of human rights violations and total defencelessness of the victims and their next of kin.'[22] The Inter-American Court has derived the duty to punish from the general guarantee of Article 1 (1) of the Convention and the duty to take domestic measures under Article 2 of the Convention.[23] This means that the state also has to adapt its internal legislation in order to make investigation and punishment possible.[24] The Court also considers that the duty to punish flows from Articles 8 (1) and 25 of the Convention in relation to Article 1 (1) of the Convention.[25] The duty to

[21] Case *Velásquez Rodríguez v Honduras*, Judgment of 29 July 1988, Series C No. 4, para 166; see also para 175.

[22] See Case *Cantoral Benavides v Peru (Reparations)*, Judgment of 3 December 2001, Series C No 88, para 69; Case *Cesti Hurtado v Peru (Reparations)*, Judgment of 31 May 2001, Series C No 78, para 63; *Villagrán Morales et al v Guatemala, "Street Children" Case, (Reparations)* Judgment of 26 May 2001, Series C No 77, para 100; Case of "*Panel Blanca*" *v Guatemala (Reparations)*, Judgment of 25 May 2001, Series C No 76, para 201; Case *Bámaca Velásquez v Guatemala (Reparations)*, Judgment of 22 February 2002, Series C No 91, para 74.

[23] Case *Velásquez Rodríguez v Honduras*, Judgment of 29 July 1988, Series C No 4, para 177; Case *Loayza Tamayo v Peru (Reparations)*, Judgment of 27 November 1998, Series C No 42, paras 168-171; Case *Castillo Páez v Peru (Reparations)*, Judgment of 27 November 1998, Series C No 43, paras 98-108; Case *Suárez Rosero v Ecuador (Reparations)*, Judgment of 20 January 1999, Series C No 44, paras 77-80; Case *Blake v Guatemala (Reparations)*, Judgment of 22 January 1999, Series C No 48, paras 59-65.

[24] Case *Velásquez Rodríguez v Honduras*, Judgment of 29 July 1988, Series C No 4, para 166.

[25] Case *Blake v Guatemala*, Judgment of 24 January 1998, Series C No 36, para 97; see also *Villagrán Morales et al v Guatemala, Street Children Case*, Judgment of 19 November 1999, para 225; Case *Durand and Ugarte v Peru*, Judgment of 16 August 2000, Series C No 68, para 130; *Case Las Palmeras v Colombia*, Judgment of 6 December 2001, Series C No 90, para 65; Case *Juan Humberto Sánchez v Honduras*, Judgment of 7 June 2003, Series C No 99, para 121-136; Case *Myrna Mack Chang v Guatemala*, Judgment of 25 November, 2003, Series C No 101, para 275.

punish also falls under the reparation to be guaranteed to victims next to material and moral damages.[26]

The Inter-American Commission on Human Rights has held that the duty to punish flows from Article 1 (1) of the American Convention on Human Rights[27] and from Articles 8 (1) and 25 (1).[28] It has, amongst other, recommended investigation and prosecution in cases of extrajudicial executions,[29] disappearances,[30] torture,[31] and domestic violence,[32] crimes against humanity and genocide.[33] In a recommendation of 1998, the Inter-American Commission on Human Rights recommended 'that the member states of the Organization of American States adopt such legislative and other measures as may be necessary to invoke and exercise universal jurisdiction in respect of individuals in matters of genocide, crimes against humanity, and war crimes.'[34] In its Recommendation on *Asylum and International*

---

[26] Case of "*Panel Blanca" v Guatemala, Reparations*, Judgment of 25 May 2001, paras 194-202; *Villagrán Morales et al v Guatemala, Street Children Case (Reparations)*, Judgment of 26 May, 2001, Series C No 77, para 98-101; Case *Cantoral Benavides v Peru (Reparations)*, Judgment of 3 December 2001, Series C No 88, paras 69, 70; Case *Durand and Ugarte v Peru (Reparations)*, Judgment of 3 December 2001, Series C No 89, para 39 c) and operative paragraph 3 c); Case *Bámaca Velásquez v Guatemala (Reparations)*, Judgment of 22 February 2002, Series C No 91, paras 73-78; Case *Trujillo Oroza v Bolovia (Reparations)*, Judgment of 27 February 2002, Series C No 92, para 99-111; Case *Bulacio v Argentina*, Judgment of 18 September 2003, Series C No 100, para 110.

[27] Report No. 136/99, *Ignacio Ellacuría S.J et al* (El Salvador), 22 December 1999, paras 170 *et seq*; *Riofrío Massacre* (Colombia), 6 April 2001, paras 77 *et seq*; Case 10.247 *et al*, *Extrajudicial Executions and Forced Disappearances of Persons* (Peru), 11 October 2001, para 247.

[28] Report No 133/99, Case 11.725, *Carmelo Soria Espinoza* (Chile), 19 November 1999, paras 92 *et seq*; Report No 34/96, Cases 11.228 (Chile), 15 October 1996, paras 72 *et seq*; Report No 36/96, Case 10843 (Chile), 15 October 1996, paras 66 *et seq*; Report No. 136/99, *Ignacio Ellacuría S.J et al* (El Salvador), 22 December 1999, paras 189 *et seq*; *Riofrío Massacre* (Colombia), 6 April 2001, paras 64 *et seq*.; Case 10.247 *et al., Extrajudicial Executions and Forced Disappearances of Persons* (Peru), 11 October 2001, paras 235 *et seq*; Report No. 36/96, Case 10.843, *Héctor Marcial Garay Hermosilla* (Chile), 15 October 1996, para 67; Report No. 34/96, Cases 11.228 *et al.* (Chile), 15 October 1996, para 70; Report No 1/99, Case 10.480, *Lucio Parada Cea et al* (El Salvador), 27 January 1999, paras 130 *et seq*.

[29] Report No. 62/01, Case 11.654, *Riofrío Massacre* (Colombia), 6 April 2001, para 84 (1).

[30] Report 52/99, Cases 10.544 *et al*, *Raúl Zevallos Loayza et al* (Perú), 13 April 1999, para 123; Report No 101/01, Cases 10.247 *et al*, *Extrajudicial Executions and Forced Disappearances of Persons* (Perú), 11 October 2001, para 253 (2).

[31] Report No. 62/01, Case 11.654, *Riofrío Massacre* (Colombia), 6 April 2001, para 84 (1).

[32] Case *Maria Da Penha Maia Fernandes* (Brazil), Report of 16 April 2001, para 61 (1).

[33] OEA/Ser/L/V/II/102 Doc. 70, 16 April 1999, Annual Report 1998, Chapter VII, Recommendation 21.

[34] OEA/Ser/L/V/II/102 Doc. 70, 16 April 1999, Annual Report 1998, Chapter VII, Recommendation 21.

Crimes, it recalled the principle that asylum should not be granted to those who flee to avoid criminal responsibility.[35]

d) European Court of Human Rights

The European Court of Human Rights has recognized since 1985 that certain acts which impede the enjoyment of a person's right to physical integrity, whether committed by public or private persons, require that the state punish such acts by criminal law. The first case, *X and Y v the Netherlands*, concerned a case of rape of a minor, which could not be prosecuted because of a procedural obstacle.[36] The Court found that the protection afforded by civil law in the case of wrongdoing of the kind inflicted on the victim was insufficient, because fundamental values and essential aspects of private life were at stake. Effective deterrence was indispensable and could be achieved only by criminal-law provisions.[37] The Court later found that the protection of the right to life,[38] the prohibition of torture[39] and cruel, inhuman or degrading treatment or punishment[40] and the prohibition of enforced disappearances[41] require the prosecution and punishment of the act. The duty to punish is embedded, in the interpretation of the Court, in the wider obligation of protection. In other words, states must 'take appropriate steps to safeguard the lives of those within its jurisdiction [...]. The state's obligation in this respect extends beyond its primary duty to secure the right to life by putting in place effective criminal-law provisions to deter the commission of offences against the person backed up by law-enforcement machinery for the prevention, suppression and sanctioning of breaches of such provisions.'[42] It has also pointed to the close link between the failure to

35 Recommendation on *Asylum and International Crimes*, 20 October 2000, Annual Report 2000, Chapter VI, OEA/Ser./L/V/II.111 Doc. 20 rev, 16 April 2001.

36 Case *X and Y v the Netherlands*, Judgment of 26 March 1985, Series A 91; see also the Judgment M.C. *v Bulgaria*, 4 December 2003, para 153.

37 Case *X and Y v the Netherlands*, Judgment of 26 March 1985, Series A 91, para 27.

38 Case *Osman v the United Kingdom*, Judgment of 28 October 1998, Reports 1998-VIII, para 116.

39 Case *Aksoy v Turkey*, Judgment of 18 December 1996, Reports 1996-VI, para 98.

40 Case A. *v the United Kingdom*, Judgment of 23 September 1998, *Reports of Judgments and Decisions* 1998-VI, paras 22, 23.

41 Case *Kurt v Turkey*, Judgment of 25 May 1998, Report 1998-III, para 140.

42 Case *Osman v the United Kingdom*, Judgment of 28 October 1998, Reports 1998-VIII, para 115; Case *Mahmut Kaya v Turkey*, Judgment of 28 March 2000, Reports 2000-III, para 85; Case *Kiliç v Turkey*, Judgment of 28 Mars 2000, Reports 2000-III, para 62.

apply the criminal laws effectively and the ensuing impunity of perpetrators and held that the defects in investigation and prosecution 'undermined the effectiveness of the protection afforded by the criminal law.' This 'permitted or fostered a lack of accountability of members of the security forces for their actions which [...] was not compatible with the rule of law in a democratic society respecting the fundamental rights and freedoms guaranteed under the Convention.'[43] The Committee of Ministers, the body in charge of supervising the implementation of the Court's judgments, has, moreover, expressed concern where the sanctions of crimes such as torture or ill-treatment resulted in light custodial sentences or were converted into fines and in most cases subsequently suspended, as it saw it as a confirmation of 'serious shortcomings in the criminal-law protection against abuses highlighted in the European Court's judgments'; it stressed the need for a 'sufficiently deterring minimum level of prison sentences for personnel found guilty of torture and ill-treatment.'[44]

The European Court of Human Rights not only holds that the obligation to prosecute and punish flows from the substantive guarantees of the Convention (such as the prohibition of torture, and cruel, inhuman and degrading treatment, the protection of the right to life or private life), but that it is part of the right to a remedy, guaranteed in Article 13 ECHR.[45]

e) *African Commission on Human and Peoples' Rights*

The African Commission on Human and Peoples' Rights has also recognized a duty to investigate, prosecute and punish. In the case of the *Malawi African Association et al v Mauritania*, the African Commission, after having found multiple gross violations of human rights, recommended that the government "arrange for the commencement of an independent enquiry in order to clarify the fate of the persons considered as disappeared, identify

---

[43] Case *Mahmut Kaya v Turkey*, Judgment of 28 March 2000, Reports 2000-III, para 98; Case *Kiliç v Turkey*, Judgment of 28 Mars 2000, Reports 2000-III, para 75; on the legal consequences of a general climate of impunity see also Case *Orhan v Turkey*, Judgment of 18 June 2002, para 330.

[44] Interim Resolution ResDH(2002)98, *Action of the security forces in Turkey, Progress achieved and outstanding problems, General measures to ensure compliance with the judgments of the European Court of Human Rights in the cases against Turkey listed in Appendix II (Follow-up to Interim Resolution DH(99)434*, 10 July 2002.

[45] Case *Aksoy v Turkey*, Judgment of 18 December 1996, Reports 1996-VI, para 98; Case *Aydin v Turkey*, Judgment of 25 September 1997, Reports 1997-VI, para 103, Case *Kaya v Turkey*, Judgment of 19 February 1998, Reports 1998-I, paras 106-107; Case *Orhan v Turkey*, Judgment of 18 June 2002, para 384.

and bring to book the authors of the violations perpetrated at the time of the facts arraigned".[46] In the case concerning human rights violations in Ogoniland in Nigeria, the Commission appealed to the Government to ensure the protection of the environment, health and livelihood of the people of Ogoniland by, *inter alia*, "[c]onducting an investigation into the human rights violations described above and prosecuting officials of the security forces, the *Nigerian National Petroleum Company* and the relevant agencies involved in human rights violations".[47]

2. Specific Rights

The obligation of states to punish certain violations of human rights is enshrined in human rights treaties with regard to very different rights. Some Conventions only speak of the duty to sanction human rights violations,[48] other treaties specifically obligate states to adopt criminal sanctions.[49] The duty to prosecute and punish can also be found in many declaratory instruments.[50] Some specific gross human rights violations shall be highlighted here.

[46] Case *Malawi African Association et al v Mauritania*, Communications 54/91, 61/91, 98/93, 164/97, 196/97, 210/98 (27th Ordinary Session, May 2000).

[47] Case *The Social and Economic Rights Action Center and the Center for Economic and Social Rights v Nigeria*, Communication 155/96 (30th Ordinary Session, October 2001).

[48] See Article 2 (b) CEDAW; Article 4 (a) CERD.

[49] Article IV of the Apartheid Convention, Articles 4 and 5 CAT, Articles 3-5 of the Optional Protocol to the Convention on the Rights of the Child on the sale of children, child prostitution and child pornography; Article 4 of the Optional Protocol to the Convention on the Rights of the Child on the involvement of children in armed conflict; Articles IV, V and VI of the Convention on the Prevention and Punishment of the Crime of Genocide; Articles 1 and 6 of the Inter-American Convention to Prevent and Punish Torture; Article 7 of the Inter-American Convention on the Prevention, Punishment and Eradication of Violence against Women; Articles I and IV of the Inter-American Convention on Forced Disappearance of Persons; Article 18 of the ILO Indigenous and Tribal Peoples Convention 1989 (No. 169) stipulates that '[a]dequate penalties shall be established by law for unauthorised intrusion upon, or use of, the lands of the peoples concerned, and governments shall take measures to prevent such offences.' See also the Convention on the Non-Applicability of Statutory Limitations to War Crimes and Crimes Against Humanity and the European Convention on the Non-Applicability of Statutory Limitation to Crimes Against Humanity and War Crimes.

[50] Article 4 (c) and (d) of the Declaration on the Elimination of Violence against Women, Article 4 of the Declaration on the Protection of All Persons from Enforced Disappearance, Art. 18 of the UN Principles on Extra-legal Executions, Principle 7 of the Basic Principles on the Use of Force and Firearms by Law Enforcement Officials, Principle 5 of the Principles of International Cooperation in the Detection, Arrest, Extradition and Punishment of Persons Guilty of War Crimes and Crimes against

a) Torture and Cruel, Inhuman or Degrading Treatment or Punishment

Article 4 of the Convention against Torture imposes an obligation on states to 'ensure that all acts of torture are offences under its criminal law.' The Committee against Torture considers that this obligation requires that states codify the crime of torture in their criminal codes.[51] It considers that the incorporation of the crime of torture is warranted to comply with all the obligations under the Convention against Torture, such as the principle of legality or the obligation of extradition[52] or to permit universal jurisdiction.[53]

Articles 5 and 7 establish a duty of the state to prosecute or extradite the offender and permits universal jurisdiction over the offence.[54] The Committee against Torture has, however, stated that the duty to prosecute and punish torture and ill-treatment is not only enshrined in the Convention, but is an obligation under customary international law.[55] It has recalled this obligation in many of its conclusions and recommendations to states parties.[56]

Humanity, Paragraphs 60, 62 of the Vienna Declaration and Programme of Action, Paragraphs 84-89 of the Programme of Action of the World Conference against Racism, Racial Discrimination, Xenophobia and Related Intolerance.

51 *Conclusions and recommendations on Zambia*, CAT/C/XXVII/Concl.4, 23 November 2001, para. 8 (a); *Conclusions and recommendations on Saudi Arabia*, CAT/C/CR/28/5, 28 May 2002, para. 8 (a); *Conclusions and recommendations on Indonesia*, CAT/C/XXVII/Concl.3, 22 November 2001, para. 10 (a); *Conclusions and recommendations on USA*, A/55/44, 15 May 2000, paras 175-180, para. 180 (a); *Conclusions and recommendations on Sweden*, 6 June 2002, CAT/C/CR/28/6, paras 5, 7; *Conclusions and recommendations on Norway*, 28 May 2002, CAT/C/CR/28/7, para 6; *Conclusions and recommendations on Slovaquia*, 11 May 2001, A/56/44, para 105; *Conclusions and recommendations on Belarus*, 20 November 2000, A/56/44, paras 45, 46; *Conclusions and recommendations on Austria*, 12 November 1999, A/55/44, para 60; *Conclusions and recommendations on Finland*, 12 November 1999, A/55/44, para 55.

52 *Conclusions and Recommendations on Armenia*, 17 November 2000, A/56/44, para 39; *Conclusions and recommendations on Senegal*, 9 July 1996, A/51/44; *Conclusions and recommendations on Kazakhstan*, 17 May 2001, A/56/44/ para 128.

53 *Conclusions and Recommendations on Namibia*, 6 May 1997, A/52/44, para 4.

54 Articles 1 and 6 of the Inter-American Convention to Prevent and Punish Torture.

55 Decision concerning communications 1/1988, 2/1988 and 3/1988 (Argentina), 23 November 1989, paragraph 7.2, A/45/44, 1990.

56 *Concluding Observations on Senegal*, 9 July 96, A/51/44, paras 102-119, at 117; *Concluding Observations on Peru*, 15 November 1999, A/55/44, paras 56-63, at 61; *Conclusions and recommendations on Azerbaijan*, 17 November 1999, A/55/44, paras 64-69, at 69; *Conclusions and recommendations on Kyrgyzstan*, 18 November 1999, A/55/44, paras 70-75, at 74 (e); *Conclusions and recommendations on Croatia*, 17 November 1998, A/54/44, paras 61-71, at 75 (c); *Conclusions and recommendations on Zambia*, CAT/C/XXVII/Concl.4, 23 November 2001, para 8 d); *Conclusions and recommendations on Saudi Arabia*, CAT/C/CR/28/5, 28 May 2002, para 8 f); *Conclusions and recommendations on Indonesia*, CAT/C/XXVII/Concl.3, 22 November 2001,

The duty to prosecute and punish torture and other cruel, inhuman or degrading treatment or punishment is also recalled by all other major human rights bodies.[57]

b) Extra-judicial, Summary and Arbitrary Executions

The UN General Assembly has stressed that impunity was often the main cause for the prevalence of extrajudicial, summary or arbitrary executions,[58] and reiterated 'the obligation of all Governments to conduct exhaustive and impartial investigations into all suspected cases of extrajudicial, summary or arbitrary executions, to identify and bring to justice those responsible, while ensuring the right of every person to a fair and public hearing by a competent, independent and impartial tribunal established by law, to grant adequate compensation within a reasonable time to the victims or their families and to adopt all necessary measures, including legal and judicial measures, in order to bring an end to impunity and to prevent the further occurrence of such executions.[59] The Resolutions of the Commission on Human Rights on 'extrajudicial, summary and arbitrary executions' also reiterate the need to bring perpetrators of such acts to justice.[60] The Special Rapporteur on extrajudicial, summary and arbitrary executions has emphasized that the prosecution of perpetrators must be part of a broader policy aimed at promoting peace, social stability, justice and the rule of law and that victims must obtain compensation.[61] In *General*

para 10 f); *Conclusions and recommendations on Brazil*, A/56/44, paras 115-120, 16 May 2001, para 120 b); *Conclusions and recommendations on USA*, A/55/44, paras 175-180, 15 May 2000, para 180 b).

[57] Resolutions on 'Torture and other cruel, inhuman or degrading treatment or punishment', E/CN.4/RES/2003/32, para 3; E/CN.4/RES/2002/38, para 3; E/CN.4/RES/2001/62, 25 April 2001, para 4; E/CN.4/RES/2000/43, 20 April 2000, para 2; *Report of the Special Rapporteur on torture*, 3 July 2001, A/56/156, para 39 (a) and (c); E/CN.4/2003/68, 17 December 2002, para 26 (k); Human Rights Committee: *General Comment No 20 on Article* 7, 10 March 1992, HRI/GEN/1/Rev.7, para 13; Human Rights Committee: *Concluding Observations on Uganda*, CCPR/CO/80/UGA, 4 May 2004, para 16; Human Rights Committee: *Concluding Observations on Suriname*, CCPR/CO/80/SUR, 30 March 2004, para 11; ECtHR: Case *Aksoy v Turkey*, Judgment of 18 December 1996, Reports 1996-VI, para 98; Case A. *v the United Kingdom*, Judgment of 23 September 1998, *Reports of Judgments and Decisions* 1998-VI, paras 22, 23; I/ACmHR: Report No. 62/01, Case 11.654, *Riofrío Massacre* (Colombia), 6 April 2001, para 84 (1).

[58] A/RES/57/214, 28 February 2003, preambular para 6 and para 4.

[59] A/RES/57/214, 28 February 2003, operative para 5; A/RES/55/111 of 4 December 2001.

[60] Resolutions E/CN.4/RES/2003/53, para 4; E/CN.4/RES/2002/36, para 4; E/CN.4/RES/2001/45, para 6; E/CN.4/RES/2000/31, para 4; E/CN.4/RES/1999/35; E/CN.4/RES/1998/68, para 4.

[61] *Interim report of the Special Rapporteur on extrajudicial, summary and arbitrary executions*, 11 August

Comment No 6 on Article 6, the Human Rights Committee held that states parties should prevent and punish deprivation of life resulting from criminal acts.[62] It has asked that perpetrators of extra-judicial executions be brought to justice in it's jurisprudence.[63] The Committee has especially emphasized states' obligations to prosecute disproportionate use of force by law enforcement personnel.[64] The European Court of Human Rights[65] and the Inter-American Court and Commission[66] have also found that authors of violations of the right to life must be prosecuted and punished. The duty to punish unlawful executions, including the principle of universal jurisdiction, is also enshrined in Article 18 of the UN Principles on Extra-legal Executions.[67]

c) Enforced Disappearances

The UN General Assembly has recalled that 'impunity with regard to enforced disappearances contributes to the perpetuation of this phenomenon and constitutes one of the obstacles to the elucidation of its manifestations, and in this respect also reminds them of the need to ensure that their competent authorities conduct prompt and impartial inquiries in all circumstances in which there is a reason to believe that an enforced disappearance has occurred in territory under their jurisdiction, and that, if allegations are confirmed, perpetrators should be prosecuted.'[68] The duty to prosecute and

2000, A/55/288, para 48; *Report of the Special Rapporteur on extrajudicial, summary and arbitrary executions*, 2 July 2002, A/57/138, paras 22-27 and *Report on the mission to Brazil*, 28 January 2004, E/CN.4/2004/7/Add.3, paras 55-64, 87.

62 *General Comment No 6 on Article 6*, 4 April 1982, HRI/GEN/1/Rev 6, para 3.

63 Case *Coronel et al v Colombia*, Views of 13 October 2000, CCPR/C/70/D/778/1997, para 10.

64 *Concluding Observations on Germany*, CCPR/CO/80/DEU, 30 March 2004, paras 15, 16; *Lithuania*, CCPR/CO/80/LTU, 1 April 2004, para 10; *Concluding Observations on Uganda*, CCPR/CO/80/UGA, 4 May 2004, para 16.

65 Case *Osman v the United Kingdom*, Judgment of 28 October 1998, Reports 1998-VIII, para 116.

66 Inter-American Commission: Report No. 62/01, Case 11.654, *Riofrío Massacre* (Colombia), 6 April 2001, para 84 (1); Report No 101/01, Cases 10.247 *et al*, *Extrajudicial Executions and Forced Disappearances of Persons* (Perú), 11 October 2001, para 253 (2); I/ACtHR: *Caracazo Case* (Reparation), Judgment of 29 August 2002, Series C No 95, para 115.

67 Principle 7 of the Basic Principles on the Use of Force and Firearms by Law Enforcement Officials.

68 A/RES/57/215, 28 February 2003, para 4; see also A/RES/49/193 of 23 December 1994, A/RES/51/94 of 12 December 1996, and A/RES/53/150 of 9 December 1998; See also the resolutions of the Commission on Human Rights on Enforced Disapearances: E/CN.4/RES/2003/38, para 5 (c); E/CN.4/RES/2002/41, para 5 (c); E/CN.4/RES/2001/46, para 5 (c); E/CN.4/RES/2000/37, para 5 (c); E/CN.4/RES/1999/38, para 5 (c); E/CN.4/RES/1998/40, para 5 (c); E/CN.4/RES/1997/28, para 5

punish enforced disappearances is also enshrined in Articles I and IV of the Inter-American Convention on Forced Disappearance of Persons and Article 4 of the UN Declaration on the Protection of All Persons from Enforced Disappearance.

The Working Group on Enforced or Involuntary Disappearances highlights the intrinsic relationship between prevention and punishment of perpetrators of enforced disappearances:

> 'Turning to consideration of preventive measures, the Group highlights the following: [...] bringing to justice all persons accused of having committed acts of enforced disappearances, guaranteeing their trial only by competent civilian courts and ensuring that they do not benefit from any special amnesty law or other similar measures likely to provide exemption from criminal proceedings or sanctions [...] The Working Group is convinced that ending impunity for the perpetrators of enforced or involuntary disappearances is a circumstance pivotal, not only to the pursuit of justice, but to effective prevention.'[69]

The duty to punish enforced disappearances has also been affirmed by the Human Rights Committee,[70] the Inter-American Commission and Court of Human Rights,[71] the European Court of Human Rights,[72] and the African Commission on Human and Peoples' Rights.[73]

(b); E/CN.4/RES/1996/30, para 14; E/CN.4/RES/1995/38, para 13; E/CN.4/RES/1994/39, para 15; E/CN.4/RES/1993/35, para 5.

[69] *Report of the Working Group on Enforced or Involuntary Disappearances*, 21 January 2003, E/CN.4/2003/70, page 3.

[70] Case *Nydia Erika Bautista v Colombia*, Views of 13 November 1995, CCPR/C/55/D/563/1993, para 8.6, 10; Case *José Vicente y Amado Villafañe Chaparro v Colombia*, 29 July 1997, CCPR/C/60/D/612/1995, para 8.2; Case *Coronel et al v Colombia*, Views of 13 October 2000, CCPR/C/70/D/778/1997, para 10; *Concluding Observations on Colombia*, 25 March 2004, CCPR/CO/80/COL, para 10.

[71] Case *Velásquez Rodríguez v Honduras*, Judgment of 29 July 1988, Series C No. 4, para 166; see also para 175; I/ACmHR: Report 52/99, Cases 10.544 *et al*, *Raúl Zevallos Loayza et al* (Peru), 13 April 1999, para 123; Report No 101/01, Cases 10.247 *et al*, *Extrajudicial Executions and Forced Disappearances of Persons* (Perú), 11 October 2001, para 253 (2).

[72] Case *Kurt v Turkey*, Judgment of 25 May 1998, Report 1998-III, para 140.

[73] Case *Malawi African Association et al v Mauritania*, Communications 54/91, 61/91, 98/93, 164/97, 196/97, 210/98 (27th Ordinary Session, May 2000).

d) Crimes against Humanity

It is beyond doubt that crimes against humanity impose an obligation on states to prosecute and punish. This was codified in the Nuremberg Charter of the International Military Tribunal,[74] and later in the Statutes of the International Tribunal for Former Yugoslavia,[75] the International Tribunal for Rwanda,[76] and the International Criminal Court.[77] It was also reaffirmed in Resolution 95 (1) of 11 December 1946 on the *Affirmation of the Principles of International Law recognized by the Charter of the Nuremberg*, the *Convention* on the Non-Applicability of Statutory Limitations to War Crimes and Crimes Against Humanity, and the Principles of international co-operation in the detention, arrest, extradition and punishment of persons guilty of war crimes and crimes against humanity, and codified in the *Draft Code of Crimes against Peace and Security of Mankind* of 1996 of the International Law Commission.[78]

It should be noted that crimes against humanity are not a category of crimes exclusively pertaining to the category of humanitarian law. Gross violations of human rights, if committed on a widespread or systematic scale, also constitute crimes against humanity. Indeed, while humanitarian law applies in times of armed conflict, crimes against humanity can also be committed in peace time. The definition of crimes against humanity does not require a link to an armed conflict. The codification of crimes against humanity in the Nuremberg Charter defines these crimes as 'murder, extermination, enslavement, deportation, and other inhumane acts committed against any civilian population, *before* or during the war; [...].'[79] The International Law Commission's *Draft Code of Crimes Against the Peace and Security of Mankind* of 1996 defines crimes against humanity as 'any of the following acts, when committed in a systematic manner or on a large scale and instigated or directed by a Government or any organization or group: [...].'[80] In

---

74 Article 6 (c).

75 Article 5.

76 Article 3.

77 Article 7.

78 ILC Report on its 48th Session (1996), A/51/10, 1996, Chapter II(2), paras 46-48.

79 Article 6 of the Charter of the International Military Tribunal, emphasis added.

80 ILC Report on its 48th Session (1996), A/51/10, 1996, Chapter II(2), paras 46-48, Article 18.

the same vein, there is no requirement of an armed conflict in the Rome Statute of the International Criminal Court, which defines crimes against humanity as 'any of the following acts, when committed as part of a widespread or systematic attack directed against any civilian population, with knowledge of the attack [...].'[81] As opposed to the definition of war crimes, which refers to the law of armed conflict, the definition of crimes against humanity does not do so, and indeed the elements of crimes state clearly that the attack to which the definition refers 'need not constitute a military attack.'[82] Similarly, the Convention on the Non-Applicability of Statutory Limitations to War Crimes and Crimes against Humanity states that crimes against humanity can be committed in time of war or in times of peace.[83]

e) Genocide

It is equally beyond doubt that the crime of genocide constitutes a crime under international law – both customary and treaty law, which carries a duty to prosecute and punish.[84] This is enshrined in Articles IV, V and VI of the Convention on the Prevention and Punishment of the Crime of Genocide. In 1994, the Security Council established the International Tribunal for Rwanda in Resolution 955 'for the sole purpose of prosecuting persons responsible for genocide and other serious violations of international humanitarian law committed in the territory of Rwanda and Rwandan citizens responsible for genocide and other such violations committed in the territory of neighbouring States.'[85] The Crime of genocide is now enshrined in Article 6 of the Rome Statute of the International Court.

f) War Crimes

Many gross human rights violations constitute war crimes when they are committed during an armed conflict.[86] As war crimes, they carry an international

[81] Article 7 of the Rome Statute, this definition has also been retaken by the UN Human Rights Committee in its *General Comment No 31 on the Nature of the General Legal Obligation Imposed on States Parties to the Covenant*, 26 May 2004, CCPR/C/21/Rev.1/Add.13, para 18.

[82] Elements of Crime, ICC-ASP/1/3, Article 7, para 3.

[83] Article I (b).

[84] See I.C.J., *Reservations to the Convention on the Prevention and Punishment of the Crime of Genocide*, Advisory Opinion of 28 May 1951, I.C.J. Reports 1951, p 15.

[85] S/RES/955 (1994) of 8 November 1994, para 1.

[86] On the application on human rights in times of armed conflict see only: I.C.J., *Legal Consequences*

duty of the state to prosecute and punish them. The duty to prosecute and punish grave breaches of the Geneva Conventions was enshrined in the Geneva Conventions in 1949 and later in Additional Protocol 1.[87] The Conventions impose an obligation to enact legislation necessary to provide effective penal sanctions for persons committing or ordering the committing of grave breaches, and a mandatory system of universal jurisdiction for crimes against protected persons such as wilful killing, torture or inhuman treatment, including biological experiments, wilfully causing great suffering or serious injury to body or health, unlawful deportation or transfer or unlawful confinement of a person, denial of the right to a fair and regular trial, and the taking of hostages.[88] The mandatory system of universal jurisdiction means that any state has a duty, and not only a right, 'to search for persons alleged to have committed, or ordered to be committed, such grave breaches, and shall bring such persons, regardless of their nationality, before its own courts. It may also, if it prefers, and in accordance with the provisions of its own legislation, hand such persons over for trial to another High Contracting Party concerned, provided such High Contracting Party has made out a *prima facie* case'. The almost universal ratification of the Geneva Conventions[89] and the implementing legislation enacted by many states[90] is evidence of state practice and *opinio juris* that allows the conclusion that the obligation to prosecute or extradite persons alleged to have committed grave breaches is a customary rule of international law.

International practice has also evolved to establish a duty to prosecute and punish other war crimes, such as breaches of the Hague Convention and

---

of the Construction of a Wall in the Occupied Palestinian Territory, Advisory Opinion of 9 July 2004; Human Rights Committee: *General Comment No 31 on Article 2 of the Covenant: The Nature of the General Legal Obligation Imposed on States Parties to the Covenant*, 21 May 2004, CCPR/C/74/CRP.4 / Rev.6, para 11; Statement by the President of the ICRC to the 60th Annual Session of the Commission on Human Rights, 17 March 2003 [available at http://www.icrc.org/Web/Eng/siteeng0.nsf/html/section_ihl_and_human_rights, visited 7 January 2005].

87 Article 49 First Geneva Convention; Article 50 Second Geneva Convention; Article 129 Third Geneva Convention; Art. 146 Fourth Geneva Convention; Article 85 (1) Protocol Additional to the Geneva Conventions.

88 Examples taken from Article 130 Third Geneva Convention and Article 147 Fourth Geneva Convention.

89 See the ratification schedule on the internet site of the ICRC [available at http://www.icrc.org, last viewed 28 June 2004].

90 See the implementation legislation on the internet site of the ICRC [available at http://www.icrc.org, last viewed 28 June 2004].

Regulations and similar violations[91] and serious violations of Article 3 common to the four Geneva Conventions of 1949 and other serious violations of the laws and customs of war committed in non-international armed conflict.[92]

g) Other Gross Human Rights Violations

The concept of gross human rights violations is dynamic and evolves in time. One of their characteristics is that they are frequently codified as crimes under international law. Thus, there are several other violations that entail the duty to prosecute and punish of states, such as slavery, trafficking in human beings,[93] child pornography,[94] or violent acts of racial discrimination.[95]

***

[91] See Article 6 (b) of the Charter of the International Military Tribunal; Principle VI (b) of the Principles of International Law Recognized in the Charter of the Nuremberg Tribunal and in the Judgment of the Tribunal adopted by the International Law Commission, Yearbook of the International Law Commission, 1950, Vol II; Article 20 of the Draft Code of Crimes against the Peace and Security of Mankind, adopted by the International Law Commission, Yearbook of the International Law Commission, 1996, Vol II(2); Article 3 of the Statute of the ICTY; Article 3 has been interpreted by the Appeals Chamber to cover violations committed both in international and in internal armed conflict: *Prosecutor v Tadic*, Appeals Chamber of the ICTY, Decision of 2 October 1995, IT-94-1, para 94; Preamble and Article 8 of the Rome Statute of the International Criminal Court.

[92] *Military and Paramilitary Activities in and against Nicaragua (Nicaragua v the United States of America)*, Merits, Judgment of 17 June 1983, ICJ Reports 1986, para 218; Article 4 of the Statute of the International Tribunal for Rwanda; *Prosecutor v Tadic*, Appeals Chamber of the ICTY, Decision of 2 October 1995, IT-94-1, para 134 with many references to State practice; *Prosecutor v Delalic ("Celibici" Case)*, Appeals Chamber of the ICTY, Decision of 20 February 2001, IT-96-21, paras 153-173; Article 8 (2) (c) and (c) of the Rome Statute of the International Criminal Court.

[93] Article 5 of the Protocol to Prevent, Suppress and Punish Trafficking in Persons, especially Women and Children, supplementing the United Nations Convention against Transnational Organized Crime.

[94] Articles 3, 4 and 5 of the Optional Protocol to the Convention on the Rights of the Child on the Sale of Children, Child Prostitution and Child Pornography.

[95] Article 4 (a) CERD; *Concluding Observations on Italy*, CERD/C/304/Add.68, 7 April 1999, paras 9 and 14; see also *Concluding Observations on Germany*, CERD/C/304/Add.115, 27 April 2001, para 14 (c); *Concluding Observations on France*, 19 April 2000, CERD/C/304/Add.91, para 11; *Concluding Observations on Czech Republic*, 10 December 2003, CERD/C/63/CO/4, para 15; *Concluding Observations on Finland*, 10 December 2003, CERD/C/63/CO/5, para 9; European Commission against Racism and Intolerance (ECRI), *General Policy Recommendation No. 7 on National Legislation to Combat Racism and Racial Discrimination*, 13 December 2002, CRI (2003) 8, paras 5-7, 1-23, 28; ECtHR: Case *Nachova and others v Bulgaria*, Judgment of 26 February 2004, paras 157, 158; see also the earlier case of *Menson and Others v the United Kingdom* (Decision), no. 47916/99, ECHR 2003-V; Paragraphs 84-89 of the Programme of Action of the World Conference against Racism, Racial Discrimination, Xenophobia and Related Intolerance.

It is beyond doubt that states have an obligation to prosecute and punish perpetrators – be they the direct or indirect authors or accomplices - of gross human rights violations, in particular the authors of acts such as torture and cruel, inhuman or degrading treatment or punishment, unlawful killings, enforced disappearances, crimes against humanity, genocide and war crimes.

II. Rights of Victims, Relatives and Witnesses in Criminal Proceedings

The prosecution and punishment constitutes a measure of redress for victims. It can only have a restorative function if victims are not treated as objects, but as subjects of the process. This has increasingly been recognized, and international law has started to define in more detail the requirements for the criminal process in order to protect the rights and interests of victims and witnesses.[96]

Many of the requirements that a criminal process has to fulfil according to international law can be derived from those standards set by international bodies with regard to investigation as described above as well as from principles of fair trial.[97] This is due to the fact that investigation is the first stage for a prosecution, so that international bodies, in the face of states' failure to either investigate or prosecute, concentrate on the modalities of the former.

Numerous international standards concerning victims of crime also apply to victims of serious violations of human rights and humanitarian law, since these violations generally constitute crimes. The Declaration of Basic Principles of Justice for Victims of Crimes and Abuse of Power adopted by the General Assembly in 1985 expressly includes into the definition of victims of crime the victims of criminal abuse of power.[98] Beyond these principles, other principles such as the Council Framework Decision on the Standing of Victims in Criminal Proceedings of the European Union[99] and the Re-

[96] The importance of participation and protection of victims and witnesses and their representatives has also been stressed by the UN Human Rights Commission: Resolution E/CN.4/RES/2003/72 (impunity), 25 April 2003, para 8; Resolution E/CN.4/RES/2003/38 (enforced or involuntary disappearances), 23 April 2003, para 4 (c).

[97] See above Chapter III, at II.

[98] Article 1.

[99] *Council Framework Decision of 15 March 2001 on the standing of victims in criminal proceedings*, Doc.cit;

commendation on the Position of Victims in Criminal Law and Criminal Procedure of the Committee of Ministers of the Council of Europe of 1985 apply in their respective Member States.[100] Finally, the Rome Statute of the International Criminal Court provides that a Victims and Witnesses Unit will be set up within the Registry.[101] The Rules of Procedure and Evidence contain further measures to be taken for the protection of victims and witnesses.

Without quoting all the measures that these instruments provide it may be summarized that they all require that:

- The victims' and witnesses' safety and right to privacy must be guaranteed, especially against ill-treatment, intimidation or reprisal.[102] Women and children must be especially protected.[103]
- Their dignity must be respected and inconvenience must be minimized in handing their cases.[104]
- Victims must be able to defend their interests, to be heard in proceedings and to present evidence, without prejudice to the rights of the

pursuant to Article 34 (2) (b) of the Treaty of the European Union, Framework decisions are binding upon Member States as to the result to be achieved but leave to the national authorities the choice of form and methods; they have no direct effect, i.e. beneficiaries cannot rely on their provisions directly.

100 Recommendation No R (85) 11 *on the position of victim in criminal law and criminal procedure*, 28 June 1985.

101 Article 43 (6).

102 Articles 13 (3) and (5) of the Declaration on the Protection of All Persons from Enforced Disappearance; Article 6 (d) of the UN Declaration of Basic Principles of Justice for Victims of Crime and Abuse of Power; Article 13 CAT; Principle 15 of the UN Principles on Extra-judicial executions; Principle 3 (b) of the UN Principles on the Investigation of Torture; Article 12(d) of the UN Principles on Reparation; Article 8 of the *Council Framework Decision of 15 March 2001 on the standing of victims in criminal proceedings*, Official Journal L 082, 22 March 2001 P. 0001 – 0004; Recommendation No. R (85) 11 on the position of victim in criminal law and criminal procedure, F.15.

103 Article 2 of the Declaration on the Rights of the Child; Articles 3(1), 19, 39 CRC; Article 8 of the Protocol to Prevent, Suppress and Punish Trafficking in Persons, especially Women and Children, supplementing the United Nations Convention against Transnational Organized Crime; Article 5(b) CEDAW.

104 Articles 10, 12 (b) of the UN Principles on Reparation; Article 4 of the UN Declaration of Basic Principles of Justice for Victims of Crime and Abuse of Power; Article 2 of the *Council Framework Decision of 15 March 2001 on the standing of victims in criminal proceedings*, Official Journal L 082, 22 March 2001 P. 0001 – 0004; Recommendation No. R (85) 11 *on the position of victim in criminal law and criminal procedure*, I.C.8.

accused.[105] They must have broad legal standing, such as *partie civile*, to defend their interests.[106] They have a right to receive information on their rights as well as on the conduct and outcome of proceedings.[107] They should also have a remedy against decisions to discontinue the case.[108]

- They must be able to claim redress through simple and accessible proceedings.[109] The proceedings must be conducted without delay.[110]
- They must have access to legal and psychological counselling and advice, and to legal aid and translation where necessary.[111]
- Police and judicial personnel must be trained to guarantee respect for the rights of victims and their relatives and witnesses.

***

[105] Article 6 (2) Protocol to Prevent, Suppress and Punish Trafficking in Persons, especially Women and Children, supplementing the United Nations Convention against Transnational Organized Crime; Article 6 (b) of the UN Declaration of Basic Principles of Justice for Victims of Crime and Abuse of Power; *Article 3 of the Council Framework Decision of 15 March 2001 on the standing of victims in criminal proceedings*, Official Journal L 082, 22 March 2001 P. 0001 - 0004; Recommendation No. R (85) 11 on the position of victim in criminal law and criminal procedure, I.D.

[106] See Principle 19 of the UN Principles on Impunity.

[107] Articles 4, 6 (a) of the UN Declaration of Basic Principles of Justice for Victims of Crime and Abuse of Power; Principle 12(a) of the UN Principles on Reparation; Recommendation No. R (85) 11 *on the position of victim in criminal law and criminal procedure*, I.D.9.

[108] Article 6 (b) of the UN Declaration of Basic Principles of Justice for Victims of Crime and Abuse of Power; Article 4 of the *Council Framework Decision of 15 March 2001 on the standing of victims in criminal proceedings*, Official Journal L 082, 22 March 2001 P. 0001 - 0004; Recommendation No. R (85) 11 *on the position of victim in criminal law and criminal procedure*, I.B.6; ECtHR: *Hugh Jordan v the United Kingdom*, Judgment of 4 May 2001, Reports 2001-III, para 122.

[109] Articles 5 and 6 of the UN Declaration of Basic Principles of Justice for Victims of Crime and Abuse of Power; Article 12(d) of the UN Principles on Reparation.

[110] Article 6 (e) of the UN Declaration of Basic Principles of Justice for Victims of Crime and Abuse of Power.

[111] Article 12(c) of the UN Principles on Reparation; Articles 14-17 of the UN Declaration of Basic Principles of Justice for Victims of Crime and Abuse of Power; Articles 6 and 7 of the *Council Framework Decision of 15 March 2001 on the standing of victims in criminal proceedings*, Official Journal L 082, 22 March 2001 P. 0001 - 0004; Recommendation No. R (85) 11 *on the position of victim in criminal law and criminal procedure*, I.A.2.

Summary

Experience has shown that the need for justice of victims of human rights violations is a fundamental and necessary part of reparation. It is a way to give evidence that other forms of reparation such as compensation are not merely granted as token measures of repentance, but that there is a genuine willingness to ban and eradicate human rights violations in a society. The elementary importance of this positive obligation of states is illustrated by the fact that while it is explicitly enshrined in only some treaties, all human rights bodies are unanimous in recognizing that it flows directly from states obligations.

Over the past decades, international bodies have interpreted and refined the duty to prosecute and punish. First, they have made clear that for certain gross human rights violations, disciplinary sanctions are not enough and criminal sanctions are required. They have also developed the rights of victims and witnesses, increasingly recognizing that their genuine involvement is an essential part of justice and of the reparation process.

While there remains some controversy as to possible exceptions to the principle of criminal responsibility for violations of humanitarian law and gross human rights violations, it is beyond doubt that the principle as such is firmly enshrined in international law. This has to be kept in mind when discussing the questions of amnesties and statutes of limitations in the following chapter.

CHAPTER IX
OBSTACLES TO PROSECUTION AND PUNISHMENT: JURISDICTION OF MILITARY TRIBUNALS – AMNESTIES – STATUTES OF LIMITATION

Justice, however, is a richer, more subtle concept. It contains within it punitive notions, to be sure, but also, at its core, the belief that there is as much redemption in the process of justice, as there is in the outcome. It vindicates truth over lies and deception. [...] The abandonment - even the postponement - of the process of justice is an affront to those who obey the law and a betrayal of those who rely on the law for their protection; it is a call for the use of force in revenge and, therefore, a bankruptcy of peace.[1]

While the duty to prosecute and punish is now firmly enshrined as a rule of customary international law with regard to serious violations of international human rights and humanitarian law, its implementation by states encounters numerous obstacles. Some of the impediments for bringing perpetrators of human rights violations to justice have been addressed in international practice and jurisprudence: trials in military courts which shield members of the armed forces from criminal responsibility; amnesties for gross human rights violations; statutes of limitations for crimes under international law.

As mentioned in the previous chapter, these obstacles can lead to situations of impunity in violation of the state's obligation to prosecute and punish perpetrators of gross human rights violations and the right to justice of victims. Impunity, in the words of the Inter-American Court of Human Rights, 'fosters chronic recidivism of human right violations, and total defenselessness of victims and their relatives.'[2] Moreover, it constitutes an ob-

---

1 *Statement by Ms Louise Arbour, UN High Commissioner for Human Rights, on the opening of the 61st session of the Commission on Human Rights*, 14 March 2005.

2 *Case of Panel Blanca v Guatemala*, Judgment of 8 March 1998, Series C No 37, para 173; Case *Bámaca Velásquez v Guatemala*, Judgment of 25 November 2000, Series C No 79, para 211.

stacle to victims' right to reparation. As the Special Rapporteur on the right to reparation has stated: 'In fact, once the State authorities fail to investigate the facts and to establish criminal responsibility, it becomes very difficult for victims or their relatives to carry on effective legal proceedings aimed at obtaining just and adequate reparation.'[3]

I. Impunity in Military Trials

Experience has shown that the judgment of gross human rights violations by military tribunals has frequently led to impunity for those violations, denial of the right to an effective remedy (especially as leading to prosecution and punishment of those responsible) and the denial of reparation to victims. This recurring phenomenon has led international bodies to hold that gross violations of human rights should be tried by civilian and not by military courts.

As far as international norms are concerned, the obligation to prosecute and punish gross human rights violations in civilian courts is found in international instruments on enforced disappearance, i.e. Article 16 (2) of the Declaration on the Protection of All Persons from Enforced Disappearance and Article IX of the Inter-American Convention on Forced Disappearance of Persons.[4]

1. United Nations System

The UN Commission on Human Rights has recommended in its Resolution on *Civil Defence Forces* that 'offences involving human rights violations by such forces shall be subject to the jurisdiction of the civilian courts.'[5] It also recommended in its resolutions on *Equatorial Guinea* that the competence of military tribunals should be limited to strictly military offences committed by military personnel and should exclude offences committed against the civilian population.[6] Many experts of the Human Rights Com-

---

[3] Theo Van Boven, *Study concerning the right to restitution, compensation and rehabilitation for victims of gross violations of human rights and fundamental freedoms*, E/CN.4/Sub.2/8, 2 July 1993, paras 126-127.

[4] See also UN Commission on Human Rights Resolution E/CN.4/RES/1994/39, 4 March 1994, para 21.

[5] Resolution E/CN.4/RES/1994/67, 9 March 1994, para 2 (f); see also E/CN.4/RES/1994/39, 4 March 1994, para 21.

[6] Resolutions E/CN.4/RES/1998/71, 21 April 1998, para 9 (a); E/CN.4/RES/1999/19, 23 April 1999, para 8 (a); E/CN.4/RES/2000/19, 18 April 2000, para 2 (e); E/CN.4/RES/2001/22, 20 April 2001, para 2 (e).

mission have pronounced themselves against judging military personnel by military courts where there are allegations of gross human rights violations: the Special Rapporteur on extrajudicial, summary and arbitrary executions,[7] the Special Rapporteur on torture,[8] the Special Rapporteur on the independence of judges and lawyers,[9] the Special Representative on the question of human rights defenders,[10] the Special Rapporteur on the situation of human rights in Guatemala,[11] the Special Rapporteur on the situation of human rights in Equatorial Guinea,[12] the Working Group on Enforced or Involuntary Disappearances,[13] and the Working Group on Arbitrary Detention[14]. The Special Rapporteur of the Sub-Commission on the question of impunity[15] and the Expert on military tribunals[16] have also recommended that gross human rights violations should not be tried in military courts and the Sub-Commission has urged states to investigate, prosecute and punish crimes against human rights defenders in ordinary courts.[17]

The Human Rights Committee has recommended that gross violations of human rights should not be tried by military courts but by civilian courts

[7] E/CN.4/1983/16, paras 75-78; E/CN.4/1984/29, paras 75- 86 and 130-131; E/CN.4/1985/17, paras 41 to 45; E/CN.4/1987/20, paras 186 and 246; E/CN.4/1989/25, para 220; E/CN.4/1990/22, para 463; E/CN.4/1991/36, para 591; E/CN.4/1993/46, para 686; E/CN.4/1994/7, para 697; E/CN.4/1994/7/Add.2, para 48; E/CN.4/1995/61, paras 93, 125,183, 402 and 403; E/CN.4/1998/68, para 97; E/CN.4/1999/39/Add.1, paras 62, 66, 72, 172 and 216; E/CN.4/2000/3/Add.3, para 44; E/CN.4/2000/3, para 89; and E/CN.4/2001/9 paras 56 and 62.

[8] E/CN.4/2002/76, 27 December 2001, Annex 1, Recommendation (j); E/CN.4/2003/68, 17 December 2002, para 26 (k).

[9] E/CN.4/1998/39/Add.2, 30 March 1998, para 7.

[10] A/57/61, 10 September 2001, para 47; E/CN.4/2002/106/Add.2, 24 April 2002, paras 183, 184.

[11] E/CN.4/1996/15, 5 December 1995, para 129; E/CN.4/1997/90, 22 January 1997, para 23.

[12] E/CN.4/2000/40, 27 January 2000, para 71.

[13] E/CN.4/1994/26, 22 December 1993, para 45 (i).

[14] E/CN.4/2002/77/Add.2, 5 March 2002, para 77; E/CN.4/1999/63, 18 December 1998, paras 49, 80 (b).

[15] Principle 29 of the UN Principles on Impunity, E/CN.4/2005/102/Add.1, 8 February 2005.

[16] *Working paper by Mr. Decaux containing an updated version of the draft principles governing the administration of justice through military tribunals*, E/CN.4/Sub.2/2005/9, Principle 8.

[17] Resolutions on the question of the violation of human rights and fundamental freedoms in all countries, E/CN.4/Sub.2/RES/1998/3 20 August 1998, para 3; E/CN.4/Sub.2/RES/1999/3, 20 August 1999, para 4.

in many of its concluding observations to countries.[18] The Committee against Torture has recommended likewise.[19]

2. Regional Systems

The Inter-American Court and Commission both have forcefully rejected the trial of gross human rights violations by military courts as one of the main causes of impunity for such violations. In the case of *Durand and Ugarte* the Court held that

> '[i]n a democratic Government of laws the penal military jurisdiction shall have a restrictive and exceptional scope and shall lead to the protection of special juridical interests, related to the functions assigned by law to the military forces. Consequently, civilians must be excluded from the military jurisdiction scope and only the military shall be judged by commission of crime or offenses that by its own nature attempt against legally protected interests of military order.'[20]

It found that the excessive use of force of the armed forces could not be considered as military offences but constituted common crimes, so that investigation and punishment had to be conducted in the ordinary courts.[21] It has reiterated this opinion in other cases concerning gross hu-

[18] *Concluding Observations on Colombia*, 25 September 1992, CCPR/C/79/Add.2, paras 5, 6, and *Concluding Observations on Colombia*, 5 May 1997, CCPR/C/79/Add.76, paras 18 y 34; *Concluding Observations on Venezuela*, 28 December 1992, CCPR/C/79/Add.13, para 7; *Concluding Observations on Croatia*, 28 December 1992, CCPR/C/79/Add.15, para 362; *Concluding Observations on Brazil*, 24 July 1996, CCPR/C/79/Add.66, para 10; *Concluding Observations on Lebanon*, 1 April 1997, CCPR/C/79/Add.78, para 14; *Concluding Observations on Chile*, 30 March 1999, CCPR/C/79/Add.104, para 9; *Concluding Observations on the Dominican Republic*, 26 April 2001, CCPR/CO/71/DOM, para 10; *Concluding Observations on Guatemala*, 27 August 2001, CCPR/CO/72/GTM, paras 10 and 20; *Concluding Observations on Bolivia*, 1 May 1997, CCPR/C/79/Add.74, para 11; *Concluding Observations on El Salvador*, 18 April 1994, CCPR/C/79/Add.34, para 5; *Concluding Observations on Ecuador*, 18 August 1998, CCPR/C/79/Add.92, para 7; *Concluding Observations on Egypt*, 9 August 1993, CCPR/C/79/Add.23, para 9; *Concluding Observations on Chile*, 30 March 1999, CCPR/C/79/Add.104, para 9; *Concluding Observations on Poland*, 29 July 1999, CCPR/C/79/Add.110, para 21; *Concluding Observations on Cameroon*, 4 November 1999, CCPR/C/79/Add.116, para 21; *Concluding Observations on Morocco*, 23 October 1991, A/47/40, para 57; *Concluding Observations on Syria*, 28 May 2001, CCPR/CO/71/SYR, para 17; *Concluding Observations on Russian Federation*, 29 July 1995, CCPR/C/79/Add.54, para 25; *Concluding Observations on Slovakia*, 4 August 1997, CCPR/C/79/Add.79, para 20; *Concluding Observations on Uzbekistan*, 26 April 2001, CCPR/CO/71/UZB, para 15.

[19] *Conclusions and recommendations on Peru*, 9 July 1996, A/51/44, paras 4 and 5; *Concluding Observations on Colombia*, 4 February 2004, CAT/C/CR/31/1, para 9 d) ii) and iii).

[20] Case *Durand and Ugarte v Peru*, Judgment of 16 August 2000, Series C No 68, para 117.

[21] *Ibid*, para 118.

man rights violations.[22] The same functional argument, which essentially limits the competence of military tribunals to service-related offences and excludes gross human rights violations from this definition, has been followed by the Inter-American Commission on Human Rights. The Commission recommended that 'pursuant to Article 2 of the Convention, the member states undertake to adopt the necessary domestic legal measures to confine the competence and jurisdiction of military tribunals to only those crimes that are purely military in nature; under no circumstances are military courts to be permitted to sit in judgment of human rights violations.'[23]

The African Commission on Human and Peoples' Rights has similarly stated that '[t]he only purpose of Military Courts shall be to determine offences of a purely military nature committed by military personnel.'[24]

***

In sum, the competence of military justice should be defined by a functional criterion. Military courts should have competence over offences of a military nature committed by military personnel. Gross human rights violations cannot be understood to ever constitute offences of a military nature and therefore should not, in principle, be tried by military courts.

***

II. AMNESTIES

Amnesties and similar measures that exempt perpetrators of gross human rights violations of responsibility can lead to situations of structural impunity, particularly after armed conflicts. International practice, however, has progressively rejected amnesties for gross human rights violations.

22 Case *Castillo Petruzzi v Peru*, Judgment of 30 May 1999, Series C No 52, paras 127-130; Case *Cantoral Benavides v Peru*, Judgment of 18 August 2000, Series C No 69, para 75.

23 Annual Report 1992-1993, OEA/Ser.L/V/II.83, doc. 14, corr. 1, 12 March 1993, Chapter V, at para VII.6; see also Annual Report 1986-1987, OAE/Ser.L/V/II.71, doc. 9, rev 1, 22 September 1987, Chapter IV (b); Annual Report 1993, OEA/Ser.L/V/II.85, Doc. 8, rev, 11 February 1994, Chapter V, at para IV, Final recommendations.

24 *Principles and Guidelines on the Right to a Fair Trial and Legal Assistance in Africa*, Principle L (a).

1. International Instruments

Because of the unprecedented gravity and scale of the crimes, amnesty was prohibited for crimes committed under the Nazi regime in Germany and other countries. Article II (5) of Control Council Law N°10, Punishment of Persons Guilty of War Crimes, Crimes Against Peace and Against Humanity of 20 December 1945 read: 'In any trial or prosecution for a crime herein referred to, the accused shall not be entitled to the benefits of any statute of limitation in respect to the period from 30 January 1933 to 1 July 1945, nor shall any immunity, pardon or amnesty granted under the Nazi regime be admitted as a bar to trial or punishment.' While this prohibition is often understood as an exceptional measure for the crimes committed during the Second World War but not as a rule of general international law, the prohibition was later taken up in some legal instruments of the United Nations. Concerning violations of human rights, it can be found in some declaratory texts such as Article 60 of the Vienna Declaration and Programme of Action, Article 18 of the Declaration on the Protection of All Persons from Enforced Disappearance or Principle 19 of the Principles on Extra-legal Executions.[25]

2. United Nations Human Rights Bodies

Increasingly, the danger that blanket, often self-granted amnesties perpetuate impunity for gross human rights violations has been recognized in international law. International human rights bodies have frequently held that amnesties contravene the rights of victims of gross human rights violations to justice and reparation and the international obligation of states to prosecute and punish their authors.

a) UN Treaty Bodies

The Human Rights Committee held in its *General Comment No 20 concerning the prohibition of torture and cruel, inhuman or degrading treatment or punishment* that '[a]mnesties are generally incompatible with the duty of States to investigate such acts; to guarantee freedom from such acts within their jurisdiction; and to ensure that they do not occur in the future.'[26] Furthermore, it has held in its observations to states party reports and in

[25] Principle 19 implicitly refers to amnesties by speaking of 'immunity'.

[26] *General Comment No 20 on Article 7*, para. 15 , 13 March 1992, HRI/GEN/1/Rev.7, para 15.

individual cases that it considers amnesty laws for gross violations of human rights incompatible with the Covenant.[27] It has also rejected amnesties for human rights violations committed during armed conflicts, including internal armed conflicts. It has stated in its concluding observations to El Salvador, Congo, Yemen, Croatia and Lebanon that amnesties are incompatible with the ICCPR,[28] clearly rejecting the argument that amnesties may be conducive to peace and democratic stability after an armed conflict when they consecrate impunity for the perpetrators.

The Committee against Torture has recommended that states 'ensure that amnesty laws exclude torture from their reach.'[29] It has repeatedly recommended that '[i]n order to ensure that perpetrators of torture do not enjoy impunity, that the state party ensure the investigation and, where appropriate, the prosecution of those accused of having committed the crime of torture, and ensure that amnesty laws exclude torture from their reach repetition.'[30]

---

[27] *Concluding Observations on Uruguay*, 5 May 1993, CCPR/C/79/Add.19, para 7; *Concluding Observations on Chile*, 30 March 1999, CCPR/C/79/Add.104, para 7; *Concluding Observations on Lebanon*, 1 April 1997, CCPR/C/79/Add.78, para 12; *Concluding Observations on El Salvador*, 18 April 1994, CCPR/C/79/Add.34, para 7; *Concluding Observations on Haiti*, 3 October 1995, A/50/40, paras 224-241, at 230; *Concluding Observations on Peru*, 15 November 2000, CCPR/CO/70/PER, para 9; *Concluding Observations on France*, 4 August 1997, CCPR/C/79/Add.80, para 13; *Concluding Observations on Argentina*, 5 April 1995, CCPR/C/79/Add.46, para 146 of 3 November 2000, CCPR/CO/70/ARG, para 9; *Concluding Observations on Croatia*, 4 April 2001, CCPR/CO/71/HRV, para 11; *Concluding Observations on Guatemala*, 27 August 2001, CCPR/CO/72/GTM, para 12; Case *Hugo Rodríguez v Uruguay*, Views of 9 August 1994, CCPR/C/51/D/322/1988, para 12.4 [torture]; Case *Celis Laureano v Peru*, Views of 16 April 1996, CCPR/C/56/D/540/1993, para 10 [disappearance].

[28] *Concluding observations on El Salvador*, 18 April 1994, CCPR/C/79/Add.34, para 7; *Concluding Observations on Yemen*, 4 February 1996, A/50/40, paras 242-265, at 252; *Concluding Observations on Lebanon*, 1 April 1997, CCPR/C/79/Add.78, para 12; *Concluding Observations on Congo*, 27 March 2000, CCPR/C/79/Add.118, para 12; *Concluding Observations on Croatia*, 30 April 2001, CCPR/CO/71/HRV, para 11; *Concluding Observations on Colombia*, 25 March 2004, CCPR/CO/80/COL, para 8.

[29] *Concluding Observations on Senegal*, 9 July 1996, A/51/44, paras 102-119, at 117; *Concluding Observations on Peru*, 15 November 1999, A/55/44, paras 56-63, at 61; *Concluding Observations on Azerbaijan*, 17 November 1999, A/55/44, paras 64-69, at 69; *Concluding Observations on Kyrgyzstan*, 18 November 1999, A/55/44, paras 70-75, at 74 (e); *Concluding Observations on Croatia*, 17 November 1998, A/54/44, paras 61-71, at 75 (c).

[30] Decision on Communications No 1/1988, 2/1988 and 3/1988 (Argentina), 23 November 1989, para 9, where the Committee considered that the amnesty laws were incompatible with the spirit of the Convention; *Conclusions and recommendations on Azerbaidjan*, 17 November 1999, A/55/44, paras 64-69, at 69 (c); · *Kyrgyzstan*, A/55/44, 18 November 1999, paras 70-75, para 75 (c); see also *Conclusions and recommendations on Senegal*, 9 July 1996, A/51/44, paras 102-119, at paras 112, 117; *Conclusions and recommendations on Peru*, A/55/44, paras 56-63, 15 November 1999, para 61 (d); *Conclusions and recom-*

b) UN Charter Bodies

The Sub-Commission on the Promotion and Protection of Human Rights[31] played a pioneering role with regard to amnesties. In 1981, it urged states to abstain from adopting laws, such as amnesty laws, which prevented the investigation of enforced disappearances.[32] In 1985, it nominated a Special Rapporteur on amnesties.[33]

The Commission on Human Rights has repeatedly recognized in its Resolutions on impunity 'that amnesties should not be granted to those who commit violations of international humanitarian and human rights law that constitute serious crimes and urges States to take action in accordance with their obligations under international law.'[34]

The Special Rapporteur on torture has recommended that '[l]egal provisions granting exemptions from criminal responsibility for torturers, such as amnesty laws (including laws in the name of national reconciliation or the consolidation of democracy and peace), indemnity laws, etc. should be abrogated.'[35] The Special Rapporteur on the independence of judges and lawyers has criticized the amnesty laws of Peru as violating the ICCPR.[36] The Special Rapporteur on extra-judicial, summary and arbitrary executions has warned that '[i]mpunity can also arise from amnesty laws passed in the interest of political stability and national reconciliation',[37] and stated that 'there should and can be no impunity for serious human rights abuses,

---

mendations on Croatia, A/54/44, paras 61-71, 11 November 1998, at para 66; *Conclusions and recommendations on Chile*, CAT/C/CR/32/5, 14 June 2004, para 7 (b).

[31] Formerly the Sub-Commission on Prevention of Discrimination and Protection of Minorities.

[32] Resolution 15 (XXXIV) 1981.

[33] See the *Study on amnesty laws and their role in the safeguard and promotion of human rights*, E/CN.4/Sub.2/1985/16/Rev.1.

[34] Resolutions E/CN.4/RES/2003/72, para 2; E/CN.4/RES/2002/79, para 2.

[35] *Second Report of the Special Rapporteur the question of torture*, E/CN.4/2003/68 of 17 December 2002, para 26 (k), reiterated in his *Third Report*, 23 December 2003, E/CN.4/2004/56, para 40.

[36] *Special Rapporteur on the Independence of Judges and Lawyers on the mission to Peru*, E/CN.4/1998/39/Add.1, 19 February 1998.

[37] *Report of the Special Rapporteur on extrajudicial, summary and arbitrary executions*, 2 July 2002, A/57/138, para 23.

particularly violations of the right to life, regardless of the past or present status or position of the alleged perpetrator.'[38]

Principle 24 of the UN Principles on Impunity stipulates that amnesties, 'even when intended to establish conditions conducive to a peace agreement or to foster national reconciliation', should not benefit perpetrators of serious crimes under international law.

3. Recent UN Practice on Amnesties for Human Rights Violations in Peace Agreements

While in earlier decisions, the Security Council and the General Assembly did not criticize amnesties in all instances,[39] more recent United Nations policy has clearly shown a change in attitude towards amnesties, not only for violations of humanitarian law, but also for human rights violations. The following examples clearly illustrate this shift in policy.

The Guatemalan Peace Accords of 1996, concluded with the assistance of the United Nations, excluded from amnesty 'crimes punishable under international treaties to which Guatemala was a party.'[40] The *Law of National Reconciliation* of December 1996 prohibits from amnesty 'the crimes of genocide, torture and enforced disappearance, as well as those crimes that may not be subject to statutes of limitations or do not allow exclusion of criminal responsibility pursuant to domestic law or international treaties ratified by Guatemala.'[41]

---

[38] *Interim report of the Report of the Special Rapporteur on extrajudicial, summary and arbitrary executions*, 11 August 2000, A/55/288, para 48.

[39] See the Statement of the President of the Security Council of 15 July 1993, 48 SCOR, at 126, S/26633 (1993), which approved the amnesty agreed in the Governors Island Agreement for Haiti of 1993; see also General Assembly Resolution A/RES/42/137 of 7 December 1987, in which the General Assembly does not pronounce itself on the amnesty law; Resolution 43/24 of 15 November 1988 on the situation in Central America: threats to international peace and security and peace initiative; in this resolution, the General Assembly endorsed the 'Agreement on procedures for the establishment of a firm and lasting peace in Central America' between the Government of Costa Rica, El Salvador, Guatemala, Honduras and Nicaragua, in which the presidents had agreed to adopt amnesties.

[40] Agreement on the Basis for the Legal Integration of the Unidad Revolucionaria Guatemalteca, UN Doc A/51/776, Doc S/1997/51, Annex II, paras 17 et seq.

[41] Decreto número 145-1996, Ley de reconciliación nacional, 27 December 1996, Article 8.

In 1999, the Lusaka ceasefire agreement, 'witnessed' by the United Nations, provided that the parties 'together with the UN' shall create conditions favourable to the arrest and prosecution of 'mass killers', 'perpetrators of crimes against humanity' and 'other war criminals'. While it acknowledges the possibility of amnesty and political asylum, it excludes 'genocidaires' from such exceptions.[42]

The Statute of the Special Court for Sierra Leone provides in its Article 10 that no amnesty can bar the prosecution of crimes under its jurisdiction, i.e. crimes against humanity, violations of Article 3 common to the Geneva Conventions and of Additional Protocol II, and other serious violations of international humanitarian law.[43] This statute was established by an Agreement between the United Nations and the Government of Sierra Leone pursuant to Security Council resolution 1315 (2000) of 14 August 2000.[44] It takes precedence over the pardon and amnesty that had been agreed to in the Lomé Peace Agreement,[45] which the Representative of Secretary General of the United Nations signed by appending a statement with 'the understanding that the amnesty provisions of the Agreement shall not apply to the international crimes of genocide, crimes against humanity, war crimes and other serious violations of humanitarian law.'[46] The possibility to overrule the Amnesty of the Lomé Agreement by the Statute of the Special Court was challenged by the defendant in the case of *Prosecutor v Morris Kallon*.[47] The Appeals Chamber of the Special Court, however, held that the Statute was 'consistent with the developing norm of international law'.[48] It held that the amnesty granted in the Lomé Agreement was 'ineffective in removing universal jurisdiction to prosecute persons accused of such

---

42 Lusaka Ceasefire Agreement of 10 July 1999, UN Doc S/1999/815 of 23 July 1999, Annex A, Chapter 9.1 and 9.2.

43 Statute of the Special Court for Sierra Leone of 16 January 2002.

44 SR/RES/1315 (2000) of 13 August 2000.

45 Peace Agreement between the Government of Sierra Leone and the Revolutionary United Front of Sierra Leone of 7 July 1999, Article IX.

46 See *Seventh Report of the Secretary General of the United Nations on the Observer Mission to Sierra Leone*, UN Doc S/1999/836, 30 July 1999, para 7; see also *Report of the Secretary-General on the establishment of a Special Court for Sierra Leone*, 4 October 2000, S/2000/915, para 22.

47 Appeals Chamber, *Prosecutor v Morris Kallon*, Case No SCSL-2004-15-AR72(E), Decision on Challenge to Jurisdiction: Lomé Accord Amnesty, 13 March 2004.

48 *Ibid*, para 63; also para 82.

crimes that other states have by reason of the nature of the crimes. It is also ineffective in depriving an international court such as the Special Court of jurisdiction.'[49]

In 2000, the Transitional Administration in East Timor adopted Regulation No 2000/15 on the Establishment of Panels with Exclusive Jurisdiction over Serious Criminal Offences. The panels of judges are vested with universal jurisdiction[50] over genocide, crimes against humanity, war crimes, torture, murder, and sexual offences.[51] The subsequently adopted regulation on the Establishment of a 'Commission for Reception, Truth and Reconciliation'[52] sees as one of the Commission's objectives the referral of human rights violations and violations of humanitarian law to the Office of the General Prosecutor with the recommendation for the prosecution of offences where appropriate,[53] and expressly leaves without prejudice the exercise of exclusive jurisdiction over serious criminal offences of the Serious Crimes Panel of judges.[54]

The *Law on the Establishment of Extraordinary Chambers in the Courts of Cambodia for the Prosecution of Crimes Committed During the Period of Democratic Kampuchea* excludes amnesties and pardons for the crimes over which the Chambers have jurisdiction, i.e. homicide, torture and religious persecution, genocide, crimes against humanity, grave breaches of the Geneva Conventions of 12 August 1949, destruction of cultural property during armed conflict, and crimes against internationally protected persons pursuant to the Vienna Convention of 1961 on Diplomatic Relations.[55]

[49] *Ibid*, para 88.

[50] Regulation n°2000/15 adopted by the UN Transitional Administration in East Timor on the Establishment of Panels with Exclusive Jurisdiction over Serious Criminal Offences UNTAET/REG/2000/15, 6 June 2000, Section 2.1.

[51] *Ibid*, Sections 1.3 and 4-9; genocide, crimes against humanity and war crimes are defined exactly as in the Rome Statute, except for Article 7 (2) (a) of the Rome Statute.

[52] Regulation n° 2001/10 on the Establishment of a Commission for Reception, Truth, and Reconciliation in East Timor, UNTAET/REG/2001/10, 13 July 2001.

[53] *Ibid*, Section 3.1. (e).

[54] *Ibid*, Section 22.2.

[55] Article 40 of the Law on the Establishment of Extraordinary Chambers in the Courts of Cambodia for the Prosecution of Crimes Committed During the Period of Democratic Kampuchea, 15 January 2001.

It is particularly interesting to see the change of the Security Council's attitude with regard to Haiti. Amnesty was negotiated in the *Governors Island* Agreement for members of the military Regime accused of committing crimes against humanity in Haiti from 1990-1993. The Security Council endorsed this agreement in 1993 as 'the only valid framework for resolving the crisis in Haiti'.[56] However, in its Resolution on the 'question concerning Haiti' of February 2004, it 'reiterates that all parties to the conflict must respect international law, *including with respect to human rights*, and that there will be individual accountability and no impunity for the violators.'[57]

Finally, the Security Council's approach to the conflict in Côte d'Ivoire is telling in its change in attitude. It emphasized 'the need to bring to justice those responsible for the *serious violations of human rights and international humanitarian law*'.[58] It then endorsed the peace agreement between the parties to the conflict in Côte d'Ivoire,[59] which reflects the view that amnesties can and should, in the spirit of Article 6 (5) of Additional Protocol II be granted to members of the parties to the conflict for taking part in the hostilities, but not to those who commit serious violations of human rights and humanitarian law. In this peace agreement, the Government of National Reconciliation commits itself to 'call for the establishment of an international board of enquiry to investigate and establish the facts throughout the national territory in order to identify cases of serious violations of human rights and international humanitarian law since 19 September 2002' and considers the perpetrators and those aiding and abetting crimes must be brought to justice before an international criminal jurisdiction.[60]

The Secretary General of the United Nations has summed up this trend in its *Report on the rule of law and transitional justice in conflict and post-conflict societies*, in which he concluded that 'United Nations-endorsed peace agreements can never promise amnesties for genocide, war crimes, crimes against humanity or gross violations of human rights.'[61]

[56] Statement of the President of the Security Council, UN SCOR, 48th Session, 329th meeting, at 26, UN Doc S/INF/49 (1993).

[57] S/RES/1529 (2004), 29 February 2004, para 7, emphasis added.

[58] S/RES/1479 of 13 May 2003, para 8.

[59] S/RES/1464 (2003) of 4 February 2003, para 1; agreement signed by the Ivorian political forces in Linas-Marcoussis of 24 January 2003, UN Doc S/2003/99.

[60] *Ibid*, paras VI.2 and VI.3.

[61] S/2004/616, 20 July 2004, para 10.

4. International Tribunals

The Special Court for Sierra Leone decided in the case of *Kallon* that a national amnesty would be contrary to the very purpose of the tribunals.[62]

The Trial Chamber of the ICTY has confirmed the unlawfulness of amnesties for torture in the case of *Furundzija,* in which it held that '[i]t would be senseless to argue, on the one hand, that on account of the *jus cogens* value of the prohibition against torture, treaties or customary rules providing for torture would be null and void *ab initio* and then be unmindful of a State say, taking national measures authorising or condoning torture or absolving its perpetrators through an amnesty [...].'[63]

5. Regional Jurisprudence

While the European Court of Human Rights has not had to pronounce itself on the legality of amnesties, the Inter-American Commission and Court of Human Rights as well as the African Commission on Human and Peoples' Rights have forcefully asserted that amnesties are incompatible with international law and particularly with the rights of victims to an effective remedy and to reparation.

a) Inter-American Commission and Court of Human Rights

The Inter-American Commission on Human Rights has found every amnesty that it has considered to be in breach of the American Convention on Human Rights. It has particularly criticized self-amnesties by *de facto* governments, which in its view lack the legal legitimacy to adopt amnesty laws.[64] It has considered that amnesty laws constitute a violation of states' obligation under Articles 1(1) and 2 ACHR.[65] It has further considered self-amnesties as violating victims' right to justice (guaranteed, amongst others, under Article 8 ACHR), their right to seek civil compensation (also guaran-

---

[62] Appeals Chamber, *Prosecutor v Morris Kallon*, Case No SCSL-2004-15-AR72(E), Decision on Challenge to Jurisdiction: Lomé Accord Amnesty, 13 March 2004, para 88; see also Y. *Naqvi, Amnesty for war crimes: Defining the limits of international recognition*, IRRC, Vol 85, September 2003, p 583, at 615.

[63] Case *Prosecutor v Anto Furundzija*, IT-95-17/1, Judgment of 10 December 1998, para 155.

[64] Report No. 36/96, Case 10.843 (Chile), 15 October 1996, para 27.

[65] Reports 28/92 (Argentina) and 29/92 (Uruguay); Report No. 36/96, Case 10.843 (Chile), 15 October 1996, paras 50, 61.

teed under Article 8 ACHR), to judicial protection (Article 25 ACHR), and the state's duty to investigate violations of human rights (Article 1(1) ACHR).[66] In more recent cases, the Inter-American Commission has also made explicit that amnesty laws violate the right to know the truth.[67] It has recommended that the state 'bring to trial and punish all of the responsible persons, *despite the decreed amnesty*.'[68] The Commission has made clear that truth commissions constitute an insufficient response to gross violations of human rights and of humanitarian law and that they cannot be a substitute for the victim's right to justice.[69]

Similarly to the Human Rights Committee, the Inter-American Commission has also declared that gross violations of human rights committed in times of armed conflict could not be subject to amnesties. It has clearly stated that Protocol II to the Geneva Conventions 'cannot be interpreted as covering violations to the fundamental human rights enshrined in the American Convention on Human Rights.'[70] It also points to the fact that 'many of the violations, such as extra-judicial executions and torture, can be put on a par with human rights violations, which are not subject to suspension according to the American Convention.'[71]

---

[66] Report Nº 28/92, Cases 10.147, 10.181, 10.240, 10.262, 10.309 and 10.311 (Argentina), 2 October 1992, paras 32-41; Case 10.843 (Chile), 15 October 1996, paras 59-93; Report No. 34/96, Cases 11.228, 11.229, 11.231 and 11.282 (Chile), 15 October 1996, para 58-92; Report No. 25/98, Cases 11.505, 11.532, 11.541, 11.546, 11.549, 11.569, 11.572, 11.573, 11.583, 11.585, 11.595, 11.652, 11.657, 11.675 and 11.705 (Chile), 7 April 1998, paras 51-97; Report No. 1/99, Case 10.480 *Lucio Parada Cea and others v El Salvador*, 27 January 1999, paras 112-158; Report No. 136/99, Case 10.488 *Ignacio Ellacuría S.J. and others v. El Salvador*, 22 December 1999, paras 197-232; Report No 37/00, Case 11.481, *Monsignor Oscar Arnulfo Romero y Galdámez v El Salvador*, 13 April 2000, paras 123-151.

[67] Report No. 25/98, Cases 11.505, 11.532, 11.541, 11.546, 11.549, 11.569, 11.572, 11.573, 11.583, 11.585, 11.595, 11.652, 11.657, 11.675 and 11.705 (Chile), 7 April 1998, paras 51-97; Report No. 1/99, Case 10.480 *Lucio Parada Cea and others v. El Salvador*, 27 January 1999, paras 112-158; Report No. 136/99, Case 10.488 *Ignacio Ellacuría S.J. and others v. El Salvador*, 22 December 1999, paras 221-232; Report No 37/00, Case 11.481, *Monsignor Oscar Arnulfo Romero y Galdámez v El Salvador*, 13 April 2000, paras 123-151.

[68] Report No. 1/99, Case 10.480 *Lucio Parada Cea and others v. El Salvador*, 27 January 1999, para 160, emphasis added.

[69] Report No. 36/96, Case 10.843, *Garay Hermonsilla et al v Chile*, para 156; Report 26/92, 24 September 1992 (El Salvador), Reports No 29/92, 2 October 1992, (Uruguay), Report No 24/92 (Argentina), 2 October 1992.

[70] *Report on the Situation of Human Rights in El Salvador*, OEA/Ser.L/II.85, Doc. 28 rev., 11 February 1994, General Conclusions. See also Report 1/99, Case 10.480, *Lucio Parada Cea et al (El Salvador)*, 27 January 1999, para 116, citing the ICRC position.

[71] Report 1/99, Case 10.480, *Lucio Parada Cea et al (El Salvador)*, 27 January 1999, para 115.

In the *Barrios Altos Case*, the Inter-American Court of Human Rights held:

> 'This Court considers that all amnesty provisions, provisions on prescription and the establishment of measures designed to eliminate responsibility are inadmissible, because they are intended to prevent the investigation and punishment of those responsible for serious human rights violations such as torture, extrajudicial, summary or arbitrary execution and forced disappearance, all of them prohibited because they violate non-derogable rights recognized by international human rights law.
>
> The Court, in accordance with the arguments put forward by the Commission and not contested by the State, considers that the amnesty laws adopted by Peru prevented the victims' next of kin and the surviving victims in this case from being heard by a judge, as established in Article 8(1) of the Convention; they violated the right to judicial protection embodied in Article 25 of the Convention; they prevented the investigation, capture, prosecution and conviction of those responsible for the events that occurred in Barrios Altos, thus failing to comply with Article 1(1) of the Convention, and they obstructed clarification of the facts of this case. Finally, the adoption of self-amnesty laws that are incompatible with the Convention meant that Peru failed to comply with the obligation to adapt internal legislation that is embodied in Article 2 of the Convention.'[72]

It has confirmed this jurisprudence in subsequent cases.[73]

b) African Commission on Human and Peoples' Rights

The African Commission on Human and Peoples' Rights has declared that 'an amnesty law adopted with the aim of nullifying suits or other actions seeking redress that may be filed by the victims or their beneficiaries [...] cannot shield that country from fulfilling its international obligations under the Charter.'[74] It also clearly held that '[t]he granting of amnesty to absolve perpetrators of human rights violations from accountability violates the right of victims to an effective remedy.'[75]

---

[72] *Case of Barrios Altos v Peru*, Judgment of 14 March 2001, Series C No. 75, paras 41, 42.

[73] *Barrios Altos Case, Interpretation of the Judgment on the Merits*, Judgment of 3 September 2001, Series C No 83, para 15; *Trujillo Oroza Case (Reparations)*, Judgment of 27 February 2002, Series C No 92, para 106; *Caracazo Case (Reparations)*, Judgment of 29 August 2002, Series C No 95, para 119.

[74] Case *Malawi African Association et al v Mauritania*, Communications 54/91 et al (27th Ordinary Session, May 2000), para 83.

[75] *Principles and Guidelines on the Right to a Fair Trial and Legal Assistance in Africa*, Principle C (d).

6. International Committee of the Red Cross

Article 6 (5) of Additional Protocol II to the Geneva Conventions is sometimes invoked, for instance by the South African Court,[76] to justify amnesties for crimes committed in internal armed conflict. According to this provision, '[a]t the end of hostilities, the authorities in power shall endeavour to grant the broadest possible amnesty to persons who have participated in the armed conflict, or those deprived of their liberty for reasons related to the armed conflict, whether they are interned or detained.' The International Committee of the Red Cross, however, has rejected this interpretation and made clear that the purpose of Article 6 (5) was intended for those who 'were detained or punished merely for having participated in the hostilities. It does not seek to be an amnesty for those who have violated international humanitarian law'.[77] The Inter-American Commission on Human Rights has followed this argument by referring to the ICRC's statement.[78]

7. Trends in National Legislation and Jurisprudence

The rejection of amnesties for gross human rights violations by the UN system appears to be confirmed by recent trends in national legislation and jurisprudence.

Several countries have chosen to prohibit amnesties or pardon for gross violations of human rights and/or humanitarian law. Thus, the Constitution of Ethiopia of 1994 states that crimes against humanity, such as genocide, summary executions, forcible disappearances or torture cannot be commuted by amnesty or pardon.[79] The Constitution of Ecuador prohibits amnesty for genocide, torture, enforced disappearance, kidnapping, and homicide for political reasons or reasons of conscience.[80] The Constitution of Venezuela states that crimes against humanity, grave violations of human rights and war crimes are not subject to amnesty or pardon.[81] The Act of

[76] See below at V.

[77] Letter of the ICRC Legal Division to the ICTY Prosecutor of 24 November 1995 and to the department of Law at the University of California of 15 April 1997.

[78] Report No. 1/99, Case 10,480 *Lucio Parada Cea and others v El Salvador*, 27 January 1999, para 115.

[79] Constitution of 1994, Article 28.

[80] Constitution of 1998, Article 23 (2).

[81] Constitution of 1998, Article 29.

National Reconciliation of Guatemala excludes amnesty for genocide, torture and enforced disappearance and all crimes considered not to be subject to statutes of limitation in treaties ratified by Guatemala.[82]

In Argentina, the National Court of Appeal for Federal Criminal and Correctional Cases confirmed a federal judge's ruling of March 2001, declaring invalid the Full Stop and Due Obedience Laws.[83] In August 2003, both Houses of Congress voted the abrogation of the two laws with retroactive effect.[84] In June 2005, the Supreme Court of Argentina declared unconstitutional both laws.[85]

In Chile, unlike in Argentina, the self-granted blanket amnesty of 1978 remains in place. As mentioned, this has been severely criticized by the Inter-American Commission on Human Rights and the Committee against Torture. The Santiago Court of Appeals ruled in January 2004 that, pursuant to Chile's obligations under the Inter-American Convention on Forced Disappearance of Persons, the 1978 amnesty could not apply in respect of kidnapping when the fate of the victim remained unclarified.[86] In this manner, at least as regards disappearances, the effects of the law have been somewhat attenuated. This Judgment has been confirmed by the Judgment of the Supreme Court of Chile of 16 November 2004.[87]

The National Court of Spain held that amnesties in the country of origin of the perpetrator do not prevent the authorities from prosecuting the authors of crimes under international law.[88]

---

82 Decreto número 145-1996, *Ley de reconciliación nacional*, 27 December 1996, Article 8.

83 *Julio Simón and Juan Antonio del Cerro, on the abduction of minors of 10 years*, Federal Criminal and Correctional Court No 4, 8686/2000, Judgment of 6 March 2001, Part VI.

84 See 'Argentina overturns amnesty laws', Story from BBC NEWS: http://news.bbc.co.uk/go/pr/fr/-/2/hi/americas/3146379.stm, Published: 2003/08/13 04:50:17 GMT and 'Argentina scraps Amnesty Laws, Story from BBC NEWS: http://news.bbc.co.uk/go/pr/fr/-/2/hi/americas/3169297.stm, Published: 2003/08/21 18:10:04 GMT.

85 *Simón, Julio Héctor y otros s/ privación ilegítima de la libertad, etc.*, Judgment of 14 June 2005 [available at http://www.csjn.gov.ar/documentos/novedades.jsp].

86 *Fernando Laureani Maturana and Miguel Krassnoff Marchenko*, Santiago Court of Appeal, Judgment of 5 January 2004.

87 See *Fallo Histórico en Chile*, Note in BBCMundo.com, [available at http://news.bbc.co.uk/go/pr/fr/-/hi/spanish/latin_america/newsid_4021000/4021207.stm, 17 November 2004].

88 National Court of Spain, *Auto de la Sala de lo Penal de la Audiencia Nacional confirmando la jurisdic-*

On the other hand, the South African Constitutional Court upheld the general national amnesty in the *Promotion of National Unity and Reconciliation Act 34 of 1995* in its judgment of 25 July 1996.[89] It considered that amnesty created an effective incentive for perpetrators to tell the truth, without which effective prosecution would remain an abstract objective. It also recalled that it had probably been the amnesty that had allowed the "historic bridge" to end apartheid to be erected.[90] The Court insisted, however, on the fact that the decision to grant amnesty was not taken solely by the perpetrators themselves,[91] and that the Act does not grant 'blanket' amnesty.[92] Indeed, amnesty was only granted under the condition that the applicant made 'a full disclosure of all relevant facts'.[93] The Committee on Amnesty has refused amnesty in certain cases where it was not satisfied that the applicant had revealed the whole truth.[94] Also, one of the key recommendations of the TRC was that 'in order to avoid a culture of impunity and to entrench the rule of law, the granting of general amnesty in whatever guise should be resisted'.[95]

While no international body has yet pronounced itself on the legality of the South African amnesty, it may be said that the process came close to a judicial process in that perpetrators had to appear and tell the truth before a Commission with *subpoena* powers, amnesty could be refused, and victims took part in the process and could make submissions in the amnesty proceedings. In this sense, it did not constitute a blanket amnesty. It is difficult to draw conclusions from this process to the legality of other amnesties. Indeed '[w]hile the TRC amnesty-for-truth process merits respect as the most honestly designed transitional arrangement short of

ción de España para conocer de los crímenes de genocidio y terrorismo cometidos durante la dictadura chilena, Judgment of 5 November 1998.

[89] *AZAPO and others v President of the Republic of South Africa and others*, Case CCT-17/96, Judgment of 25 July 1996.

[90] *Ibid*, para 19.

[91] *Ibid*, para 24.

[92] *Ibid*, para 32.

[93] Section 20 of the Act.

[94] See, for instance, the cases *Victor Mthandeni Mthembu* (AM1707/96), AC/2001/092; *Roelof Jacobus Venter* (AM2774/96), ACC/2001/107.

[95] Report of the Truth and Reconciliation Commission, Volume 6, Chapter 5, Section 7, Recommendation No 31.

"real" justice (i.e., prosecution), most of its counterparts around the world are producing or promising a lot more amnesty than truth'.[96]

Another interesting amnesty process is contained in the '*Good Friday Agreement*' in Northern Ireland. This peace agreement provides that prisoners may be released in advance. However, the Agreement does not in any way grant blanket amnesty: it only benefits prisoners, i.e. those who have already been tried and punished; and only prisoners affiliated to organisations committed to 'a complete and unequivocal ceasefire' can benefit from the measure; this condition is kept under review; account is taken of 'the seriousness of the offences for which the person was convicted and the need to protect the community'.[97] Under the *Northern Ireland (Sentences) Act* of July 1998, prisoners convicted of offences related to terrorism and attracting a sentence of five years or more became eligible to apply for early release from the Independent Sentence Review Commissioners, but only after having completed a third of their sentence or two thirds in case of life imprisonment.[98] It is important to note that licences for release can and have been suspended and even revoked and prisoners returned to prison.[99]

***

In sum, international practice and jurisprudence show that amnesties for perpetrators of serious human rights and humanitarian law violations violate the international duty of the state to prosecute and punish them and are incompatible with victims' right to justice.

It is important to note the unanimity with which the trend within different United Nations organs has evolved to reject amnesties for such violations. Indeed, both the bodies charged with ensuring respect for human rights as well as the Security Council, the body charged with guaranteeing international peace and security, converge in their opinion. This is a strong indicator that the dichotomy often asserted that amnesties may be violating victims' rights but are necessary for the establishment or maintenance of peace and

[96] Reed Brody, *Justice: The First Casualty of Truth*, in The Nation, 30 April 2001.

[97] Agreement between the Government of the United Kingdom of Great Britain and Northern Ireland and the Government of the Republic or Ireland, Annex B, 'Prisoners'.

[98] *Northern Ireland (Sentences) Act 1998* of 28 July 1998, Sections 4 (1) (a) and 6 (1).

[99] *Ibid*, Section 8.

stability is flawed and erroneously formulated. Rather, stability and peace can only be achieved in the framework of respect for justice and law.

***

III. Statutes of Limitations

A statute of limitation is a legal procedural obstacle to preclude the initiation or continuation of legal proceedings because of the passage of time. They can apply in criminal, civil or administrative proceedings. In criminal law, they can constitute an obstacle to the prosecution of perpetrators of gross human rights violations when the offence lies too far back in time. They can also be obstacles for compensation or other reparations claims. This is the case when these claims are made in civil or administrative courts and are subject to statutes of limitation. But statutes of limitation in the criminal proceedings can also affect reparation claims. For example, if such claims are pursued in criminal proceedings in domestic courts (such as through the figure of *partie civile*, private prosecution or a tort claim as part of the criminal process), statutes of limitations for the crime will also affect these proceedings. A statute of limitation for the crime may also, in certain systems, extend to civil or administrative claims. Even if they do not do so legally, the lack of investigation and prosecution will have an indirect effect on the reparation claim in the civil or administrative jurisdiction, because they have different, and often weaker, capacity for gathering evidence.

The UN Principles on Impunity stipulate that prescription in criminal cases shall not run for such period as no effective remedy is available; it shall not apply to serious crimes under international law, which are by their nature not subject to prescription; when it does apply, prescription shall not be effective against civil or administrative actions brought by victims seeking reparation for their injuries.[100] Similarly, in his final report to the Sub-Commission, the Special Rapporteur on the right to reparation, Theo van Boven, addressed the problem of statutes of limitation for reparation claims:

> 'It is sometimes contended that as a result of passage of time the need for reparations is outdated and therefore no longer pertinent. [...] the application of statutory limitations often deprives victims of gross violations of human rights of the reparations that

[100] Principle 23; see also Article 17 (2) of the Declaration on the Protection of All Persons from Enforced Disappearance.

are due to them. The principles should prevail that claims relating to reparations for gross violations of human rights shall not be subject to a statute of limitations. In this connection, it should be taken into account that the effects of gross violations of human rights are linked to the most serious crimes to which, according to authoritative legal opinion, statutory limitations shall not apply. Moreover, it is well established that for many victims of gross violations of human rights, the passage of time has no attenuating effect; on the contrary, there is an increase in post-traumatic stress, requiring all necessary material, medical, psychological and social assistance and support over a long period of time.'[101]

There is, as far as can be seen, little jurisprudence on statutes of limitation for compensation claims. However, as statutes of limitation in criminal proceedings affect these claims and, as obstacles to prosecution, the right to justice of victims, they shall briefly be discussed. As will be shown, widespread practice shows that customary international law excludes war crimes, crimes against humanity and genocide from statutory limitations. Further, there appears to be an emerging tendency in international law to prohibit statutory limitation for other gross human rights violations.

1. War Crimes, Crimes against Humanity and Genocide

There appears to be an emerging rule of custom prohibiting statutes of limitation for war crimes and crimes against humanity, including genocide.

Control Council Law No 10 on the Punishment of Persons Guilty of War Crimes, Crimes Against Peace and Against Humanity of December 1945 prohibited the application of statutes of limitations for the crimes mentioned in the Law for the period from 30 January 1933 to 1 July 1945.[102] Subsequently, the General Assembly adopted the Convention on the Non-Applicability of Statutory Limitations to War Crimes and Crimes against Humanity in 1968. The Rome Statute of the International Criminal Court of 17 July 1998 consecrates the principle in its Article 29 which reads: 'The

[101] *Final report submitted by the Special Rapporteur on the right to restitution, compensation and rehabilitation for victims of gross violations of human rights and fundamental freedoms*, E/CN.4/Sub.2/1993/8, 2 July 1993, para 135.

[102] Control Council Law N°10, Punishment of Persons Guilty of War Crimes, Crimes Against Peace and Against Humanity, December 20, 1945, Article II, 5: 'In any trial or prosecution for a crime herein referred to, the accused shall not be entitled to the benefits of any statute of limitation in respect to the period from 30 January 1933 to 1 July 1945, nor shall any immunity, pardon or amnesty granted under the Nazi regime be admitted as a bar to trial or punishment'.

crimes within the jurisdiction of the Court shall not be subject to any statute of limitations'.

In Europe, a similar treaty was adopted by the Council of Europe, with the European Convention on the Non-Applicability of Statutory Limitation to Crimes against Humanity and War Crimes of 25 January 1974.[103]

Recent practice of the United Nations, particularly on conflicts, also appears to accept that crimes under international law are not subject to prescription. This follows from the legislation implemented by UN transitional authorities or under UN auspices. In East Timor, section 17 of Regulation 2000/15 provides that genocide, war crimes, crimes against humanity and torture 'shall not be subject to any statute of limitation'.[104] The Law on the Establishment of Extraordinary Chambers in the Courts of Cambodia for the Prosecution of Crimes Committed During the Period of Democratic Kampuchea of 15 January 2001 'extends for an additional period of 20 years the statute of limitation set forth in the 1956 Penal Code for homicide, torture and religious persecution',[105] and excludes statutes of limitation for acts of genocide and crimes against humanity.[106]

In the light of this international practice, the International Committee of the Red Cross (ICRC) considers that 'several elements contribute to the emerging customary character of non-applicability of statutes of limitations to war crimes and crimes against humanity'.[107] Indeed, there appears to be a rule of customary law on these crimes, despite the objection of some countries.

[103] This treaty entered into force on 27 June 2003, but has only been ratified by very few States.

[104] Regulation n° 2000/15 adopted by the UN Transitional Administration in East Timor on the Establishment of Panels with Exclusive Jurisdiction over Serious Criminal Offences, UNTAET/REG/2000/15, 6 June 2000, Section 17.1.

[105] Law on the Establishment of Extraordinary Chambers in the Courts of Cambodia for the Prosecution of crimes Committed During the Period of Democratic Kampuchea, 15 January 2001, Article 3

[106] *Ibid*, Articles 4, 5.

[107] *Répression nationale des violations du droit international humanitaire*, Dossier d'information, CICR, Décembre 2003.

2. Gross Human Rights Violations (General)

Beyond the prohibition of statutes of limitations for war crimes, crimes against humanity and genocide, there is an emerging trend in international jurisprudence to extend this prohibition to other gross human rights violations.

The Human Rights Committee held in its *Concluding Observations on Argentina* that '[g]ross violations of civil and political rights during military rule should be prosecutable for as long as necessary, with applicability as far back in time as necessary to bring their perpetrators to justice.'[108] In its *General Comment No 31 on Article 2* it considered that 'impediments to the establishment of legal responsibility should be removed, such as [...] unreasonably short periods of statutes of limitation in cases where such limitations are applicable.'[109]

Likewise, the Committee against Torture noted as a positive aspect in the Venezuelan legislation that the '[...] Constitution [...] requires the State to investigate and impose penalties on human rights offences, declares that action to punish them is not subject to a statute of limitations and excludes any measure implying impunity, such as an amnesty or a general pardon.'[110]

The clearest rejection of prescription for gross human rights violations was voiced by the Inter-American Court of Human Rights in the *Barrios Altos Case*, in which it held:

> 'This Court considers that all amnesty provisions, provisions on prescription and the establishment of measures designed to eliminate responsibility are inadmissible, because they are intended to prevent the investigation and punishment of those responsible for serious human rights violations such as torture, extrajudicial, summary or arbitrary execution and forced disappearance, all of them prohibited because they violate non-derogable rights recognized by international human rights law.'[111]

---

[108] *Concluding Observations on Argentina*, 3 November 2000, CCPR/CO/70/ARG, para 9.

[109] *General Comment No 31 on the Nature of the General Legal Obligation Imposed on States Parties to the Covenant*, 26 May 2004, CCPR/C/21/Rev.1/Add.13, para 18.

[110] *Conclusions and recommendations on Venezuela*, 23 December 2002, CAT/C/CR/29/2, Positive aspects, para 6(c).

[111] *Case of Barrios Altos v Peru*, Judgment of 14 March 2001, Series C No 75, para 41.

The Court reiterated this finding in subsequent cases.[112]

3. Torture

In the *Furundzija case*, the International Criminal Tribunal for the Former Yugoslavia stated that one of the consequences of the peremptory nature of the prohibition of torture was '[...] the fact that torture may not be covered by a statute of limitations [...].'[113]

It is also clear from more recent observations by the Committee against Torture that it rejects the applicability of statutes of limitation to the crime of torture.[114] Similarly, the Special Rapporteur on torture criticized statutes of limitation which lead to the exemption of perpetrators from legal responsibility.[115]

4. The Special Case of Disappearances

While enforced disappearances are not explicitly excluded under existing international human rights treaties from statutory limitation, international law nevertheless makes clear that prescription for these crimes cannot begin to run while the victims have no effective remedy. Disappearances, in that sense, are considered as continuing offences. The Declaration on the Protection of All Persons from Enforced Disappearance seeks to limit the applicability of statutes of limitations: disappearances shall be considered a continuing offence as long as the perpetrators continue to conceal the fate and the whereabouts of persons who have disappeared and these facts remain unclarified; they shall not run for the time that there are no effective

[112] *Barrios Altos Case, Interpretation of the Judgment on the Merits*, Judgment of 3 September 2001, Series C No 83, para 15; Case *Trujillo Oroza v Bolivia (Reparations)*, Judgment of 27 February 2002, Series C No 92, para 106; *Case Caracazo v Venezuela (Reparations)*, Judgment of 29 August 2002, Series C No 95, para 119.

[113] *Furundzija Case*, Judgment of 10 December 1998, IT-95-17/1, paras 155, 157.

[114] *Conclusions and recommendations on Turkey*, 27 May 2003, CAT/C/CR/30/5, Recommendation, para 7(c); *Conclusions and recommendations on Slovenia*, 27 May 2003, CAT/C/CR/30/4, Recommendation, para 6(b); *Conclusions and recommendations on Chile*, May 2004, CAT/C/CR/32/5, para 7 (f).

[115] Report of visit to Spain, E/CN.4/2004/56/Add.2, para 45: 'The length of the judicial process is reportedly often so great that by the time a trial opens, accused officers may not be tried because the statute of limitations for the offence has expired.'

remedies in the sense of Article 2 ICCPR, and where they exist, they shall be substantial and commensurate with the extreme seriousness of the offence. Article 7 of the Inter-American Convention on Enforced Disappearances of Persons reads: 'Criminal prosecution for the forced disappearance of persons and the penalty judicially imposed on its perpetrator shall not be subject to statutes of limitations. However, if there should be a norm of a fundamental character preventing application of the stipulation contained in the previous paragraph, the period of limitation shall be equal to that which applies to the gravest crime in the domestic laws of the corresponding State Party.'

The judgment of the Supreme Court of Mexico on criminal responsibility for disappearance follows the principle laid down in the Declaration on the Protection of All Persons from Enforced Disappearance. It held that in the case of an illegal deprivation of liberty, the statute of limitation could not begin to run until the time the body of the detained person was recovered, for until then the crime constituted a continuing offence.[116]

5. Trends in National Legislation and Jurisprudence

There appears to be a widespread practice to exclude statutes of limitations for genocide, crimes against humanity and war crimes, either explicitly[117] or

[116] Supreme Court of Justice of the Nation, *Jesus Ibarra Case*, Judgment of 5 November 2003.

[117] Bosnia and Herzegovina: criminal offences of genocide, crimes against humanity and war crimes, or for other criminal offences pursuant to international law (Article 19 of the Criminal Code); Bulgaria: crimes against peace and humanity (Art. 31 (7) of the Constitution of Bulgaria of 1991; Croatia: genocide, war of aggression, war crimes or other criminal offences which are not subject to statutes of limitation pursuant to international law (Articles 18 and 24 of the Criminal Code); Czech Republic: certain crimes such as war crimes and crimes against humanity (Section 67a of the Criminal Code); Hungary: war crimes, crimes against humanity, certain serious cases of homicide, certain cases of kidnapping and of violence against a superior officer or service official, and certain acts of terrorism (Section 33 (2) of the Criminal Code); Estonia: crimes against humanity and war crimes (Section 5 (4) of the Criminal Code); Poland: war crimes and crimes against humanity (Article 43 of the Constitution of 1997 and Article105 of the Criminal Code of 6 June 1997); Slovenia: genocide, war crimes and 'criminal offences the prosecution of which may not be prevented under international agreements' (Article 116 of the Criminal Code); Slovakia: genocide, crimes against humanity and war crimes (Article 67 of the Criminal Code); Russian Federation: crimes against peace and security of mankind (Article 60 (8) of the Criminal Code); Kyrgyzstan: crimes against peace and security of mankind and war crimes (Article 67 (6) of the Criminal Code); Republic of Moldova: 'crimes against peace and security of mankind, war crimes or other crimes mentioned in the international treaties the Republic of Moldova is a party to' (Article 60 (8) of the Criminal Code); Tajikistan: crimes against peace and security of mankind (Article 75 (6) and 81 (5) of the Criminal Code), Armenia: 'crimes against peace and human security' and also crimes envisaged in international agreements to which Armenia is a party (Art. 75 (5) Criminal code);

by reference to the international obligations of the state.[118] A number of countries, often common law countries, are silent about statutes of limitation, because they do not use the legal concept of statutes of limitation.[119] The prohibition of prescription for the crimes of genocide, crimes against humanity and war crimes has also been confirmed in national case law.[120]

Some countries have gone further and have prohibited statutes of limitations for other gross human rights violations and crimes. For example, the

Azerbaidjan: 'crimes against peace and security of humanity and war crimes' (Art. 75(5) of the Criminal code), Belarus: crimes against peace, crimes against the security of humanity and war crimes (Article 85 of the Criminal Code); Burkina Faso: genocide and crimes against humanity (Article 317 of the Criminal Code); Mali: genocide, crimes against humanity and war crimes (Article 32 of the Criminal Code); Rwanda: Article 20 of the Law Nº 33 bis/2003 of 06/09/2003 repressing the crime of genocide, crimes against humanity and war crimes; France: genocide and crimes against humanity (Article 213-5 of the Criminal Code of 1994); Italy: crimes punishable with life imprisonment (Article 157 of the Criminal Code); Switzerland: genocide, war crimes, and certain other crimes against the physical integrity of persons (Article 75bis of the Criminal Code); Belgium: "Loi de 1993 telle que modifiée par la loi du 23 avril 2003 relative à la répression des violations graves du droit international humanitaire et l'article 144 ter du Code judiciaire" (the law was amended through loi du 5 août 2003 relative aux violations du droit international humanitaire, but which left the provision on statutes of limitation unchanged).

[118] Georgia: Articles 71, 76 of the Criminal Code; Moldova: Article 60 (8) of the Criminal Code; Armenia: Art. 75 (5) of the Criminal Code; Bosnia and Herzegovina: Article 19 of the Criminal Code; Guatemala: Article 8 of the Act of National Reconciliation (*Ley de reconciliación nacional*); Croatia: Articles 18 and 24 of the Criminal Code; Slovenia: Article 116 of the Criminal Code; South Africa: Implementation of the Rome Statute of the ICC Act (N° 27 of 2002) (Article 29 of the Rome Statute is incorporated in the Act); Argentina: Law 25.778 of 20 August 2003 (gives constitutional rank to the Convention on the Non-Applicability of Statutory Limitations to War Crimes and Crimes against Humanity); Spain: Article 131 (4) of the Criminal Code has been amended by Ley Orgánica 15/2003 of 25 November 2003; Germany: Section 5 of the Act to introduce the Code of Crimes of International Law of 26 June 2002; Netherlands: Section 13 of the International Crimes Act of 19 June 2003; New Zealand: International Crimes and International Criminal Court Act 2000 (Article 29 of the Rome Statute is replicated in section 12).

[119] Australia: ICC (Consequential Amendments) Act 2002, n°42 of 27 June 2002: no mention of statutes of limitation. There is no limitation period for the ICC crimes under Australian law; Ireland: International Criminal Court Law 2003 (silent on statute of limitations); United Kingdom: International Criminal Court Act 2001 (no mention of statutes of limitation; no limitation period for the ICC crimes under UK law); Canada: Crimes Against Humanity and War Crimes Act of 29 June 2000 (no mention of statutes of limitation in this Act. There is no limitation period for the ICC crimes under Canadian law).

[120] District Tribunal of Jerusalem, *Eichman* case, arrêt du 12 décembre 1961, para 53; crimes against humanity and war crimes; Cour de Cassation, affaire *Klaus Barbie*, Judgment of 20 December 1985: crimes against humanity; Rome Military Court of Appeal, Judgement of 22 July 1997, *Haas and Priebke* cases: crimes against humanity; this judgement was upheld by the Military Court of Appeal on 7 March 1998 and by the Supreme Court of Cassation on 16 November 1998; Supreme Court of Argentina: *Erich Priebke* case N°16.063/94, 2 November 1995: crimes against humanity.

Constitution of Ecuador prohibits statutes of limitation for genocide, torture, enforced disappearance, kidnapping, homicide for political reasons or reasons of conscience.[121] In Guatemala, the Law on National Reconciliation excludes statutes of limitation for genocide, torture, enforced disappearance and 'those offences which are not subject to prescription or to extinction of criminal responsibility, in conformity with internal law and international treaties ratified by Guatemala'.[122] Article 29 of the Constitution of the Bolivarian Republic of Venezuela of 1999 prohibits prescription for crimes against humanity, gross human rights violations and war crimes; the Criminal Code also prohibits prescription for the crime of enforced disappearance.[123] In El Salvador, there is no prescription for torture, acts of terrorism, kidnapping, genocide, violations of the laws and customs of war, enforced disappearance of persons, political, ideological, racial, gender or religious persecution.[124] The Constitution of Paraguay states that genocide, torture, forced disappearance of persons, kidnapping, or homicide for political reasons shall not be subject to statutes of limitation.[125] In Ethiopia, there is no statute of limitation for 'crimes against humanity, so defined by international agreements ratified by Ethiopia and by other laws of Ethiopia, such as genocide, summary executions, forcible disappearances or torture'.[126] In Hungary, statutes of limitation are prohibited for war crimes, crimes against humanity, certain serious cases of homicide, certain cases of kidnapping and of violence against a superior officer or service official, and certain acts of terrorism.[127] Italy excludes statutes of limitations for all crimes punishable with life imprisonment.[128] Switzerland prohibits statutes of limitations not only for genocide and war crimes, but also certain other crimes against the physical integrity of persons.[129]

---

[121] Article 23 of the Constitution of 1998

[122] Article 8 of the Act of National Reconciliation (*Ley de reconciliación nacional*), original in Spanish, own translation; Guatemala has not ratified the Convention on the Non-Applicability of Statutory Limitations to War Crimes and Crimes against Humanity of 1968 or the Rome Statute.

[123] Article 181 of the Criminal Code of 2000

[124] Article 99 of the Criminal Code: it also retroactively prohibits prescription for genocide, torture and enforced disappearance for crimes committed before the coming into force of the Code.

[125] Article 5 of the Constitution of 1992 and Article 102 (3) of the Criminal Code of 1997.

[126] Article 28 of the Constitution of 1994.

[127] Section 33 (2) of the Criminal Code.

[128] Article 157 of the Criminal Code.

[129] Article 75bis of the Criminal Code.

The prohibition of prescription for the crimes of genocide, crimes against humanity and war crimes has also been confirmed in national case law.

In the Judgment concerning *Eichmann*, the District Tribunal of Jerusalem confirmed the validity of the *Nazis and Nazi Collaborators (Punishment) Law*, which did not allow prescription for offences against the Jewish People, crimes against humanity and war crimes on account of the extreme gravity of these offences.[130]

In France, the Cassation Court held in the judgment concerning *Klaus Barbie* that crimes against humanity were not subject to statutes of limitation.[131]

The Rome Military Court of Appeal and Supreme Court of Cassation sentenced *Priebke* to 15 years in prison. It described the principle of non-applicability of statutes of limitation to war crimes as a peremptory norm of general international law.[132]

The Supreme Court of Argentina considered in the case concerning the extradition of *Erich Priebke* to Italy in 1995 that the qualification of offences as crimes against humanity did not depend on the will of states but on peremptory norms of international law and that under those conditions there was no statute of limitation for them.[133]

In 1999, the Federal Criminal and Correctional Court of Buenos Aires recalled in the case concerning the appeals against the preventive detention of former generals that forced disappearance of persons constitutes a crime against humanity, and as such is not subject to statutory limitation, whatever the date of its commission.[134] The Supreme Court of Paraguay has equally held that crimes against humanity are not subject to prescription.[135]

[130] District Tribunal of Jerusalem, *Eichmann* case, Judgment of 12 December 1961, para 53.

[131] Cour de Cassation, affaire *Klaus Barbie*, Judgment of 20 December 1985.

[132] Rome Military Court of Appeal, judgment of 22 July 1997, *Haas and Priebke* cases; This judgment was upheld by the Military Court of Appeal on 7 March 1998 and by the Supreme Court of Cassation on 16 November 1998.

[133] Supreme Court of Argentina, *Erich Priebke* Extradition, Case No 16.063/94, Judgment of 2 November 1995.

[134] Federal Criminal and Correctional Court of Argentina, Case No 30514, *in the Process against Massera and others on Exceptions*, Judgment of 9 September 1999.

[135] Supreme Court of Justice, Case No 585/96, *Capitán de Caballería Modesto Napoleón Ortigoza*,

In a related case, in May 2005 the Chilean Supreme Court suspended a deadline for investigations into human rights violations committed under the regime of former president Pinochet.[136]

***

- Domestic legislation in numerous countries as well as international and national jurisprudence provides evidence that there is a customary rule on the non-applicability of statutes of limitation to genocide and crimes against humanity.
- There also appears to be an emerging rule that gross human rights violations, particularly torture, should not be subject to prescription.
- With regard to disappearances, the UN Declaration and the Inter-American Convention as well as national case law make clear that statutes of limitation cannot run for as long as the person remains disappeared, since the offence continues as long as the person remains disappeared.

Acuerdo y sentencia of 31 December 1996 [summary available at: http://www.derechos.org/nizkor/paraguay/1997/6.html, viewed 9 December 2004].

[136] BBC News, Chile rights deadline suspended, 6 May 2005.

SUMMARY

The international legal principles on the right to a remedy and reparation can be summarized as follows:

- Victims of gross human rights violations have a right to truth, to justice and to reparation, to which the duty of the state is to provide effective remedies, to investigate the violation and to reveal the truth, to prosecute and punish perpetrators and to combat impunity, to cease the violation and to guarantee its non-repetition, and the duty to provide full reparation are corollaries.

- Persons entitled to reparation are not only the direct victims, but also other persons who have suffered harm as a result of the violation, be it physical, mental or economic harm, such as members of the family of the victim. When a great number of persons have suffered from human rights violations, there should be collective procedures to enforce their rights. In some instances, collective reparation may be warranted.

- Victims of gross human rights violations have a right to a prompt, effective and accessible remedy before an independent authority. They should have access to legal counsel and if necessary to free legal assistance. The remedy must be capable of leading to relief, including reparation and compen-sation. It must be expeditious and enforceable by the competent authorities. The remedy must be judicial in cases of gross human rights violations.

- Victims and relatives of human rights violations have a right to a prompt, thorough, independent, and impartial official investigation, capable of leading to the identification and, if appropriate, the punishment of the authors. The investigating authority must be personally and institutionally independent and vested with the necessary powers and resources to conduct a meaningful investigation. Victims and their relatives have a right to effective participation in the investigation. Officials who are under investigation should be suspended during the time of the investigation.

- The right to truth entails the right of victims and relatives to know the truth not only about the facts and circumstances surrounding human rights violation, but also the reasons that led to them and the implicated authors. This knowledge must be disclosed and made public not only to the victims and their relatives but also, unless it causes harm to them, for the benefit of society as a whole.

- State responsibility for human rights violations entails the obligation to cease the violation if it is ongoing and to provide guarantees of non-repetition. Guarantees of non-repetition may take varying forms, such as ensuring civilian control over military and security forces, strengthening the independence of the judiciary, protection of legal, medical, media and related personnel and human rights defenders, and human rights training, or removal of officials implicated in gross human rights violations from office.

- The term reparation can be understood as the general term for different measures of redress, such as restitution (*restitutio in integrum*), compensation, rehabilitation and satisfaction. The right to seek reparation should not be subject to statutes of limitations.

- Restitution means the restoration of the situation prior to the violation. However, while restitution is, in principle, the primary form of reparation, in practice it is the least frequent, because it is mostly impossible to completely return to the situation before the violation, especially because of the moral damage caused to victims and their relatives. When restitution is not possible or only partially possible, the state has to provide compensation covering the damage arisen from the loss of the *status quo ante.*

- The state has to provide compensation for material or moral damage caused by the violation to all persons who suffer harm as a consequence of the violation, i.e. the victim and his or her relatives, and other person close to the victim if they can show that they have suffered harm.

- As far as material damage is concerned, it emerges from the jurisprudence that no economically assessable loss is excluded *per se* from compensation, as long as the conditions for reparation are fulfilled. If the existence of material damage can be demonstrated, the award does not depend on whether the victim can give detailed evidence of the precise amounts, as it is frequently impossible to prove such exact figures. In the absence of detailed information, compensation is granted on the basis of equity.

- Compensation must also encompass financial reparation for physical or mental suffering. As this is not as such economically quantifiable, it must rest on an assessment in equity.

- Rehabilitation should seek to physically and mentally help victims to overcome the damage suffered by the violation, and to rehabilitate their dignity and their social and legal situation.

- Satisfaction should help to restore a person's dignity, mental well-being, and reputation.

- States have an obligation to prosecute and punish perpetrators of gross human rights violations. In order to comply with their obligation to avoid and combat impunity, members of the armed forces who committed gross human rights violations should not be tried in military tribunals.

- Amnesties for perpetrators of serious human rights and humanitarian law violations violate the international duty of the state to prosecute and punish them and are incompatible with victims' right to justice.

- Statutes of limitation for criminal proceedings are incompatible with international law for crimes against humanity, genocide and war crimes. There also appears to be an emerging rule that gross human rights violations, particularly torture, should not be subject to prescription.

ANNEX I

Selection of International Norms and Standards

I. United Nations Standards

- Article 8 of the Universal Declaration of Human Rights;
- Articles 2 (3), (5), 14 (6) of the International Covenant on Civil and Political Rights;
- Articles 13, 14 of the Convention against Torture and Other Cruel, Inhuman or Degrading Treatment or Punishment;
- Article 6 of the Convention on the Elimination of Racial Discrimination;
- Article 39 of the Convention of the Rights of the Child;
- Principles 4, 5 of the Declaration of Basic Principles of Justice for Victims of Crime and Abuse of Power;
- Principles 4, 16 and 20 of the Principles on the Effective Prevention and Investigation of Extra-Legal, Arbitrary or Summary Executions;
- Article 9 of the Declaration on the Protection of All Persons from Enforced Disappearance;
- Article 27 of the Vienna Declaration and Programme of Action;
- Article 9 of the Declaration on Human Rights Defenders;
- Principles 1, 2 of the Principles on the Effective Investigation and Documentation of Torture and Other Cruel, Inhuman or Degrading Treatment or Punishment;
- Articles 68, 75, 79 of the Statute of the International Criminal Court;

- Articles 28-39 of the Draft Articles on Responsibility of States for Internationally Wrongful Acts as adopted by the International Law Commission.

II. Humanitarian Law Standards

- Article 3 of the Fourth Hague Convention respecting the Laws and Customs of War on Land of 1907;
- Article 91 of the Protocol Additional to the Geneva Conventions and relating to the Protection of Victims of International Armed Conflict.

III. Regional Standards

- Articles 7 (a), 21 (2) of the African Charter on Human and Peoples' Rights;
- Article 27 of the Protocol to the African Charter on Human and Peoples' Rights on the Establishment of an African Court on Human and Peoples' Rights;
- Article 9 of the Arab Charter on Human Rights;
- Articles 5 (5), 13, 41 of the European Convention on Human Rights;
- Article 47 of the Charter of Fundamental Rights of the European Union;
- Articles 25, 63 (1) of the American Convention on Human Rights;
- Article XVIII of the American Declaration of the Rights and Duties of Man;
- Article 8 (1) of the Inter-American Convention to Prevent and Punish Torture.

I. UNITED NATIONS STANDARDS

Universal Declaration of Human Rights

Article 8

Everyone has the right to an effective remedy by the competent national tribunals for acts violating the fundamental rights granted him by the constitution or by law.

International Covenant on Civil and Political Rights

Article 2 (3)

Each State Party to the present Covenant undertakes:

(a) To ensure that any person whose rights or freedoms as herein recognized are violated shall have an effective remedy, notwithstanding that the violation has been committed by persons acting in an official capacity;

(b) To ensure that any person claiming such a remedy shall have his right thereto determined by competent judicial, administrative or legislative authorities, or by any other competent authority provided for by the legal system of the State, and to develop the possibilities of judicial remedy;

(c) To ensure that the competent authorities shall enforce such remedies when granted.

Article 9 (5)

Anyone who has been the victim of unlawful arrest or detention shall have an enforceable right to compensation.

Convention against Torture and Other Cruel, Inhuman or Degrading Treatment or Punishment

Article 13

Each State Party shall ensure that any individual who alleges he has been subjected to torture in any territory under its jurisdiction has the right to complain to, and to have his case promptly and impartially examined by, its competent authorities. Steps shall be taken to ensure that the complainant and witnesses are protected against all ill-treatment or intimidation as a consequence of his complaint or any evidence given.

Article 14

1. Each State Party shall ensure in its legal system that the victim of an act of torture obtains redress and has an enforceable right to fair and adequate compensation, including the means for as full rehabilitation as possible. In the event of the death of the victim as a result of an act of torture, his dependants shall be entitled to compensation.

2. Nothing in this article shall affect any right of the victim or other persons to compensation which may exist under national law.

Convention on the Elimination of Racial Discrimination

Article 6

States Parties shall assure to everyone within their jurisdiction effective protection and remedies, through the competent national tribunals and other State institutions, against any acts of racial discrimination which violate his human rights and fundamental freedoms contrary to this Convention, as well as the right to seek from such tribunals just and adequate reparation or satisfaction for any damage suffered as a result of such discrimination.

Convention of the Rights of the Child

Article 39

States Parties shall take all appropriate measures to promote physical and psychological recovery and social reintegration of a child victim of: any form of neglect, exploitation, or abuse; torture or any other form of cruel, inhuman or degrading treatment or punishment; or armed conflicts. Such recovery and reintegration shall take place in an environment which fosters the health, self-respect and dignity of the child.

Declaration of Basic Principles of Justice for Victims of Crime and Abuse of Power

Principle 4

Victims should be treated with compassion and respect for their dignity. They are entitled to access to the mechanisms of justice and to prompt redress, as provided for by national legislation, for the harm that they have suffered.

Principle 5

Judicial and administrative mechanisms should be established and strengthened where necessary to enable victims to obtain redress through formal or informal procedures that are expeditious, fair, inexpensive and accessible. Victims should be informed of their rights in seeking redress through such mechanisms.

Principles on the Effective Prevention and Investigation of Extra-Legal, Arbitrary or Summary Executions

Principle 4

Effective protection through judicial or other means shall be guaranteed to individuals and groups who are in danger of extra-legal, arbitrary or summary executions, including those who receive death threats.

Principle 16

Families of the deceased and their legal representatives shall be informed of, and have access to any hearing as well as to all information relevant to the investigation, and shall be entitled to present other evidence. The family of the deceased shall have the right to insist that a medical or other qualified representative be present at the autopsy. When the identity of a deceased person has been determined, a notification of death shall be posted, and the family or relatives of the deceased shall be informed immediately. The body of the deceased shall be returned to them upon completion of the investigation.

Principle 20

The families and dependents of victims of extra-legal, arbitrary or summary executions shall be entitled to fair and adequate compensation within a reasonable period of time.

Declaration on the Protection of All Persons from Enforced Disappearance

Article 9

1. The right to a prompt and effective judicial remedy as a means of determining the whereabouts or state of health of persons deprived of their liberty and/or identifying the authority ordering or carrying out the deprivation of liberty is required to prevent enforced disappearances under all circumstances, including those referred to in article 7 above.

2. In such proceedings, competent national authorities shall have access to all places where persons deprived of their liberty are being held and to each part of those places, as well as to any place in which there are grounds to believe that such persons may be found.

3. Any other competent authority entitled under the law of the State or by any international legal instrument to which the State is a party may also have access to such places.

Vienna Declaration and Programme of Action

Article 27

Every State should provide an effective framework of remedies to redress human rights grievances or violations. The administration of justice, including law enforcement and prosecutorial agencies and, especially, an independent judiciary and legal profession in full conformity with applicable standards contained in international human rights instruments, are essential to the full and non-discriminatory realization of human rights and indispensable to the processes of democracy and sustainable development. In this context, institutions concerned with the administration of justice should be properly funded, and an increased level of both technical and financial assistance should be provided by the international community. It is incumbent upon the United Nations to make use of special programmes of advisory services on a priority basis for the achievement of a strong and independent administration of justice.

Declaration on Human Rights Defenders

Article 9

1. In the exercise of human rights and fundamental freedoms, including the promotion and protection of human rights as referred to in the present Declaration, everyone has the right, individually and in association with others, to benefit from an effective remedy and to be protected in the event of the violation of those rights.

2. To this end, everyone whose rights or freedoms are allegedly violated has the right, either in person or through legally authorized representation, to complain to and have that complaint promptly reviewed in a public hearing before an independent, impartial and competent judicial or other authority established by law and to obtain from such an authority a decision, in accordance with law, providing redress, including any compensation due, where there has been a violation of that person's rights or freedoms, as well as enforcement of the eventual decision and award, all without undue delay.

3. To the same end, everyone has the right, individually and in association with others, inter alia:

(a) To complain about the policies and actions of individual officials and governmental bodies with regard to violations of human rights and fundamental freedoms, by petition or other appropriate means, to competent domestic judicial, administrative or legislative authorities or any other competent authority provided for by the legal system of the State, which should render their decision on the complaint without undue delay;

(b) To attend public hearings, proceedings and trials so as to form an opinion on their compliance with national law and applicable international obligations and commitments;

(c) To offer and provide professionally qualified legal assistance or other relevant advice and assistance in defending human rights and fundamental freedoms.

4. To the same end, and in accordance with applicable international instruments and procedures, everyone has the right, individually and in association with others, to unhindered access to and communication with international bodies with general or special competence to receive and consider communications on matters of human rights and fundamental freedoms.

5. The State shall conduct a prompt and impartial investigation or ensure that an inquiry takes place whenever there is reasonable ground to believe that a violation of human rights and fundamental freedoms has occurred in any territory under its jurisdiction.

Principles on the Effective Investigation and Documentation of Torture and Other Cruel, Inhuman or Degrading Treatment or Punishment

Principle 1

The purposes of effective investigation and documentation of torture and other cruel, inhuman or degrading treatment or punishment (hereinafter "torture or other ill-treatment") include the following:

(a) Clarification of the facts and establishment and acknowledgement of individual and State responsibility for victims and their families;

(b) Identification of measures needed to prevent recurrence;

(c) Facilitation of prosecution and/or, as appropriate, disciplinary sanctions for those indicated by the investigation as being responsible and demonstration of the need for full reparation and redress from the State, including fair and adequate financial compensation and provision of the means for medical care and rehabilitation.

Principle 2

States shall ensure that complaints and reports of torture or ill-treatment are promptly and effectively investigated. Even in the absence of an express complaint, an investigation shall be undertaken if there are other indications that torture or ill-treatment might have occurred. The investigators, who shall be independent of the suspected perpetrators and the agency they serve, shall be competent and impartial. They shall have access to, or be empowered to commission investigations by, impartial medical or other experts. The methods used to carry out such investigations shall meet the highest professional standards and the findings shall be made public.

Rome Statute of the International Criminal Court

Article 68

1. The Court shall take appropriate measures to protect the safety, physical and psychological well-being, dignity and privacy of victims and witnesses. In so doing, the Court shall have regard to all relevant factors, including age, gender as defined in article 7, paragraph 3, and health, and the nature of the crime, in particular, but not limited to, where the crime involves sexual or gender violence or violence against children. The Prosecutor shall take such measures particularly during the investigation and prosecution of such crimes. These measures shall not be prejudicial to or inconsistent with the rights of the accused and a fair and impartial trial.

2. As an exception to the principle of public hearings provided for in article 67, the Chambers of the Court may, to protect victims and witnesses or an accused, conduct any part of the proceedings in camera or allow the presentation of evidence by electronic or other special means. In particular, such measures shall be implemented in the case of a victim of sexual violence or a child who is a victim or a witness, unless otherwise ordered by the Court, having regard to all the circumstances, particularly the views of the victim or witness.

3. Where the personal interests of the victims are affected, the Court shall permit their views and concerns to be presented and considered at stages of the proceedings determined to be appropriate by the Court and in a manner which is not prejudicial to or inconsistent with the rights of the accused and a fair and impartial trial. Such views and concerns may be presented by the legal representatives of the victims where the Court considers it appropriate, in accordance with the Rules of Procedure and Evidence.

4. The Victims and Witnesses Unit may advise the Prosecutor and the Court on appropriate protective measures, security arrangements, counselling and assistance as referred to in article 43, paragraph 6.

5. Where the disclosure of evidence or information pursuant to this Statute may lead to the grave endangerment of the security of a witness or his or her family, the Prosecutor may, for the purposes of any proceedings conducted prior to the commencement of the trial, withhold such evidence or information and instead submit a summary thereof. Such measures shall be exer-

cised in a manner which is not prejudicial to or inconsistent with the rights of the accused and a fair and impartial trial.

6. A State may make an application for necessary measures to be taken in respect of the protection of its servants or agents and the protection of confidential or sensitive information.

Article 75

1. The Court shall establish principles relating to reparations to, or in respect of, victims, including restitution, compensation and rehabilitation. On this basis, in its decision the Court may, either upon request or on its own motion in exceptional circumstances, determine the scope and extent of any damage, loss and injury to, or in respect of, victims and will state the principles on which it is acting.

2. The Court may make an order directly against a convicted person specifying appropriate reparations to, or in respect of, victims, including restitution, compensation and rehabilitation. Where appropriate, the Court may order that the award for reparations be made through the Trust Fund provided for in article 79.

3. Before making an order under this article, the Court may invite and shall take account of representations from or on behalf of the convicted person, victims, other interested persons or interested States.

4. In exercising its power under this article, the Court may, after a person is convicted of a crime within the jurisdiction of the Court, determine whether, in order to give effect to an order which it may make under this article, it is necessary to seek measures under article 93, paragraph 1.

5. A State Party shall give effect to a decision under this article as if the provisions of article 109 were applicable to this article.

6. Nothing in this article shall be interpreted as prejudicing the rights of victims under national or international law.

Article 79

1. A Trust Fund shall be established by decision of the Assembly of States Parties for the benefit of victims of crimes within the jurisdiction of the Court, and of the families of such victims.

2. The Court may order money and other property collected through fines or forfeiture to be transferred, by order of the Court, to the Trust Fund.

3. The Trust Fund shall be managed according to criteria to be determined by the Assembly of States Parties.

Draft Articles on Responsibility of States for Internationally Wrongful Acts as adopted by the International Law Commission

Article 28
Legal consequences of an internationally wrongful act

The international responsibility of a State which is entailed by an internationally wrongful act in accordance with the provisions of Part One involves legal consequences as set out in this Part.

Article 29
Continued duty of performance

The legal consequences of an internationally wrongful act under this Part do not affect the continued duty of the responsible State to perform the obligation breached.

Article 30
Cessation and non-repetition

The State responsible for the internationally wrongful act is under an obligation:

(a) To cease that act, if it is continuing;

(b) To offer appropriate assurances and guarantees of non-repetition, if circumstances so require.

Article 31
Reparation

1. The responsible State is under an obligation to make full reparation for the injury caused by the internationally wrongful act.

2. Injury includes any damage, whether material or moral, caused by the internationally wrongful act of a State.

Article 32
Irrelevance of internal law

The responsible State may not rely on the provisions of its internal law as justification for failure to comply with its obligations under this Part.

Article 33
Scope of international obligations set out in this Part

1. The obligations of the responsible State set out in this Part may be owed to another State, to several States, or to the international community as a whole, depending in particular on the character and content of the international obligation and on the circumstances of the breach.

2. This Part is without prejudice to any right, arising from the international responsibility of a State, which may accrue directly to any person or entity other than a State.

Article 34
Forms of reparation

Full reparation for the injury caused by the internationally wrongful act shall take the form of restitution, compensation and satisfaction, either singly or in combination, in accordance with the provisions of this chapter.

Article 35
Restitution

A State responsible for an internationally wrongful act is under an obligation to make restitution, that is, to re-establish the situation which existed before the wrongful act was committed, provided and to the extent that restitution:

(a) Is not materially impossible;

(b) Does not involve a burden out of all proportion to the benefit deriving from restitution instead of compensation.

Article 36
Compensation

1. The State responsible for an internationally wrongful act is under an obligation to compensate for the damage caused thereby, insofar as such damage is not made good by restitution.

2. The compensation shall cover any financially assessable damage including loss of profits insofar as it is established.

Article 37
Satisfaction

1. The State responsible for an internationally wrongful act is under an obligation to give satisfaction for the injury caused by that act insofar as it cannot be made good by restitution or compensation.

2. Satisfaction may consist in an acknowledgement of the breach, an expression of regret, a formal apology or another appropriate modality.

3. Satisfaction shall not be out of proportion to the injury and may not take a form humiliating to the responsible State.

Article 38
Interest

1. Interest on any principal sum due under this chapter shall be payable when necessary in order to ensure full reparation. The interest rate and mode of calculation shall be set so as to achieve that result.

2. Interest runs from the date when the principal sum should have been paid until the date the obligation to pay is fulfilled.

Article 39
Contribution to the injury

In the determination of reparation, account shall be taken of the contribution to the injury by willful or negligent action or omission of the injured State or any person or entity in relation to whom reparation is sought.

II. HUMANITARIAN LAW

Fourth Hague Convention respecting the Laws and Customs of War on Land

Article 3

A belligerent party which violates the provisions of the said Regulations shall, if the case demands, be liable to pay compensation. It shall be responsible for all acts committed by persons forming part of its armed forces.

Protocol Additional to the Geneva Conventions and relating to the Protection of Victims of International Armed Conflict

Article 91

A Party to the conflict which violates the provisions of the Conventions or of this Protocol shall, if the case demands, be liable to pay compensation. It shall be responsible for all acts committed by persons forming part of its armed forces.

III. REGIONAL INSTRUMENTS

African Charter on Human and Peoples' Rights

Article 7 (1)(a)

Every individual shall have the right to have his cause heard. This comprises:

(a) the right to an appeal to competent national organs against acts of violating his fundamental rights as recognized and guaranteed by conventions, laws, regulations and customs in force.

Article 21 (2)

In case of spoliation the dispossessed people shall have the right to the lawful recovery of its property as well as to an adequate compensation.

Protocol to the African Charter on Human and Peoples' Rights on the Establishment of an African Court on Human and Peoples' Rights

Article 27

1. If the Court finds that there has been violation of a human or peoples' right, it shall make appropriate orders to remedy the violation, including the payment of fair compensation or reparation.

2. In cases of extreme gravity and urgency, and when necessary to avoid irreparable harm to persons, the Court shall adopt such provisional measures as it deems necessary.

European Convention on Human Rights

Article 5 (5)

Everyone who has been the victim of arrest or detention in contravention of the provisions of this article shall have an enforceable right to compensation.

Article 13

Everyone whose rights and freedoms as set forth in this Convention are violated shall have an effective remedy before a national authority notwithstanding that the violation has been committed by persons acting in an official capacity.

Article 41

If the Court finds that there has been a violation of the Convention or the protocols thereto, and if the internal law of the High Contracting Party concerned allows only partial reparation to be made, the Court shall, if necessary, afford just satisfaction to the injured party.

Charter of Fundamental Rights of the European Union

Article 47

Everyone whose rights and freedoms guaranteed by the law of the Union are violated has the right to an effective remedy before a tribunal in compliance with the conditions laid down in this Article.

Everyone is entitled to a fair and public hearing within a reasonable time by an independent and impartial tribunal previously established by law. Everyone shall have the possibility of being advised, defended and represented.

Legal aid shall be made available to those who lack sufficient resources in so far as such aid is necessary to ensure effective access to justice.

American Convention on Human Rights

Article 25

1. Everyone has the right to simple and prompt recourse, or any other effective recourse, to a competent court or tribunal for protection against acts that violate his fundamental rights recognized by the constitution or laws of the state concerned or by this Convention, even though such violation may have been committed by persons acting in the course of their official duties.

2. The States Parties undertake:

a. to ensure that any person claiming such remedy shall have his rights determined by the competent authority provided for by the legal system of the state;

b. to develop the possibilities of judicial remedy; and

c. to ensure that the competent authorities shall enforce such remedies when granted.

Article 63 (1)

1. If the Court finds that there has been a violation of a right or freedom protected by this Convention, the Court shall rule that the injured party be ensured the enjoyment of his right or freedom that was violated. It shall also rule, if appropriate, that the consequences of the measure or situation that constituted the breach of such right or freedom be remedied and that fair compensation be paid to the injured party.

American Declaration of the Rights and Duties of Man

Article XVIII

Every person may resort to the courts to ensure respect for his legal rights. There should likewise be available to him a simple, brief procedure whereby the courts will protect him from acts of authority that, to his prejudice, violate any fundamental constitutional rights.

Inter-American Convention to Prevent and Punish Torture

Article 8

The States Parties shall guarantee that any person making an accusation of having been subjected to torture within their jurisdiction shall have the right to an impartial examination of his case.

Arab Charter on Human Rights

Article 9

All persons are equal before the law and everyone within the territory of the State has a guaranteed right to legal remedy.

ANNEX II

UN Principles on Reparation and Impunity

Basic principles and guidelines on the right to a remedy and reparation for victims of gross violations of international human rights law and serious violations of international humanitarian law[1]

PREAMBLE

Recalling the provisions providing a right to a remedy for victims of violations of international human rights law found in numerous international instruments, in particular the Universal Declaration of Human Rights at article 8, the International Covenant on Civil and Political Rights at article 2, the International Convention on the Elimination of All Forms of Racial Discrimination at article 6, the Convention against Torture and Other Cruel, Inhuman or Degrading Treatment or Punishment at article 14, the Convention on the Rights of the Child at article 39, and of international humanitarian law as found in article 3 of the Hague Convention of 18 October 1907 concerning the Laws and Customs of War and Land (Convention No. IV of 1907), article 91 of Protocol Additional to the Geneva Conventions of 12 August 1949 relating to the Protection of Victims of International Armed Conflicts (Protocol I), and articles 68 and 75 of the Rome Statute of the International Criminal Court,

[1] Adopted by Commission on Human Rights resolution E/CN.4/RES/2005/35 of 19 April 2005 and by the General Assembly Resolution A/RES/60/147 of 16 December 2005.

Recalling the provisions providing a right to a remedy for victims of violations of international human rights found in regional conventions, in particular the African Charter on Human and Peoples' Rights at article 7, the American Convention on Human Rights at article 25, and the European Convention for the Protection of Human Rights and Fundamental Freedoms at article 13,

Recalling the Declaration of Basic Principles of Justice for Victims of Crime and Abuse of Power emanating from the deliberations of the Seventh United Nations Congress on the Prevention of Crime and the Treatment of Offenders, and resolution 40/34 of 29 November 1985 by which the General Assembly adopted the text recommended by the Congress,

Reaffirming the principles enunciated in the Declaration of Basic Principles of Justice for Victims of Crime and Abuse of Power, including that victims should be treated with compassion and respect for their dignity, have their right to access to justice and redress mechanisms fully respected, and that the establishment, strengthening and expansion of national funds for compensation to victims should be encouraged, together with the expeditious development of appropriate rights and remedies for victims,

Noting that the Rome Statute of the International Criminal Court requires the establishment of "principles relating to reparation to, or in respect of, victims, including restitution, compensation and rehabilitation" and requires the Assembly of States Parties to establish a trust fund for the benefit of victims of crimes within the jurisdiction of the Court, and of the families of such victims, and mandates the Court "to protect the safety, physical and psychological well-being, dignity and privacy of victims" and to permit the participation of victims at all "stages of the proceedings determined to be appropriate by the Court",

Affirming that the Principles and Guidelines contained herein are directed at gross violations of international human rights law and serious violations of international humanitarian law which, by their very grave nature, constitute an affront to human dignity,

Emphasizing that the Principles and Guidelines do not entail new international or domestic legal obligations but identify mechanisms, modalities, procedures and methods for the implementation of existing legal obligations under international human rights law and international humanitarian law which are complementary though different as to their norms,

Recalling that international law contains the obligation to prosecute perpetrators of certain international crimes in accordance with international obligations of States and the requirements of national law or as provided for in the applicable statutes of international judicial organs, and that the duty to prosecute reinforces the international legal obligations to be carried out in accordance with national legal requirements and procedures and supports the concept of complementarity,

Noting further that contemporary forms of victimization, while essentially directed against persons, may nevertheless also be directed against groups of persons who are targeted collectively,

Recognizing that, in honouring the victims' right to benefit from remedies and reparation, the international community keeps faith with the plight of victims, survivors and future human generations, and reaffirms the international legal principles of accountability, justice and the rule of law,

Convinced that, in adopting a victim-oriented perspective, the international community affirms its human solidarity with victims of violations of international law, including violations of international human rights law and international humanitarian law, as well as with humanity at large, in accordance with the following Basic Principles and Guidelines.

I. OBLIGATION TO RESPECT, ENSURE RESPECT FOR AND IMPLEMENT INTERNATIONAL HUMAN RIGHTS LAW AND INTERNATIONAL HUMANITARIAN LAW

1. The obligation to respect, ensure respect for and implement international human rights law and international humanitarian law as provided for under the respective bodies of law emanates from:

(a) Treaties to which a State is a party;

(b) Customary international law;

(c) The domestic law of each State.

2. If they have not already done so, States shall, as required under international law, ensure that their domestic law is consistent with their international legal obligations by:

(a) Incorporating norms of international human rights law and international humanitarian law into their domestic law, or otherwise implementing them in their domestic legal system;

(b) Adopting appropriate and effective legislative and administrative procedures and other appropriate measures that provide fair, effective and prompt access to justice;

(c) Making available adequate, effective, prompt, and appropriate remedies, including reparation, as defined below; and

(d) Ensuring that their domestic law provides at least the same level of protection for victims as required by their international obligations.

II. SCOPE OF THE OBLIGATION

3. The obligation to respect, ensure respect for and implement international human rights law and international humanitarian law as provided for under the respective bodies of law, includes, inter alia, the duty to:

(a) Take appropriate legislative and administrative and other appropriate measures to prevent violations;

(b) Investigate violations effectively, promptly, thoroughly and impartially and, where appropriate, take action against those allegedly responsible in accordance with domestic and international law;

(c) Provide those who claim to be victims of a human rights or humanitarian law violation with equal and effective access to justice, as described below, irrespective of who may ultimately be the bearer of responsibility for the violation; and

(d) Provide effective remedies to victims, including reparation, as described below.

III. GROSS VIOLATIONS OF INTERNATIONAL HUMAN RIGHTS LAW AND SERIOUS VIOLATIONS OF INTERNATIONAL HUMANITARIAN LAW THAT CONSTITUTE CRIMES UNDER INTERNATIONAL LAW

4. In cases of gross violations of international human rights law and serious violations of international humanitarian law constituting crimes under in-

ternational law, States have the duty to investigate and, if there is sufficient evidence, the duty to submit to prosecution the person allegedly responsible for the violations and, if found guilty, the duty to punish her or him. Moreover, in these cases, States should, in accordance with international law, cooperate with one another and assist international judicial organs competent in the investigation and prosecution of these violations.

5. To that end, where so provided in an applicable treaty or under other international law obligations, States shall incorporate or otherwise implement within their domestic law appropriate provisions for universal jurisdiction. Moreover, where it is so provided for in an applicable treaty or other international legal obligations, States should facilitate extradition or surrender offenders to other States and to appropriate international judicial bodies and provide judicial assistance and other forms of cooperation in the pursuit of international justice, including assistance to, and protection of, victims and witnesses, consistent with international human rights legal standards and subject to international legal requirements such as those relating to the prohibition of torture and other forms of cruel, inhuman or degrading treatment or punishment.

IV. STATUTES OF LIMITATIONS

6. Where so provided for in an applicable treaty or contained in other international legal obligations, statutes of limitations shall not apply to gross violations of international human rights law and serious violations of international humanitarian law which constitute crimes under international law.

7. Domestic statutes of limitations for other types of violations that do not constitute crimes under international law, including those time limitations applicable to civil claims and other procedures, should not be unduly restrictive.

V. VICTIMS OF GROSS VIOLATIONS OF INTERNATIONAL HUMAN RIGHTS LAW AND SERIOUS VIOLATIONS OF INTERNATIONAL HUMANITARIAN LAW

8. For purposes of this document, victims are persons who individually or collectively suffered harm, including physical or mental injury, emotional

suffering, economic loss or substantial impairment of their fundamental rights, through acts or omissions that constitute gross violations of international human rights law, or serious violations of international humanitarian law. Where appropriate, and in accordance with domestic law, the term "victim" also includes the immediate family or dependants of the direct victim and persons who have suffered harm in intervening to assist victims in distress or to prevent victimization.

9. A person shall be considered a victim regardless of whether the perpetrator of the violation is identified, apprehended, prosecuted, or convicted and regardless of the familial relationship between the perpetrator and the victim.

VI. TREATMENT OF VICTIMS

10. Victims should be treated with humanity and respect for their dignity and human rights, and appropriate measures should be taken to ensure their safety, physical and psychological well-being and privacy, as well as those of their families. The State should ensure that its domestic laws, to the extent possible, provide that a victim who has suffered violence or trauma should benefit from special consideration and care to avoid his or her re-traumatization in the course of legal and administrative procedures designed to provide justice and reparation.

VII. VICTIMS' RIGHT TO REMEDIES

11. Remedies for gross violations of international human rights law and serious violations of international humanitarian law include the victim's right to the following as provided for under international law:

(a) Equal and effective access to justice;
(b) Adequate, effective and prompt reparation for harm suffered; and
(c) Access to relevant information concerning violations and reparation mechanisms.

VIII. ACCESS TO JUSTICE

12. A victim of a gross violation of international human rights law or of a serious violation of international humanitarian law shall have equal access

to an effective judicial remedy as provided for under international law. Other remedies available to the victim include access to administrative and other bodies, as well as mechanisms, modalities and proceedings conducted in accordance with domestic law. Obligations arising under international law to secure the right to access justice and fair and impartial proceedings shall be reflected in domestic laws. To that end, States should:

(a) Disseminate, through public and private mechanisms, information about all available remedies for gross violations of international human rights law and serious violations of international humanitarian law;

(b) Take measures to minimize the inconvenience to victims and their representatives, protect against unlawful interference with their privacy as appropriate and ensure their safety from intimidation and retaliation, as well as that of their families and witnesses, before, during and after judicial, administrative, or other proceedings that affect the interests of victims;

(c) Provide proper assistance to victims seeking access to justice;

(d) Make available all appropriate legal, diplomatic and consular means to ensure that victims can exercise their rights to remedy for gross violations of international human rights law or serious violations of international humanitarian law.

13. In addition to individual access to justice, States should endeavour to develop procedures to allow groups of victims to present claims for reparation and to receive reparation, as appropriate.

14. An adequate, effective and prompt remedy for gross violations of international human rights law or serious violations of international humanitarian law should include all available and appropriate international processes in which a person may have legal standing and should be without prejudice to any other domestic remedies.

IX. REPARATION FORM HARM SUFFERED

15. Adequate, effective and prompt reparation is intended to promote justice by redressing gross violations of international human rights law or serious violations of international humanitarian law. Reparation should be proportional to the gravity of the violations and the harm suffered. In ac-

cordance with its domestic laws and international legal obligations, a State shall provide reparation to victims for acts or omissions which can be attributed to the State and constitute gross violations of international human rights law or serious violations of international humanitarian law. In cases where a person, a legal person, or other entity is found liable for reparation to a victim, such party should provide reparation to the victim or compensate the State if the State has already provided reparation to the victim.

16. States should endeavour to establish national programmes for reparation and other assistance to victims in the event that the party liable for the harm suffered is unable or unwilling to meet their obligations.

17. States shall, with respect to claims by victims, enforce domestic judgements for reparation against individuals or entities liable for the harm suffered and endeavour to enforce valid foreign legal judgements for reparation in accordance with domestic law and international legal obligations. To that end, States should provide under their domestic laws effective mechanisms for the enforcement of reparation judgements.

18. In accordance with domestic law and international law, and taking account of individual circumstances, victims of gross violations of international human rights law and serious violations of international humanitarian law should, as appropriate and proportional to the gravity of the violation and the circumstances of each case, be provided with full and effective reparation, as laid out in principles 19 to 23, which include the following forms: restitution, compensation, rehabilitation, satisfaction and guarantees of non-repetition.

19. *Restitution* should, whenever possible, restore the victim to the original situation before the gross violations of international human rights law or serious violations of international humanitarian law occurred. Restitution includes, as appropriate: restoration of liberty, enjoyment of human rights, identity, family life and citizenship, return to one's place of residence, restoration of employment and return of property.

20. *Compensation* should be provided for any economically assessable damage, as appropriate and proportional to the gravity of the violation and the circumstances of each case, resulting from gross violations of international human rights law and serious violations of international humanitarian law, such as:

(a) Physical or mental harm;

(b) Lost opportunities, including employment, education and social benefits;

(c) Material damages and loss of earnings, including loss of earning potential;

(d) Moral damage;

(e) Costs required for legal or expert assistance, medicine and medical services, and psychological and social services.

21. *Rehabilitation* should include medical and psychological care as well as legal and social services.

22. *Satisfaction* should include, where applicable, any or all of the following:

(a) Effective measures aimed at the cessation of continuing violations;

(b) Verification of the facts and full and public disclosure of the truth to the extent that such disclosure does not cause further harm or threaten the safety and interests of the victim, the victim's relatives, witnesses, or persons who have intervened to assist the victim or prevent the occurrence of further violations;

(c) The search for the whereabouts of the disappeared, for the identities of the children abducted, and for the bodies of those killed, and assistance in the recovery, identification and reburial of the bodies in accordance with the expressed or presumed wish of the victims, or the cultural practices of the families and communities;

(d) An official declaration or a judicial decision restoring the dignity, the reputation and the rights of the victim and of persons closely connected with the victim;

(e) Public apology, including acknowledgement of the facts and acceptance of responsibility;

(f) Judicial and administrative sanctions against persons liable for the violations;

(g) Commemorations and tributes to the victims;

(h) Inclusion of an accurate account of the violations that occurred in international human rights law and international humanitarian law training and in educational material at all levels.

23. *Guarantees of non-repetition* should include, where applicable, any or all of the following measures, which will also contribute to prevention:

(a) Ensuring effective civilian control of military and security forces;

(b) Ensuring that all civilian and military proceedings abide by international standards of due process, fairness and impartiality;

(c) Strengthening the independence of the judiciary;

(d) Protecting persons in the legal, medical and health-care professions, the media and other related professions, and human rights defenders;

(e) Providing, on a priority and continued basis, human rights and international humanitarian law education to all sectors of society and training for law enforcement officials as well as military and security forces;

(f) Promoting the observance of codes of conduct and ethical norms, in particular international standards, by public servants, including law enforcement, correctional, media, medical, psychological, social service and military personnel, as well as by economic enterprises;

(g) Promoting mechanisms for preventing and monitoring social conflicts and their resolution;

(h) Reviewing and reforming laws contributing to or allowing gross violations of international human rights law and serious violations of international humanitarian law.

X. ACCESS TO RELEVANT INFORMATION CONCERNING VIOLATIONS AND REPARATION MECHANISMS

24. States should develop means of informing the general public and, in particular, victims of gross violations of international human rights law and serious violations of international humanitarian law of the rights and remedies addressed by these Principles and Guidelines and of all available legal, medical, psychological, social, administrative and all other services to which victims may have a right of access. Moreover, victims and their representatives should be entitled to seek and obtain information on the causes leading to their victimization and on the causes and conditions pertaining to the gross violations of international human rights law and serious violations of international humanitarian law and to learn the truth in regard to these violations.

XI. NON-DISCRIMINATION

25. The application and interpretation of these Principles and Guidelines must be consistent with international human rights law and international humanitarian law and be without any discrimination of any kind or ground, without exception.

XII. NON-DEROGATION

26. Nothing in these Principles and Guidelines shall be construed as restricting or derogating from any rights or obligations arising under domestic and international law. In particular, it is understood that the present Principles and Guidelines are without prejudice to the right to a remedy and reparation for victims of all violations of international human rights law and international humanitarian law. It is further understood that these Principles and Guidelines are without prejudice to special rules of international law.

XIII. RIGHTS OF OTHERS

27. Nothing in this document is to be construed as derogating from internationally or nationally protected rights of others, in particular the right of an accused person to benefit from applicable standards of due process.

Updated Set of principles for the protection and promotion of human rights through action to combat impunity[2]

PREAMBLE

Recalling the Preamble to the Universal Declaration of Human Rights, which recognizes that disregard and contempt for human rights have resulted in barbarous acts which have outraged the conscience of mankind,

Aware that there is an ever-present risk that such acts may again occur,

Reaffirming the commitment made by Member States under Article 56 of the Charter of the United Nations to take joint and separate action, giving full importance to developing effective international cooperation for the achievement of the purposes set forth in Article 55 of the Charter concerning universal respect for, and observance of, human rights and fundamental freedoms for all,

Considering that the duty of every State under international law to respect and to secure respect for human rights requires that effective measures should be taken to combat impunity,

Aware that there can be no just and lasting reconciliation unless the need for justice is effectively satisfied,

Equally aware that forgiveness, which may be an important element of reconciliation, implies, insofar as it is a private act, that the victim or the victim's beneficiaries know the perpetrator of the violations and that the latter has acknowledged his or her deeds,

Recalling the recommendation set forth in paragraph 91 of Part II of the Vienna Declaration and Programme of Action, wherein the World Confer-

[2] E/CN.4/2005/102/Add.1, 8 February 2005, recommended by Commission on Human Rights resolution E/CN.4/RES/2005/81 of 21 April 2005.

ence on Human Rights (June 1993) expressed its concern about the impunity of perpetrators of human rights violations and encouraged the efforts of the Commission on Human Rights to examine all aspects of the issue,

Convinced, therefore, that national and international measures must be taken for that purpose with a view to securing jointly, in the interests of the victims of violations, observance of the right to know and, by implication, the right to the truth, the right to justice and the right to reparation, without which there can be no effective remedy against the pernicious effects of impunity,

Pursuant to the Vienna Declaration and Programme of Action, the following principles are intended as guidelines to assist States in developing effective measures for combating impunity.

Definitions

A. Impunity

"Impunity" means the impossibility, de jure or de facto, of bringing the perpetrators of violations to account - whether in criminal, civil, administrative or disciplinary proceedings since they are not subject to any inquiry that might lead to their being accused, arrested, tried and, if found guilty, sentenced to appropriate penalties, and to making reparations to their victims.

B. Serious crimes under international law

As used in these principles, the phrase "serious crimes under international law" encompasses grave breaches of the Geneva Conventions of 12 August 1949 and of Additional Protocol I thereto of 1977 and other violations of international humanitarian law that are crimes under international law, genocide, crimes against humanity, and other violations of internationally protected human rights that are crimes under international law and/or which international law requires States to penalize, such as torture, enforced disappearance, extrajudicial execution, and slavery.

C. Restoration of or transition to democracy and/or peace

This expression, as used in these principles, refers to situations leading, within the framework of a national movement towards democracy or peace negotiations aimed at ending an armed conflict, to an agreement, in whatever form, by which the actors or parties concerned agree to take measures against impunity and the recurrence of human rights violations.

D. Truth commissions

As used in these principles, the phrase "truth commissions" refers to official, temporary, non-judicial fact-finding bodies that investigate a pattern of abuses of human rights or humanitarian law, usually committed over a number of years.

E. Archives

As used in these principles, the word "archives" refers to collections of documents pertaining to violations of human rights and humanitarian law from sources including

(a) national governmental agencies, particularly those that played significant roles in relation to human rights violations; (b) local agencies, such as police stations, that were involved in human rights violations; (c) State agencies, including the office of the prosecutor and the judiciary, that are involved in the protection of human rights; and (d) materials collected by truth commissions and other investigative bodies.

I. COMBATING IMPUNITY: GENERAL OBLIGATIONS

PRINCIPLE 1. GENERAL OBLIGATIONS OF STATES TO TAKE EFFECTIVE ACTION TO COMBAT IMPUNITY

Impunity arises from a failure by States to meet their obligations to investigate violations; to take appropriate measures in respect of the perpetrators, particularly in the area of justice, by ensuring that those suspected of criminal responsibility are prosecuted, tried and duly punished; to provide victims with effective remedies and to ensure that they receive reparation for the injuries suffered; to ensure the inalienable right to know the truth about violations; and to take other necessary steps to prevent a recurrence of violations.

II. THE RIGHT TO KNOW

A. General principles

PRINCIPLE 2. THE INALIENABLE RIGHT TO THE TRUTH

Every people has the inalienable right to know the truth about past events concerning the perpetration of heinous crimes and about the circumstances and reasons that led, through massive or systematic violations, to the perpetration of those crimes. Full and effective exercise of the right to the truth provides a vital safeguard against the recurrence of violations.

PRINCIPLE 3. THE DUTY TO PRESERVE MEMORY

A people's knowledge of the history of its oppression is part of its heritage and, as such, must be ensured by appropriate measures in fulfilment of the State's duty to preserve archives and other evidence concerning violations of human rights and humanitarian law and to facilitate knowledge of those violations. Such measures shall be aimed at preserving the collective memory from extinction and, in particular, at guarding against the development of revisionist and negationist arguments.

PRINCIPLE 4. THE VICTIMS' RIGHT TO KNOW

Irrespective of any legal proceedings, victims and their families have the imprescriptible right to know the truth about the circumstances in which violations took place and, in the event of death or disappearance, the victims' fate.

PRINCIPLE 5. GUARANTEES TO GIVE EFFECT TO THE RIGHT TO KNOW

States must take appropriate action, including measures necessary to ensure the independent and effective operation of the judiciary, to give effect to the right to know. Appropriate measures to ensure this right may include non-judicial processes that complement the role of the judiciary. Societies that have experienced heinous crimes perpetrated on a massive or systematic basis may benefit in particular from the creation of a truth commission or other commission of inquiry to establish the facts surrounding those violations so that the truth may be ascertained and to prevent the disappearance of evidence. Regardless of whether a State establishes such a body, it must ensure the preservation of, and access to, archives concerning violations of human rights and humanitarian law.

B. Commissions of inquiry

PRINCIPLE 6. THE ESTABLISHMENT AND ROLE OF TRUTH COMMISSIONS

To the greatest extent possible, decisions to establish a truth commission, define its terms

f reference and determine its composition should be based upon broad public consultations in which the views of victims and survivors especially are sought. Special efforts should be made to ensure that men and women participate in these deliberations on a basis of equality.

In recognition of the dignity of victims and their families, investigations undertaken by truth commissions should be conducted with the object in particular of securing recognition of such parts of the truth as were formerly denied.

PRINCIPLE 7. GUARANTEES OF INDEPENDENCE, IMPARTIALITY AND COMPETENCE

Commissions of inquiry, including truth commissions, must be established through procedures that ensure their independence, impartiality and competence. To this end, the terms of reference of commissions of inquiry, including commissions that are international in character, should respect the following guidelines:

(a) They shall be constituted in accordance with criteria making clear to the public the competence and impartiality of their members, including expertise within their membership in the field of human rights and, if relevant, of humanitarian law. They shall also be constituted in accordance with conditions ensuring their independence, in particular by the irremovability of their members during their terms of office except on grounds of incapacity or behaviour rendering them unfit to discharge their duties and pursuant to procedures ensuring fair, impartial and independent determinations;

(b) Their members shall enjoy whatever privileges and immunities are necessary for their protection, including in the period following their mission, especially in respect of any defamation proceedings or other civil or criminal action brought against them on the basis of facts or opinions contained in the commissions' reports;

(c) In determining membership, concerted efforts should be made to ensure adequate representation of women as well as of other appropriate groups whose members have been especially vulnerable to human rights violations.

PRINCIPLE 8. DEFINITION OF A COMMISSION'S TERMS OF REFERENCE

To avoid conflicts of jurisdiction, the commission's terms of reference must be clearly defined and must be consistent with the principle that commissions of inquiry are not intended to act as substitutes for the civil, administrative or criminal courts. In particular, criminal courts alone have jurisdiction to establish individual criminal responsibility, with a view as appropriate to passing judgement and imposing a sentence.

In addition to the guidelines set forth in principles 12 and 13, the terms of reference of a commission of inquiry should incorporate or reflect the following stipulations:

(a) The commission's terms of reference may reaffirm its right: to seek the assistance of law enforcement authorities, if required, including for the purpose, subject to the terms of principle 10 (a), of calling for testimonies; to inspect any places concerned in its investigations; and/or to call for the delivery of relevant documents;

(b) If the commission has reason to believe that the life, health or safety of a person concerned by its inquiry is threatened or that there is a risk of losing an element of proof, it may seek court action under an emergency procedure or take other appropriate measures to end such threat or risk;

(c) Investigations undertaken by a commission of inquiry may relate to all persons alleged to have been responsible for violations of human rights and/or humanitarian law, whether they ordered them or actually committed them, acting as perpetrators or accomplices, and whether they are public officials or members of quasi-governmental or private armed groups with any kind of link to the State, or of non-governmental armed movements. Commissions of inquiry may also consider the role of other actors in facilitating violations of human rights and humanitarian law;

(d) Commissions of inquiry may have jurisdiction to consider all forms of violations of human rights and humanitarian law. Their investigations should focus as a matter of priority on violations constituting serious crimes under international law, including in particular violations of the fundamental rights of women and of other vulnerable groups;

(e) Commissions of inquiry shall endeavour to safeguard evidence for later use in the administration of justice;

(f) The terms of reference of commissions of inquiry should highlight the importance of preserving the commission's archives. At the outset of their work, commissions should clarify the conditions that will govern access to their documents, including conditions aimed at preventing disclosure of confidential information while facilitating public access to their archives.

PRINCIPLE 9. GUARANTEES FOR PERSONS IMPLICATED

Before a commission identifies perpetrators in its report, the individuals concerned shall be entitled to the following guarantees:

(a) The commission must try to corroborate information implicating individuals before they are named publicly;

(b) The individuals implicated shall be afforded an opportunity to provide a statement setting forth their version of the facts either at a hearing convened by the commission while conducting its investigation or through submission of a document equivalent to a right of reply for inclusion in the commission's file.

PRINCIPLE 10. GUARANTEES FOR VICTIMS AND WITNESSES TESTIFYING ON THEIR BEHALF

Effective measures shall be taken to ensure the security, physical and psychological well-being, and, where requested, the privacy of victims and witnesses who provide information to the commission.

(a) Victims and witnesses testifying on their behalf may be called upon to testify before the commission only on a strictly voluntary basis;

(b) Social workers and/or mental health-care practitioners should be authorized to assist victims, preferably in their own language, both during and after their testimony, especially in cases of sexual assault;

(c) All expenses incurred by those giving testimony shall be borne by the State;

(d) Information that might identify a witness who provided testimony pursuant to a promise of confidentially must be protected from disclosure. Victims providing testimony and other witnesses should in any event be informed of rules that will govern disclosure of information provided by them to the commission. Requests to provide information to the commission anonymously should be given serious consideration, especially in cases of sexual assault, and the commission should establish procedures to guarantee anonymity in appropriate cases, while allowing corroboration of the information provided, as necessary.

PRINCIPLE 11. ADEQUATE RESOURCES FOR COMMISSIONS

The commission shall be provided with:

(a) Transparent funding to ensure that its independence is never in doubt;

(b) Sufficient material and human resources to ensure that its credibility is never in doubt.

PRINCIPLE 12. ADVISORY FUNCTIONS OF THE COMMISSIONS

The commission's terms of reference should include provisions calling for it to include in its final report recommendations concerning legislative and other action to combat impunity.

The terms of reference should ensure that the commission incorporates women's experiences in its work, including its recommendations. When establishing a commission of inquiry, the Government should undertake to give due consideration to the commission's recommendations.

PRINCIPLE 13. PUBLICIZING THE COMMISSION'S REPORTS

For security reasons or to avoid pressure on witnesses and commission members, the commission's terms of reference may stipulate that relevant portions of its inquiry shall be kept confidential. The commission's final report, on the other hand, shall be made public in full and shall be disseminated as widely as possible.

C. Preservation of and access to archives bearing witness to violations

PRINCIPLE 14. MEASURES FOR THE PRESERVATION OF ARCHIVES

The right to know implies that archives must be preserved. Technical measures and penalties should be applied to prevent any removal, destruction, concealment or falsification of archives, especially for the purpose of ensuring the impunity of perpetrators of violations of human rights and/or humanitarian law.

PRINCIPLE 15. MEASURES FOR FACILITATING ACCESS TO ARCHIVES

Access to archives shall be facilitated in order to enable victims and their relatives to claim their rights. Access shall be facilitated, as necessary, for persons implicated, who request it for their defence. Access to archives should also be facilitated in the interest of historical research, subject to reasonable restrictions aimed at safeguarding the privacy and security of victims and other individuals. Formal requirements governing access may not be used for purposes of censorship.

PRINCIPLE 16. COOPERATION BETWEEN ARCHIVE DEPARTMENTS AND THE COURTS AND NON-JUDICIAL COMMISSIONS OF INQUIRY

Courts and non-judicial commissions of inquiry, as well as investigators reporting to them, must have access to relevant archives. This principle must be implemented in a manner that respects applicable privacy concerns, including in particular assurances of confidentiality provided to victims and other witnesses as a precondition of their testimony. Access may not be denied on grounds of national security unless, in exceptional circumstances, the restriction has been prescribed by law; the Government has demonstrated that the restriction is necessary in a democratic society to protect a legitimate national security interest; and the denial is subject to independent judicial review.

PRINCIPLE 17. SPECIFIC MEASURES RELATING TO ARCHIVES CONTAINING NAMES

(a) For the purposes of this principle, archives containing names shall be understood to be those archives containing information that makes it possible, directly or indirectly, to identify the individuals to whom they relate;

(b) All persons shall be entitled to know whether their name appears in State archives and, if it does, by virtue of their right of access, to challenge the validity of the information concerning them by exercising a right of reply. The challenged document should include a cross-reference to the document challenging its validity and both must be made available together whenever the former is requested. Access to the files of commissions of inquiry must be balanced against the legitimate expectations of confidentiality of victims and other witnesses testifying on their behalf in accordance with principles 8 (f) and 10 (d).

PRINCIPLE 18. SPECIFIC MEASURES RELATED TO THE RESTORATION OF OR TRANSITION TO DEMOCRACY AND/OR PEACE

(a) Measures should be taken to place each archive centre under the responsability of a specifically designated office;

(b) When inventorying and assessing thereliability of stored archives, special attention should be given to archives relating to places of detention and other sites of serious violations of human rights and/or humanitarian law such as torture, in particular when the existence of such places was not officially recognized;

(c) Third countries shall be expected to cooperate with a view to communicating or restituting archives for the purpose of establishing the truth.

III. THE RIGHT TO JUSTICE

A. General principles

PRINCIPLE 19. DUTIES OF STATES WITH REGARD TO THE ADMINISTRATION OF JUSTICE

States shall undertake prompt, thorough, independent and impartial investigations of violations of human rights and international humanitarian law and take appropriate measures in respect of the perpetrators, particularly in the area of criminal justice, by ensuring that those responsible for serious crimes under international law are prosecuted, tried and duly punished. Although the decision to prosecute lies primarily within the competence of the State, victims, their families and heirs should be able to institute proceedings, on either an individual or a collective basis, particularly as *parties civiles* or as persons conducting private prosecutions in States whose law of criminal procedure recognizes these procedures. States should guarantee broad legal standing in the judicial process to any wronged party and to any person or non-governmental organization having a legitimate interest therein.

B. Distribution of jurisdiction between national, foreign, international and internationalized courts

PRINCIPLE 20. JURISDICTION OF INTERNATIONAL AND INTERNATIONALIZED CRIMINAL TRIBUNALS

It remains the rule that States have primary responsibility to exercise jurisdiction over serious crimes under international law. In accordance with the terms of their statutes, international and internationalized criminal tribunals may exercise concurrent jurisdiction when national courts cannot offer satisfactory guarantees of independence and impartiality or are materially unable or unwilling to conduct effective investigations or prosecutions.

States must ensure that they fully satisfy their legal obligations in respect of international and internationalized criminal tribunals, including where necessary through the enactment of domestic legislation that enables States to fulfil obligations that arise through their adherence to the Rome Statute of the International Criminal Court or under other binding instruments, and through implementation of applicable obligations to apprehend and surrender suspects and to cooperate in respect of evidence.

PRINCIPLE 21. MEASURES FOR STRENGTHENING THE EFFECTIVENESS OF INTERNATIONAL LEGAL PRINCIPLES CONCERNING UNIVERSAL AND INTERNATIONAL JURISDICTION

States should undertake effective measures, including the adoption or amendment of internal legislation, that are necessary to enable their courts to exercise universal jurisdiction over serious crimes under international law in accordance with applicable principles of customary and treaty law.

States must ensure that they fully implement any legal obligations they have assumed to institute criminal proceedings against persons with respect to whom there is credible evidence of individual responsibility for serious crimes under international law if they do not extradite the suspects or transfer them for prosecution before an international or internationalized tribunal.

C. Restrictions on rules of law justified by action to combat impunity

PRINCIPLE 22. NATURE OF RESTRICTIVE MEASURES

States should adopt and enforce safeguards against any abuse of rules such as those pertaining to prescription, amnesty, right to asylum, refusal to extradite, *non bis in idem*, due obedience, official immunities, repentance, the jurisdiction of military courts and the irremovability of judges that fosters or contributes to impunity.

PRINCIPLE 23. RESTRICTIONS ON PRESCRIPTION

Prescription - of prosecution or penalty - in criminal cases shall not run for such period as no effective remedy is available. Prescription shall not apply to crimes under international law that are by their nature imprescriptible.

When it does apply, prescription shall not be effective against civil or administrative actions brought by victims seeking reparation for their injuries.

PRINCIPLE 24. RESTRICTIONS AND OTHER MEASURES RELATING TO AMNESTY

Even when intended to establish conditions conducive to a peace agreement or to foster national reconciliation, amnesty and other measures of clemency shall be kept within the following bounds:

(a) The perpetrators of serious crimes under international law may not benefit from such measures until such time as the State has met the obligations to which principle 19 refers or the perpetrators have been prosecuted before a court with jurisdiction – whether international, internationalized or national - outside the State in question;

(b) Amnesties and other measures of clemency shall be without effect with respect to the victims' right to reparation, to which principles 31 through 34 refer, and shall not prejudice the right to know;

(c) Insofar as it may be interpreted as an admission of guilt, amnesty cannot be imposed on individuals prosecuted or sentenced for acts connected with the peaceful exercise of their right to freedom of opinion and expression. When they have merely exercised this legitimate right, as guaranteed by articles 18 to 20 of the Universal Declaration of Human Rights and 18, 19, 21 and 22 of the International Covenant on Civil and Political Rights, the law shall consider any judicial or other decision concerning them to be null and void; their detention shall be ended unconditionally and without delay;

(d) Any individual convicted of offences other than those to which paragraph (c) of this principle refers who comes within the scope of an amnesty is entitled to refuse it and request a retrial, if he or she has been tried without benefit of the right to a fair hearing guaranteed by articles 10 and 11 of the Universal Declaration of Human Rights and articles 9, 14 and 15 of the International Covenant on Civil and Political Rights, or if he or she was convicted on the basis of a statement established to have been made as a result of inhuman or degrading interrogation, especially under torture.

PRINCIPLE 25. RESTRICTIONS ON THE RIGHT OF ASYLUM

Under article 1, paragraph 2, of the Declaration on Territorial Asylum, adopted by the General Assembly on 14 December 1967, and article 1 F of the Convention relating to the Status of Refugees of 28 July 1951, States may not extend such protective status, including diplomatic asylum, to persons with respect to whom there are serious reasons to believe that they have committed a serious crime under international law.

*PRINCIPLE 26. RESTRICTIONS ON EXTRADITION/*NON BIS IN IDEM

(a) Persons who have committed serious crimes under international law may not, in order to avoid extradition, avail themselves of the favourable provisions generally relating to political offences or of the principle of non-extradition of nationals. Extradition should always be denied, however, especially by abolitionist countries, if the individual concerned risks the death penalty in the requesting country. Extradition should also be denied where there are substantial grounds for believing that the suspect would be in danger of being subjected to gross violations of human rights such as torture; enforced disappearance; or extra-legal, arbitrary or summary execution. If extradition is denied on these grounds, the requested State shall submit the case to its competent authorities for the purpose of prosecution;

(b) The fact that an individual has previously been tried in connection with a serious crime under international law shall not prevent his or her prosecution with respect to the same conduct if the purpose of the previous proceedings was to shield the person concerned from criminal responsibility, or if those proceedings otherwise were not conducted independently or impartially in accordance with the norms of due process recognized by international law and were conducted in a manner that, in the circumstances, was inconsistent with an intent to bring the person concerned to justice.

PRINCIPLE 27. RESTRICTIONS ON JUSTIFICATIONS RELATED TO DUE OBEDIENCE, SUPERIOR RESPONSIBILITY, AND OFFICIAL STATUS

(a) The fact that the perpetrator of violations acted on the orders of his or her Government or of a superior does not exempt him or her from responsibility, in particular criminal, but may be regarded as grounds for reducing the sentence, in conformity with principles of justice;

(b) The fact that violations have been committed by a subordinate does not exempt that subordinate's superiors from responsibility, in particular criminal, if they knew or had at the time reason to know that the subordinate was committing or about to commit such a crime and they did not take all the necessary measures within their power to prevent or punish the crime;

(c) The official status of the perpetrator of a crime under international law - even if acting as head of State or Government - does not exempt him or her from criminal or other responsibility and is not grounds for a reduction of sentence.

PRINCIPLE 28. RESTRICTIONS ON THE EFFECTS OF LEGISLATION ON DISCLOSURE OR REPENTANCE

The fact that a perpetrator discloses the violations that he, she or others have committed in order to benefit from the favourable provisions of legislation on disclosure or repentance cannot exempt him or her from criminal or other responsibility. The disclosure may only provide grounds for a reduction of sentence in order to encourage revelation of the truth. When disclosures may subject a perpetrator to persecution, principle 25 notwithstanding, the person making the disclosure may be granted asylum - not refugee status - in order to facilitate revelation of the truth.

PRINCIPLE 29. RESTRICTIONS ON THE JURISDICTION OF MILITARY COURTS

The jurisdiction of military tribunals must be restricted solely to specifically military offences committed by military personnel, to the exclusion of human rights violations, which shall come under the jurisdiction of the ordinary domestic courts or, where appropriate, in the case of serious crimes under international law, of an international or internationalized criminal court.

PRINCIPLE 30. RESTRICTIONS ON THE PRINCIPLE OF THE IRREMOVABILITY OF JUDGES

The principle of irremovability, as the basic guarantee of the independence of judges, must be observed in respect of judges who have been appointed in conformity with the requirements of the rule of law. Conversely, judges unlawfully appointed or who derive their judicial power from an act of allegiance may be relieved of their functions by law in accordance with the principle of parallelism. They must be provided an opportunity to challenge their dismissal in proceedings that meet the criteria of independence and impartiality with a view toward seeking reinstatement.

IV. THE RIGHT TO REPARATION/GUARANTEES OF NON-RECURRENCE

A. The right to reparation

PRINCIPLE 31. RIGHTS AND DUTIES ARISING OUT OF THE OBLIGATION TO MAKE REPARATION

Any human rights violation gives rise to a right to reparation on the part of the victim or his or her beneficiaries, implying a duty on the part of the State to make reparation and the possibility for the victim to seek redress from the perpetrator.

PRINCIPLE 32. REPARATION PROCEDURES

All victims shall have access to a readily available, prompt and effective remedy in the form of criminal, civil, administrative or disciplinary proceedings subject to the restrictions on prescription set forth in principle 23. In exercising this right, they shall be afforded protection against intimidation and reprisals.

Reparations may also be provided through programmes, based upon legislative or administrative measures, funded by national or international sources, addressed to individuals and to communities. Victims and other sectors of civil society should play a meaningful role in the design and implementation of such programmes. Concerted efforts should be made to ensure that women and minority groups participate in public consultations aimed at developing, implementing, and assessing reparations programmes.

Exercise of the right to reparation includes access to applicable international and regional procedures.

PRINCIPLE 33. PUBLICIZING REPARATION PROCEDURES

Ad hoc procedures enabling victims to exercise their right to reparation should be given the widest possible publicity by private as well as public communication media. Such dissemination should take place both within and outside the country, including through consular services, particularly in countries to which large numbers of victims have been forced into exile.

PRINCIPLE 34. SCOPE OF THE RIGHT TO REPARATION

The right to reparation shall cover all injuries suffered by victims; it shall include measures of restitution, compensation, rehabilitation, and satisfaction as provided by international law.

In the case of forced disappearance, the family of the direct victim has an imprescriptible right to be informed of the fate and/or whereabouts of the disappeared person and, in the event of decease, that person's body must be returned to the family as soon as it has been identified, regardless of whether the perpetrators have been identified or prosecuted.

B. Guarantees of non-recurrence of violations

PRINCIPLE 35. GENERAL PRINCIPLES

States shall ensure that victims do not again have to endure violations of their rights. To this end, States must undertake institutional reforms and other measures necessary to ensure respect for the rule of law, foster and sustain a culture of respect for human rights, and restore or establish public trust in government institutions. Adequate representation of women and minority groups in public institutions is essential to the achievement of these aims. Institutional reforms aimed at preventing a recurrence of violations should be developed through a process of broad public consultations, including the participation of victims and other sectors of civil society.

Such reforms should advance the following objectives:

(a) Consistent adherence by public institutions to the rule of law;

(b) The repeal of laws that contribute to or authorize violations of human rights and/or humanitarian law and enactment of legislative and other measures necessary to ensure respect for human rights and humanitarian law, including measures that safeguard democratic institutions and processes;

(c) Civilian control of military and security forces and intelligence services and disbandment of parastatal armed forces;

(d) Reintegration of children involved in armed conflict into society.

PRINCIPLE 36. REFORM OF STATE INSTITUTIONS

States must take all necessary measures, including legislative and administrative reforms, to ensure that public institutions are organized in a manner that ensures respect for the rule of law and protection of human rights. At a minimum, States should undertake the following measures:

(a) Public officials and employees who are personally responsible for gross violations of human rights, in particular those involved in military, security, police, intelligence and judicial sectors, shall not continue to serve in State institutions. Their removal shall comply with the requirements of due process of law and the principle of non-discrimination. Persons formally charged with individual responsibility for serious crimes under international law shall be suspended from official duties during the criminal or disciplinary proceedings;

(b) With respect to the judiciary, States must undertake all other measures necessary to assure the independent, impartial and effective operation of courts in accordance with international standards of due process. Habeas corpus, by whatever name it may be known, must be considered a non-derogable right;

(c) Civilian control of military and security forces as well as of intelligence agencies must be ensured and, where necessary, established or restored. To this end, States should establish effective institutions of civilian oversight over military and security forces and intelligence agencies, including legislative oversight bodies;

(d) Civil complaint procedures should be established and their effective operation assured;

(e) Public officials and employees, in particular those involved in military, security, police, intelligence and judicial sectors, should receive comprehensive and ongoing training in human rights and, where applicable, humanitarian law standards and in implementation of those standards.

PRINCIPLE 37. DISBANDMENT OF PARASTATAL ARMED FORCES/ DEMOBILIZATION AND SOCIAL REINTEGRATION OF CHILDREN

Parastatal or unofficial armed groups shall be demobilized and disbanded. Their position in or links with State institutions, including in particular the army, police, intelligence and security forces, should be thoroughly investigated and the information thus acquired made public. States should draw up a reconversion plan to ensure the social reintegration of the members of such groups.

Measures should be taken to secure the cooperation of third countries that might have contributed to the creation and development of such groups, particularly through financial or logistical support.

Children who have been recruited or used in hostilities shall be demobilized or otherwise released from service. States shall, when necessary, accord these children all appropriate assistance for their physical and psychological recovery and their social integration.

PRINCIPLE 38. REFORM OF LAWS AND INSTITUTIONS ONTRIBUTING TO IMPUNITY

Legislation and administrative regulations and institutions that contribute to or legitimize human rights violations must be repealed or abolished. In particular, emergency legislation and courts of any kind must be repealed or abolished insofar as they infringe the fundamental rights and freedoms guaranteed in the Universal Declaration of Human Rights and the International Covenant on Civil and Political Rights. Legislative measures necessary to ensure protection of human rights and to safeguard democratic institutions and processes must be enacted.

As a basis for such reforms, during periods of restoration of or transition to democracy and/or peace States should undertake a comprehensive review of legislation and administrative regulations.

INDEX

Legislative measures

Military Tribunals

Moral damages, 127-128, 134-138, 157

Non-repetition